THE COLLEGE PRESS NIV COMMENTARY

1, 2 TIMOTHY & TITUS

THE COLLEGE PRESS NIV COMMENTARY

1, 2 TIMOTHY & TITUS

C. MICHAEL MOSS, Ph.D.

New Testament Series Co-Editors:

Jack Cottrell, Ph.D.
Cincinnati Bible Seminary

Tony Ash, Ph.D.
Abilene Christian University

COLLEGE PRESS
PUBLISHING COMPANY
Joplin, Missouri

Copyright © 1994
College Press Publishing Company
2nd Printing 1997

Scripture taken from the HOLY BIBLE,
NEW INTERNATIONAL VERSION®.
NIV®. Copyright© 1973, 1978, 1984 by
International Bible Society. Used by
permission of Zondervan Publishing House.
All rights reserved.

Printed and Bound in the
United States of America
All Rights Reserved

Library of Congress Catalog Card Number: 93-7434-2
International Standard Book Number: 0-89900-625-6

A WORD FROM THE PUBLISHER

Years ago a movement was begun with the dream of uniting all Christians on the basis of a common purpose (world evangelism) under a common authority (The Word of God). The College Press NIV Commentary Series is a serious effort to join the scholarship of two branches of this unity movement so as to speak with one voice concerning the Word of God. Our desire is to provide a resource for your study of the New Testament that will benefit you whether you are preparing a Bible School lesson, a sermon, a college course or your own personal devotions. Today as we survey the wreckage of a broken world, we must turn again to the Lord and his Word, unite under his banner and communicate the life-giving message to those who are in desperate need. This is our purpose.

FOREWORD

A movement which prides itself in its back-to-the-Bible underpinnings and its plea for unity should welcome any effort of the stature of the College Press NIV Bible Commentary. The exegesis of the biblical text must always be at the heart of who we are, and the effort to do so in a way that reaches across lines that have divided our movement signals an emphasis on the original hallmarks of the movement.

Having taught Bible and Greek at David Lipscomb University for eleven years, I have come to appreciate how many good commentaries there are on nearly every book in the New Testament. I am, in some ways, reluctant about adding another book to that pile. All of those commentaries have helped to shape my understanding of the biblical text for its original audiences and its import for Christians today.

I especially want to thank my family who have supported me and encouraged me when I spend hours at my computer typing away, my students whose questions have always caused me to look at the biblical text in fresh ways, and my colleagues who have always served as a constant encouragement.

When I was asked to participate as an author in this project, I was hesitant. When I was asked to write on Timothy and Titus, I was even more hesitant. To be a part of this series is an honor. To undertake writing a commentary on 1 and 2 Timothy and Titus is a challenging task. This is, after all, the section of Scripture that has fueled the debate about the role of women, has been at the heart of effort to redefine church leadership, and has provided encouragement to those who feel as if they "have fought the good fight" and are about to "finish the course." I began the study hoping for wonderful insights, and, although I gained a few, I came out of the study convinced that many of the more traditional interpretations were still reasonable. I discovered that, although I did not have all the answers, Paul's advice to those two young preachers and to their churches still made sense both for Paul's original audiences and for the preacher and his church today. May we today heed the words of Paul to "guard what has been entrusted to" our care and to "preach the Word."

ABBREVIATIONS

BAGD .... Bauer-Arndt-Gingrich-Danker Greek Lexicon (2nd. ed.)
DSB .... Daily Study Bible
ICC .... International Critical Commentary
JBL .... Journal of Biblical Literature
JETS .... Journal of the Evangelical Theological Society
JSNT .... Journal of Studies for the New Testament
KJV .... King James Version
LWC .... Living Word Commentary
LXX .... Septuagint
MNTC .... Moffatt New Testament Commentary
NAC .... New American Commentary
NCB .... New Clarendon Bible
NCBC .... New Century Bible Commentary
NEB .... New English Bible
NIBC .... New International Bible Commentary
NIGTC .... New International Greek Testament Commentary
NRSV .... New Revised Standard Version
NTC .... New Testament Commentary
NTS .... New Testament Studies
PNTC .... Pelican New Testament Commentary
RSV .... Revised Standard Version
TBC .... Torch Bible Commentaries
TDNT .... Theological Dictionary of the New Testament, ed. by Gerhard Kittel and Gerhard Friedrich
TEV .... Today's English Version

GENERAL INTRODUCTION

While several passages in 1 and 2 Timothy and Titus have provided the fodder for tomes of theological discussion (e.g., 1 Tim 2:9-15 and the role of women; 1 Tim 3:11 and deaconesses; 1 Tim 3:1-8 and Titus 1:6-9 and the characteristics of those to serve as elders), the real value of these epistles lies in their message to two young ministers, to second generation believers in Ephesus and to a young church facing a pagan world in Crete. These epistles provide teaching which the church in the twentieth and twenty-first centuries needs to hear.

The two letters to Timothy and the letter to Titus stand in a very close relationship to one another. They are written to fellow workers of the Apostle Paul; they are bound together by similar content: false teachers who bear similar characteristics, a discussion of church leaders, similar situations for the churches addressed, and the same basic time frame.

1 and 2 Timothy and Titus have been known as the Pastoral Epistles since the eighteenth century. As early as the thirteenth century Thomas Aquinas referred to 1 Timothy as a "pastoral rule." In 1703 D.N. Berdot described Titus as a "Pastoral Epistle," based on the assumption that it was an instruction manual for a pastor.[1] In reality, neither the term "pastor" nor its equivalent, "shepherd," appears in any of the three epistles. Paul Anton popularized the term in lectures he delivered on Timothy and Titus published posthumously in 1753-1755. Anton applied the term "Pastoral Epistles" to all three epistles.[2]

---

[1] D.N. Berdot, *Exercitatio theologica-exegetica in epistulam Pauli ad Titum*, pp. 3f.
[2] Paul Anton, *Exegetische Abhandlung der Pastoralbriefe S. Pauli* (Halle, 1753-1755).

Although the term "the Pastoral Epistles" has become a convenient designation for these three epistles which have much in common, it can be misleading. These epistles are not really a manual of pastoral theology. Only a fraction of these books contains what could be termed ecclesiastical teaching (1 Tim 3:1-13; 5:3-22; Titus 1:5-9). The three epistles are very different. There is nothing within the epistles that would indicate they were written from the same place and time or that the author intended them to be studied together.

AUTHORSHIP

A crucial issue in the Pastoral Epistles (PE)[3] is the authorship of the epistles. Despite widespread denial of Pauline authorship in modern times, ancient authors generally accepted the works as authentic epistles of the Apostle Paul. Serious challenges to Pauline authorship of the Pastoral Epistles began in the nineteenth century, especially with the forceful challenge espoused by Schleiermacher in 1807.[4]

Testimony of the Books Themselves

The letters claim to be by Paul, an apostle of Christ Jesus (1 Tim 1:1; Titus 1:1; 2 Tim 1:1). This assertion matches claims of the other Pauline letters. The author describes himself as "a blasphemer, a persecutor and a violent man" (1 Tim 1:13), a description which fits the account of Paul's pre-Christian life as seen in Acts. The author describes Timothy and Titus as his spiritual sons (1 Tim 1:2; Titus 1:4); this too is in full accord with their relationship to Paul as seen in Acts

---

[3]In some footnotes, we will be using the abbreviation "PE" for "Pastoral Epistles."

[4]F. Schleiermacher, *Über den sogenannten Brief des Paulos an den Timotheos: Sendschrieben an J.C., Gass* (Berlin, 1807); reprinted in *Sämtliche Werke*, I, 1 (1836), pp. 221ff.

and the other Pauline epistles. The epistles frequently refer to events in the Apostle's life and mention co-workers like Tychicus, Apollos, Barnabas, and Mark who are known from the other Pauline epistles.

With all of this data in mind, it is little wonder that there was almost unanimous agreement regarding Pauline authorship of the Pastoral Epistles for nearly 1800 years.

Attestation by the Early Church

The early church clearly regarded Paul as the author of the Pastoral Epistles.[5] Clement of Alexandria (ca. 155–ca. 220) frequently referred to and cited the Pastoral Epistles. He even cited 1 Tim 6:20, "what is falsely called knowledge," and ascribed the passage to "the apostle."[6] Similarly Origen, his student, ascribed 1 Tim 1:15 to Paul: "Moreover, Paul, who himself also at a later time became an apostle of Jesus, says in his epistle to Timothy, 'This is a faithful saying, that Jesus Christ came into the world to save sinners, of whom I am chief.'"[7] Eusebius (ca. 265–ca. 339) attributed the Pastoral Epistles to Paul. He said, "The epistles of Paul are fourteen, all well known and beyond doubt. It should not, however, be overlooked that some have set aside the epistle to the Hebrews."[8] The Muratorian Canon (ca. 200) refers to the Pastoral Epistles as Pauline. The extensive citations of the Pastoral Epistles by the church fathers, including Justin Martyr, Polycarp, Ignatius, and Irenaeus, demonstrate the early consensus that the Pastoral Epistles are Pauline.[9]

---

[5]For a thorough examination of the patristic evidence see J.D. James, *The Genuineness and Authorship of the Pastoral Epistles* (London, 1909).

[6]Clement of Alexandria, *Stromata*, Ante-Nicene Fathers (hereafter, ANF) 2.11.

[7]Origen, *Against Celsus*, ANF 1.63.

[8]Eusebius, *Church History*, Nicene & Post-Nicene Fathers (hereafter, NPNF) 3.3.

[9]J.H. Bernard, *The Pastoral Epistles* (1899; reprint, Grand Rapids: Baker, 1980), pp. xiii-xxi.

The evidence is not, however, all positive. According to Tertullian, Marcion (ca. 140) excluded the Pastoral Epistles from his canon.[10] Marcion, of course, rejected any book which did not fit his heretical view of Christianity. He omitted Matthew, Mark, and John; and he accepted only a mutilated copy of Luke. It seems likely that Marcion objected to the Pastoral Epistles because of their denunciation of tenets of his brand of Christianity (cf. 1 Tim 1:8; 6:20; 2 Tim 3:16).

An additional bit of negative evidence is seen in the apparent absence of the Pastoral Epistles from $\mathfrak{P}^{46}$ of the Chester Beatty papyri. The codex dates from the mid-third century and contains Pauline epistles. Portions of the manuscript are missing. It lacks a portion of Romans which stood at the beginning of the codex, a portion of 1 Thessalonians, and all of 2 Thessalonians. Most scholars feel that the manuscript did not have room for the Pastoral Epistles and Philemon, which are also missing.

If one looks only at external evidence, the victory would clearly be won in favor of acceptance of the Pastoral Epistles as Pauline.

Modern Times

Until the nineteenth century the Pastoral Epistles were deemed authentic and Pauline. The first attack on apostolic authorship was made by Schmidt (1804) and Schleiermacher (1807).

Today Pauline authorship of the Pastoral Epistles is disputed on five grounds:

Historical Allusions. Scott has said, "That Paul cannot have been the author [of the PE] is most clearly apparent when we examine the historical framework of the letters."[11]

---

[10]Tertullian, *Against Marcion*, ANF 5.21.

[11]E.F. Scott, *The Pastoral Epistles*, The Moffatt New Testament Commentary, 1936, pp. xvi, xvii.

The problem may be summarized as follows: the Pastoral Epistles do not fit into the historical framework of Acts and the Pauline epistles. Acts mentions only two imprisonments: Caesarea and Rome.[12]

The modern reader is not provided with many of the details of Paul's early life (i.e., the period described in Acts). Nowhere in Acts, or for that matter anywhere in the Pauline corpus outside 2 Corinthians, can one find Paul's frequent imprisonments, his five beatings, or his three shipwrecks (2 Cor 11:23-27). Also one is not bound to place the events described in the Pastoral Epistles into the period described in Acts. In fact the situation there seems to indicate likelihood of Paul's being released from prison.[13] The traditional interpretation which proposes a release from the imprisonment mentioned in Acts during which 1 Timothy and Titus were written and a subsequent Roman imprisonment as described in 2 Timothy has much to offer and provides few difficulties.[14] There is nothing improbable about Paul being released from prison, engaging in the kind of ministry indicated in 1 Timothy and Titus, and then later being imprisoned again with death being imminent.

Ecclesiastical Situation. It is argued that the church situation described in the Pastoral Epistles is akin to the second century and far too developed for Paul. At this juncture it is worth noting that very little of the Pastoral Epistles can really be termed "ecclesiastical teaching."[15]

Paul does have an interest in ecclesiastical matters: he and Barnabas appoint elders (Acts 14:23); Paul addresses the

---

[12]Recently an Ephesian imprisonment has been postulated on the basis of 1 Cor 15:32. The evidence for the traditional Roman imprisonment remains strong.

[13]Acts 15:25; 26:32; 28:16, 30.

[14]The external evidence for such a historical reconstruction includes Clement of Rome (Paul preaching to the boundaries of the West) and Eusebius (Paul preaching after his first defense).

[15]As little as one-tenth of the content of the PE relates to "church order" (1 Tim 3:1-13; 5:3-22; Titus 1:5-9).

bishops and deacons at Philippi (Phil 1:1); Paul lists pastor-teachers among the divine gifts provided to the early church (Eph 4:11-13); and Paul calls for the elders at Ephesus on his way to Rome, calling upon them to oversee (verb from which the noun "bishop" comes) and shepherd (verb from which the noun "pastor" comes) their flocks (Acts 20:13-35).

Nothing in the Pastoral Epistles would demand the later phenomenon of monarchical bishops. As Carson, Moo, and Morris have noted, "Clearly none of this amounts to much in the way of organization, certainly to nothing more than can have appeared in the church in comparatively early days."[16]

The Nature of the False Teaching. It is usually assumed that all three Pastoral Epistles face the same false teaching, an assumption which has been questioned in recent years. Many have wanted to see the Pastoral Epistles addressing a heresy seen only after the early second century and therefore as being non-Pauline. Easton argued that the Pastoral Epistles painted a picture of Christianity threatened by a "coherent and powerful heresy," a heresy which claimed to be more profound than the revelation of the Church.[17] That the heresy seen here is "coherent and powerful" and that one must see it as second century Gnosticism is still to be demonstrated. The heresy or heresies seen in the Pastoral Epistles betray a strong Jewish element much akin to what one meets in the Qumran literature and the apocryphal work, Jubilees.[18] There are no real grounds to see the false teaching confronted in the Pastoral Epistles as something which would not, indeed did not (cf. Colossians), arise in Paul's lifetime.

It does seem that the false teaching and false teachers encountered in all three of the Pastoral Epistles are of the

---

[16]Donald Carson, Douglas Moo, and Leon Morris, *An Introduction to the New Testament* (Grand Rapids: Zondervan, 1992), p. 364.

[17]B.S. Easton, *The Pastoral Epistles* (New York), pp. 2-3.

[18]See especially 1 Tim 1:7; Titus 1:10, 14; 3:9. When seen in this light, 1 Tim 1:4 and 6 seem less Gnostic. Indeed the heresy or heresies one meets in the PE bear resemblance to later Gnosticism but may be no more than what has been termed "incipient gnosticism."

same sort. They have similar tendencies and use similar language even though every element seen in one book may not appear in the other. One must simply piece together the elements that compose this heresy: emphasis on myths and genealogies (1 Tim 1:4; Titus 1:14; 3:9; 2 Tim 4:4); concern for the Law and Jewishness (1 Tim 1:7; Titus 1:10, 14; 3:9); emphasis on "knowledge" (1 Tim 6:20; 2 Tim 3:6-9); controversy, speculation and arguments (1 Tim 1:4, 6; 6:4, 20; Titus 1:10; 3:9; 2 Tim 2:14, 16, 23; 3:1-5); immorality (1 Tim 1:19, 20; Titus 1:15, 16; 2 Tim 2:16, 19; 3:1-5); deception (1 Tim 4:1-3; Titus 1:10-13; 2 Tim 3:6-13); some ascetic practices (1 Tim 4:1-5); and teaching for material gain (1 Tim 6:5; Titus 1:11; 2 Tim 3:2-4).

Vocabulary and Style. As Guthrie has noted, "the majority of those who favor the non-Pauline authorship of the Epistles are swayed more by linguistic considerations than by any of the objections mentioned above."[19] Perhaps no scholar has presented this argument for non-Pauline authorship in stronger fashion than P.N. Harrison. Harrison built upon the work of previous scholars to argue that the vocabulary and style of the Pastoral Epistles indicated that they did not share the same author as the ten epistles generally accepted as Pauline.

Harrison noted that well over one third of the words, excluding proper names, used in the Pastoral Epistles occur nowhere else in the New Testament. Many of the words used in the Pastoral Epistles and the universally accepted Pauline epistles have different meanings. Many of the words used only in the Pastoral Epistles are found in the early church fathers and in the apologists.[20] On the surface Harrison's arguments seem most convincing; however, Carson, Moo, and Morris have noted that one could use the same line of

---

[19]Donald Guthrie, *New Testament Introduction*, 3rd ed., (Downers Grove, IL: InterVarsity, 1970), p. 209.
[20]P.N. Harrison, *The Problem of the Pastoral Epistles* (London: Oxford University Press, 1921), pp. 20ff.

argument to suggest that the three Pastoral Epistles were themselves written by different authors.[21]

In examining the style of the Pastoral Epistles, Harrison gives special emphasis to particles, prepositions, and pronouns — elements that are indicative of style which an imitator might not follow. After noting a drastic difference in usage, he concludes that it is unlikely that "within a very few years we should find the same writer producing three epistles without once happening to use a single word in all that list — *one or the other of which has hitherto appeared on the average nine times to every page that Paul wrote.*"[22] Guthrie, however, has noted that Harrison's data is selective and "would seem to be invalid."[23]

One must allow any author to use differing vocabulary and styles which would fit a differing situation, audience, purpose, and time frame. Arguments offered thus far on the basis of vocabulary and style neither prove nor disprove Pauline authorship of the Pastoral Epistles.

The Theology of the Pastoral Epistles. It has been argued that the theology of the Pastoral Epistles is not that of Paul: the cross is no longer the center of theology, and there is undue emphasis on works. This argument fails to take into consideration the whole of the teaching, both in the ten epistles generally accepted as Pauline and in the Pastoral Epistles as a whole. Hendriksen has rightly noted, "The truth is that the doctrine taught and presupposed in the Pastorals is clearly the same as that which is held before us in the ten [Pauline epistles]."[24] Hendriksen goes on to list nine theological concepts, including salvation by grace through faith, which are central to the ten epistles generally accepted as Pauline and

---

[21]Carson, Moo, and Morris, p. 361.

[22]Harrison, *Problem*, p. 35 (italics in Harrison's work).

[23]Donald Guthrie, *The Pastoral Epistles and the Mind of Paul* (London, 1956), p. 13.

[24]William Hendriksen, *Thessalonians, Timothy and Titus*, New Testament Commentary (Grand Rapids: Baker, 1979), p. 17.

then delineates their occurrence in the Pastoral Epistles.[25]

Modern Solutions to These Issues. Several solutions have been offered to these apparent inconsistencies by serious critics. Some have suggested one must simply opt for non-apostolic authorship. Others, like Harrison (1921), Scott (1936), and Easton (1948), have suggested non-Pauline authorship for the documents as a whole while allowing for a few genuine Pauline fragments.

A central issue in the discussion is the attitude of the early church toward the pseudepigrapher. Carson, Moo, and Morris have noted that the contention that pseudonymous epistles circulated freely and were widely accepted by early Christians cannot be supported.[26] Tertullian spoke of a church leader who composed writings which wrongly bore the name of Paul. Even though this was done out of love, the man was dismissed from his office.[27] Similarly, the Muratorian Canon says that forgeries in Paul's name were to be rejected. As Carson, Moo, and Morris have noted, "Nowhere is evidence cited that any member of the New Testament church accepted the idea that a pious believer could write something in the name of an apostle and expect the writing to be welcomed."[28] Indeed discussion of canonicity tended to focus on the issue of authorship.

The traditional position of Pauline authorship of the Pastoral Epistles fits the data. One who deems these works to be authentic Pauline epistles is not without support from a good number of excellent scholars (cf. Carson, Fee, Guthrie, Hendriksen, Johnson, Moo, and Morris). When one accepts Pauline authorship, the issues of language and style remain.

---

[25]Hendriksen, p. 18.
[26]Carson, Moo, Morris, p. 367. For a thorough discussion of this issue see pages 267-371 of their work and Thomas D. Lea and Hayne P. Griffin, *1, 2 Timothy, Titus*, The New American Commentary, vol. 34 (Nashville: Broadman, 1992), pp. 37-38.
[27]Tertullian, *On Baptism*, 17.
[28]Ibid., 380.

They are still more like Paul than different from Paul. Is the change due simply to subject? Can it be an aging Paul? Should one see an amanuensis as the one responsible for the differences? The final words of Fee on the issue of authorship of the Pastoral Epistles are worth repeating:

> To say that Paul is the author of the Pastoral Epistles means that the letters ultimately come from him in the historical settings contained within them. It does not say how they came from him; the final answer to that question is not available to us.[29]

---

[29]Fee, *1, 2 Timothy, Titus*, p. 26.

THE BOOK OF
1 TIMOTHY

INTRODUCTION

PLACE OF ORIGIN AND DATE

Little can be said with certainty of Paul's location when he penned 1 Timothy.[1] Although Paul does not say explicitly that he was in Macedonia, he appears to indicate that he had been in Ephesus with Timothy, had left Timothy behind, and had gone on to Macedonia: "As I urged you when I went into Macedonia, stay there in Ephesus" (1:3).

If Paul was released from "house arrest" in Rome as the data in Acts 28:30 and the prison epistles might suggest and wrote this epistle at a subsequent time, the date for 1 Timothy would likely be 63-66. A chronology of Paul's life from Acts would indicate his imprisonment lasted until 61/62. The Neronian persecution of 64 would indicate that his release should precede that date. Eusebius recorded that Paul died in 67. If one accepts those dates, Paul would have penned 1 Timothy between 63 and 66.

Other suggestions are given by those who would contend that Paul died at the height of the Neronian persecution of 64. Some would, therefore, provide a date of 62-63 for composition of 1 Timothy. Robinson has suggested Paul's departure for Macedonia, leaving behind Timothy in Ephesus (1:3), reflects the situation seen in Acts 20:1-4. He, therefore, places 1 Timothy within the historical data of Acts and suggests a date of 55.[2] Scholars who argue for pseudonymity

---

[1] The discussion of the epistles in this commentary will follow a basic chronological arrangement — 1 Timothy, Titus, 2 Timothy.
[2] Robinson, *Redating*, pp. 82-83.

generally date the epistle during the second century (cf. Kümmel).

A date of 63–66 seems best to fit the data currently available.

DESTINATION AND AUDIENCE

Although on the surface 1 Timothy seems to be personal correspondence between Paul and Timothy, his son in the faith, there is much in the epistle that indicates Paul intended the letter to be read and heeded by the congregation at Ephesus. "Grace be with you" in 6:21 is plural. Many of Paul's admonitions to Timothy (e.g., "Don't let anyone look down on you because you are young," 4:21) may also have served to advise the church of their correct path of action.

Timothy is well known from Acts and the epistles of Paul. He was a native of Lystra; his mother was Jewish and his father a Gentile. About A.D. 49 he became a co-worker of Paul. As a young man likely converted and trained by Paul, Paul found a special place in his heart for him (1 Cor 4:17; Phil 2:22; 1 Tim 1:2). Timothy appears alongside Paul in the opening greetings of several epistles (2 Cor 1:1; Phil 1:1; Col 1:1; 1 Thess 1:1; 2 Thess 1:1). He was undoubtedly considered a trusted colleague and co-worker (1 Thess 3:2) who could be trusted to be sent on special missions (1 Cor 16:10; Phil 2:20). If one accepts the traditional site for the place of writing of the prison epistles, Timothy was with Paul in Rome (Col 1:1; Phlm 1). He has, at this juncture, been left behind in Ephesus to set things in order. He is a young man (see the discussion of 1 Tim 4:12) who was perhaps not in the best of health (1 Tim 5:23).

The church where Timothy was laboring found itself in the midst of the fourth largest city in the Roman Empire. Ephesus housed a famous shrine to Artemis, the great mother goddess, known by the Romans as Diana of the Ephesians. Upon arriving at Ephesus Paul met a group of disciples whose knowledge of the gospel was so incomplete that it would seem they were still looking for the Messiah and they clearly knew nothing of the Holy Spirit (Acts 19:1-7). Paul's next encounter was with a group of Jews, the seven sons of Sceva, a Jewish chief priest. These men were seeking to do exorcisms in the name of Jesus (Acts 19:8-16). The citizens of Ephesus were so impressed with what happened to these men and with the preaching of Paul that many came to belief. Some who had previously practiced sorcery even burned their books (Acts 19:17-20). During this stay Timothy worked with Paul at Ephesus before being sent by Paul on to Macedonia (Acts 19:21-22). Feeling the pinch of their pocketbooks, the silversmiths, who made their livelihood selling images of Artemis, instigated a riot that led to Paul's moving on to other fields (Acts 19:23-20:1). Paul's love and concern for the Ephesian church did not end there. As Paul headed along the coast of Asia Minor on his way to Jerusalem, he summoned the elders from that church to meet him at Miletus. Paul warns them of the impending dangers, especially the false teachers, and charges them to watch after the flock (Acts 20:13-38). These dangers facing the church are a recurrent theme whenever the church at Ephesus is mentioned (1 Cor 16:8-9; Eph 4:14, 17-24; 5:6-14; Rev 2:6). The nature of Paul's correspondence with Timothy in the two epistles addressed to him follows this same theme.

THE CONTRIBUTION OF 1 TIMOTHY

Perhaps the greatest contribution 1 Timothy makes is the insight it provides into Paul's view of ministry: his own, that of Timothy, and that of the church (elders/bishops, deacons, women, and believers called to godliness). The church today needs to heed that call to ministry and godliness. Paul's emphasis on prayer (2:8), the demeanor of women in worship (2:9-15), the relationships between the old and the young (5:1-2), the treatment of widows (5:3-16), the response of slaves to their masters and ultimately to the Lord (6:1-2), and the warning against arrogance and trusting in wealth (6:17-19) produce a book rich in wisdom for the believer.

Paul does warn of needless controversies which do not produce growth. While the "godless myths" (1:4), forbidding of marriage, and enforcing of food laws (4:3) may seem far removed from the issues facing the church today, it is not immune from "an unhealthy interest in controversies and arguments that result in envy, quarreling, malicious talk, evil suspicions and constant friction" (6:4-5). Similarly the modern church should give heed to Paul's warning against those "who think that godliness is a means to financial gain" (6:5).

OUTLINE

I. THE SALUTATION — 1:1-2
II. PAUL'S CHARGE TO TIMOTHY — 1:3-20
    A. The Charge and the False Teachers — 1:3-7
    B. The Lawful Use of the Law — 1:8-11
    C. Paul's Own Ministry, A Positive Example — 1:12-17
    D. The Negative Example of Hymenaeus and Alexander — 1:18-20
III. DIRECTION FOR PUBLIC WORSHIP — 2:1-15
    A. Prayers by All for All — 2:1-7
    B. Respective Roles of Men and Women — 2:8-15
IV. DIRECTIONS FOR CHURCH LEADERS — 3:1-16
    A. Qualifications of Bishops/Overseers — 3:1-7
    B. Qualifications of Deacons and "Women" — 3:8-13
    C. The Basis for These Directions — 3:14-16
V. SPECIAL INSTRUCTIONS FOR TIMOTHY — 4:1-16
    A. The Apostasy Timothy Was to Face — 4:1-5
    B. The Discipline of a Good Minister — 4:6-16
VI. RELATIONSHIPS WITHIN THE CHRISTIAN COMMUNITY — 5:1-6:2
    A. The Minister and the Church — 5:1-2
    B. The Care of Widows — 5:3-16
        1. Family Responsibilities — 5:3-8
        2. Widows to Be Enrolled — 5:9-10
        3. Younger Widows — 5:11-15
        4. Women and Widows — 5:16
    C. Elders — 5:17-25
    D. Slaves — 6:1-2

VII. FINAL EXHORTATIONS — 6:3-21
   A. An Indictment of False Teachers — 6:3-5
   B. Godliness, Contentment, and Money — 6:6-10
   C. A Charge to Timothy — 6:11-16
   D. Instructions for the Rich — 6:17-19
   E. Paul's Final Charge to Timothy — 6:20-21

1 TIMOTHY 1

I. THE SALUTATION (1:1-2)

¹**Paul, an apostle of Christ Jesus by the command of God our Savior and of Christ Jesus our hope, ²To Timothy my true son in the faith:**

Grace, mercy and peace from God the Father and Christ Jesus our Lord.

1:1 Paul, an apostle of Christ Jesus

Paul follows the normal pattern of the Hellenistic letter by first introducing himself as the author and then moving to address his audience. In 1 Timothy Paul calls himself an "apostle," a designation that is common in letters where his authority is in question or where he wishes to give added weight to his exhortations (1 Corinthians, 2 Corinthians, Galatians, Ephesians, Colossians). On other occasions he will indicate his work as "servant" (Philippians) or "prisoner" (Philemon). It may on the surface seem strange that Paul will use such a designation to write to his "true son in the faith." That designation takes on special meaning, however, when one remembers that 1 Timothy was written to be read not only by Timothy but also by the entire church at Ephesus, a church facing false teachers who would likely have emphasized their authority.

by the command of God our Savior and of Christ Jesus our hope,

Paul notes that his authority was not self-acquired but rather came "by the command of God." Ordinarily Paul will indicate that he is an apostle "by the will of God" (2 Tim 1:1).

One cannot help but wonder whether Paul is preparing Timothy for the charge or command to instruct the church to live as Christians ought by indicating that he himself has been issued a command by God.

The source of this command is "God our Savior and Christ." God is frequently referred to as "Savior" in the OT, indicating that he is the powerful deliverer. In the Roman world the term "savior" (σωτήρ, *sōtēr*) was applied to the emperor in the emperor cult, in particular to Nero. Outside the Pastoral Epistles Paul never uses the term "savior" to refer to God the Father, rather reserving the term to describe the work of Jesus. In the Pastoral Epistles both God the Father (1 Tim 1:1; 2:3; 4:10; Titus 1:3; 2:10; 3:4) and Jesus Christ the Son (Titus 1:4; 2:13; 3:6; 2 Tim 1:10) are designated "savior." Although Paul does not use the word savior to describe the Father in his other epistles, he still does designate the work of the Father as providing salvation for believers (1 Cor 1:21; 1 Thess 5:9).

Jesus is the source of the Christian's hope. Hope is not merely wishful thinking but indicates the desire of one who is earnestly expecting something. Here there is an eschatological note of the completion of the salvation that is offered through Jesus when he returns.

1:2 To Timothy my true son in the faith:

Paul both indicates the closeness of his relationship with Timothy and points to Timothy's authority by declaring him to be his "true son in the faith." He is Paul's "true," i.e., "legitimate" son. Knight has suggested three options for understanding the father-son relationship between Paul and Timothy: (1) Timothy may well have received the gospel through the preaching of Paul; (2) Paul may be describing his nurturing relationship with Timothy; he is an adopted son; or (3) Paul is simply indicating that he is older than Timothy both in physical years and in the faith. Knight is probably correct in concluding that Paul's primary emphasis is (1), but (2) and (3) may be included as well.[1]

---

[1] George W. Knight, III, *Commentary on the Pastoral Epistles*, New International Greek Testament Commentary (Grand Rapids: Eerdmans, 1992), pp. 63-64.

Not only is Paul encouraging Timothy with these words but perhaps also ensuring his positive reception by the church at Ephesus. Note that Timothy is Paul's son "in the faith." Is Paul referring to Timothy's faith in Christ which has produced this unique relationship, to his faithfulness to Christ as the sphere in which the relationship exists, or to the cause or belief system for which he and Paul labor? The middle option seems best to describe Paul's intent.

Grace, mercy and peace from God the Father and Christ Jesus our Lord.
The threefold salutation of Paul, "grace, mercy and peace," is used by Paul only here and in 2 Tim 1:2 (cf. 2 John 3; Jude 2). Paul's normal greeting is simply "grace and peace." "Grace" (χάρις, *charis*) represents the noun form of the Greek verb normally used in a greeting.[2] It indicates the unmerited goodness of God. "Mercy" (ἔλεος, *eleos*) is God's help to the discouraged, the down-and-out. The verb form appears in 1 Tim 1:13, 16 where the plight of sinners and their need for divine favor is the focus. "Peace" (εἰρήνη, *eirēnē*) represents the normal greeting among Jews, שׁלם (*shalom*) in Hebrew. The term refers not to absence of warfare, but to the wholeness of the relationship between a person and God.

II. PAUL'S CHARGE TO TIMOTHY (1:3-20)

A. THE CHARGE AND THE FALSE TEACHERS (1:3-7)

³As I urged you when I went into Macedonia, stay there in Ephesus so that you may command certain men not to teach false doctrines any longer ⁴nor to devote themselves to myths and endless genealogies. These promote controversies rather than God's work — which is by faith. ⁵The goal of this command is love, which comes from a pure heart and a good conscience and a sincere faith.

---

[2] The normal Greek greeting would be χαίρειν (*chairein*), "to rejoice."

⁶Some have wandered away from these and turned to meaningless talk. ⁷They want to be teachers of the law, but they do not know what they are talking about or what they so confidently affirm.

Paul's primary concern in the remainder of this section is that "certain men" be instructed "not to teach false doctrines." He reminds Timothy of the real message of the gospel and warns against these false teachers' abuse of the law. Timothy must fight on and not follow the bad example of Hymenaeus and Alexander, whom Paul will mention in v. 20.

1:3 As I urged you when I went into Macedonia,

The NIV translation of vv. 3-4 conceals the fact that the Greek text is a bit awkward. The text begins with "as," with no conclusion to the sentence: "As I urged you, journeying into Macedonia to stay . . . to command certain people not to teach. . . ." The KJV completes Paul's thought with "so do." Paul had previously warned the Ephesian elders about the coming of false teachers (Acts 20:29-30). That heresy has now arisen, and Paul instructs Timothy how he is to deal with it.

stay there in Ephesus

Paul's apparent ministry at Ephesus after being released from imprisonment at the end of Acts provides an interesting postscript to his telling the Ephesian elders that he would not see them again in Acts 20. It would seem that he does indeed see them and work with them. Timothy has stayed on at Ephesus at Paul's urging. This may indicate some reluctance on Timothy's part to stay on rather than travel with Paul. It may also be Paul's way of indicating to the Ephesian church that Timothy is acting on his behalf with his authority.

so that you may command certain men not to teach false doctrines any longer

The word "command"[3] is a very strong word. When fol-

---

[3] The Greek word is παραγγέλλω (*parangellō*), a military term used for the passing on of orders.

lowed by the word "not" and an infinitive, it carries the idea "forbid." Timothy is thus to forbid these people from teaching falsehood and devoting themselves to "myths and endless genealogies." The false teachers are spreading their falsehoods and spending their time in speculations that are both irrelevant and contrary to the gospel.

1:4 nor to devote themselves to myths and endless genealogies.

Many scholars have argued that the "endless genealogies" refer to the second century Gnostic emanations that proceed like a progression of ripples from the one true God. One need not propose such a drastic solution. Such speculative exploration of genealogies and myths can clearly be seen in Judaism.[4] The occurrence of the same word "myths" (μύθοι, *mythoi*) in Titus 1:14 with the clarifying adjective "Jewish" supports this conclusion. The term "myths" also appears in 1 Tim 4:7 where Paul terms them "old wives' tales." Myths are seen as enticing and attractive snares which would lure hearers from the truth. In Titus 3:9 Paul reflects on genealogies that are "unprofitable and useless."

These promote controversies rather than God's work — which is by faith.

All of this speculation was bound to promote "controversies rather than God's work — which is by faith." The phrase "God's work" (οἰκονομία, *oikonomia*) refers to the stewardship of another's property, here God's.[5] The work of God which had been entrusted to believers, his plan for redeeming his people, was being perverted by this heresy. In a manner that is characteristic of Paul, he informs his readers that God's work is accomplished through faith.

---

[4]See Philo, *Biblical Antiquities*; the apocryphal work, *Jubilees* (e.g., the story of Abraham in 11.18-24); and writings from the Qumran community (e.g., 1QS 3:13-15).
[5]Cf. Luke 16:2; Eph 3:2, 9.

1:5 The goal of this command is love, which comes from a pure heart and a good conscience and a sincere faith.

The goal of Timothy's "command" (παραγγελία, *parangelia*) is love, a quality which is not likely to be found among the false teachers. This love issues from (1) a pure heart, (2) a good conscience, and (3) a sincere faith. From a biblical perspective the heart is the seat of the will. A "pure heart" is then the conscience which wills to do what is right and noble. For Paul the "conscience" is the inner awareness of moral right and wrong (Rom 13:5; 1 Cor 8:10). Since the conscience can become calloused and marred (1 Tim 4:2; Titus 1:15), the Christian must so live within the will of God that his conscience is trained (1 Cor 8:7-12). "Sincere faith" refers to a genuine faith. In fact the Greek word behind "sincere" (ἀνυπόκριτος, *anypokritos*) could well be rendered "unhypocritical."

1:6 Some have wandered away from these and turned to meaningless talk.

The "some" of v. 6 were the same persons as the "certain men" of v. 3. The false teachers have wandered away from the pure heart, good conscience, and sincere faith of v. 5. "Wandered away" comes from a Greek word (ἀστοχέω, *astocheō*) which means "to miss the mark" or "to go beyond the goal." The false teachers have missed the mark set for them by a pure heart, a good conscience, and a sincere faith. Instead they have turned to meaningless talk. "Meaningless talk" (ματαιολογία, *mataiologia*) represents a single word in the original which could literally be rendered "empty or useless discourse." All of the talk of the false teachers leads nowhere. It may draw some followers, but it does not produce the godly life.

1:7 They want to be teachers of the law, but they do not know what they are talking about or what they so confidently affirm.

These false teachers want to be known as "teachers of the law." Like many of the Jewish rabbis of the day, they suggest extravagant interpretations of the Old Testament stories and laws pretending to be scholars. These men have no real grasp of the intent of the sacred Scriptures and little concern with regard to the gospel's implications for Christian living. Here one can see the Jewish character of the false teaching at Ephesus. Like some modern day preachers these men may hide the gospel with senseless minutiae.

B. THE LAWFUL USE OF THE LAW (1:8-11)

⁸We know that the law is good if one uses it properly. ⁹We also know that law[a] is made not for the righteous but for lawbreakers and rebels, the ungodly and sinful, the unholy and irreligious; for those who kill their fathers or mothers, for murderers, ¹⁰for adulterers and perverts, for slave traders and liars and perjurers — and for whatever else is contrary to the sound doctrine ¹¹that conforms to the glorious gospel of the blessed God, which he entrusted to me.

[a]9 Or *that the law*

1:8 We know that the law is good

Paul does not want his readers to misunderstand his last statement about the false teachers and their relationship with the law.[6] The law is "good" (καλος, *kalos*) because it reflects the will of God. The difficulty is not in the law but in the false teachers' ignorance of its intent and their misuse of it. "Ignorance" and "mindlessness" are recurring descriptions of the false teachers in the Pastoral Epistles (1 Tim 6:4, 20; Titus 1:15; 3:9; 2 Tim 2:23). The law (Paul is here using that term in a much broader sense than the Ten Commandments or law of Moses) is itself an honorable and valuable resource for the Christian. Paul himself uses adjectives like "holy," "spiritual,"

---

[6]To what is Paul referring when he uses "law" (νόμος, *nomos*)? Several factors in the text itself point to the Mosaic Law when that term is allowed to include all of the Old Testament: (1) the use of "teachers of the law;" (2) the ethical demands of vv. 9-10 which parallel the Decalogue; (3) parallel passages elsewhere in Paul (cf. Rom 3:19ff; 7-8; 13:9ff; Gal 3-4; Phil 3:7ff).

"just," and "good" to describe it (Rom 7:12-14; cf. Gal 3:23-26 for Paul's understanding of its value).

if one uses it properly.
Proper use of the law was to make it clear that actions or sins like those in vv. 9-10 were wrong. The adverb "properly" (νομίμως, *nomimōs*, sometimes literally rendered "lawfully"[7]) appears only here and in 2 Tim 2:5. God intended that the law bring human beings to a consciousness of sin (Rom 5:12; 6:23; 7:11, 13).

1:9 We also know that law is made not for the righteous but for lawbreakers and rebels, the ungodly and sinful, the unholy and irreligious;
The purpose of law is the restraint of evil-doing. The purpose of the law is to be seen not in what it does to or for the "righteous," but rather in relation to those who practice evil. Paul begins his vice list by using three pairs of adjectives which describe these sinful people in terms of their relationship with God and may well be seen as paralleling the earlier section of the Decalogue:[8] "lawbreakers and rebels" (those who willfully break the law and rebel against it); "the ungodly and sinful" (those whose disobedient lifestyle indicates that God has no place in their lives); and "the unholy and irreligious" (those who have no sense of the sacred).

for those who kill their fathers or mothers, for murderers, 1:10 for adulterers and perverts, for slave traders and liars and perjurers
As Fee has noted, Paul's catalogue of vices bears a striking resemblance to the Ten Commandments (the fifth commandment through the ninth).[9] These lawless people are "those who kill their fathers or mothers," a very gruesome way to

---

[7]Paul's use of law (*nomos*) and lawfully (*nomimōs*) provide a word play which is difficult to duplicate in English. This word play is the reason for the heading for this section, "Lawful Use of the Law."
[8]Knight, pp. 83-84.
[9]Fee, pp. 45-46.

break the fifth commandment (Exod 20:12; cf. Exod 21:15); "murderers" (literally "man-slayers," i.e., those who break the sixth commandment; cf. Exod 21:13); "adulterers" (literally "the sexually immoral") and "perverts" ("homosexuals"[10]), both groups would break commandment seven (Exod 21:14); "slave traders" (literally "those who catch a man by the foot"), perhaps not too far a stretch to be seen as breakers of the eighth commandment (Exod 21:15); and "liars and perjurers," those who bear false witness and break the ninth commandment (Exod 21:16). The order of these vices is hardly accidental. Paul is demonstrating that God gave the law, not for idle speculation and meaningless talk, but to prohibit sin.

— and for whatever else is contrary to the sound doctrine

Paul completes his list with a phrase designed to cover all the bases: "and for whatever else is contrary to the sound doctrine."[11] A final summation of this sort is quite common for Paul (Rom 13:9; Gal 5:21). The term "sound doctrine" will appear regularly in the Pastoral Epistles (1 Tim 1:10; 6:3; Titus 1:9, 13; 2:2, 8). Literally, the phrase (ὑγιαινούσῃ διδασκαλίᾳ, *hygiainousē didaskalia*; cf. the English word "hygiene") might be translated "healthy teaching." This metaphor provides a clear contrast with the sick, "unhealthy interest" or craving of the false teachers in 6:4 and the teaching of these folks which "will spread like gangrene" in 2 Tim 2:17. Knight suggests that his metaphorical use of medical language may be the result of Paul's association with Luke the physician.[12] While this may be true, it is also possible that Paul is simply using a common figure of speech.

---

[10]While the root of the word is "male-sex" the term does not refer exclusively as some have suggested either to male homosexuality or sexual activity with boys. It simply refers to homosexuality in general. Such activity is for Paul sin (Rom 1:26, 27; 1 Cor 6:9-11). Cf. D.F. Wright, "Homosexuals or Prostitutes? The Meaning of *ARSENOKOITAI* (1 Cor 6:9; 1 Tim 1:10)," *Vigilae Christianae* 38 (1984), 125-153.

[11]This could be the intent of the tenth commandment as well, a final summation of the attitude behind the breaking of the other commandments.

[12]Knight, p. 89.

1:11 that conforms to the glorious gospel of the blessed God,

This sound doctrine is teaching which "conforms to the glorious gospel of the blessed God." The original reads literally "to the gospel of the glory of the blessed God," providing the translator with two alternatives: 1) a descriptive genitive, "the glorious gospel"; or 2) a genitive of content, "the gospel which is the manifestation of God's glory." The differences between the two choices are minimal. The gospel is glorious because it manifests the glory of God. "Blessed" (μακάριος, *makarios*) is used of God only here and in 6:15 although it is frequently used in such a fashion by Philo. Paul probably intends to indicate that "blessedness" rests in and comes from God.

which he entrusted to me.

Paul concludes this section by noting that God had "entrusted" (πιστεύω, *pisteuō*) him with the gospel and the doctrine. His use of this verb indicates that God had faith in him and that the gospel was a trust given to his care (cf. Rom 3:2; 1 Cor 9:17; Gal 2:4; 1 Thess 2:4; 1 Tim 2:7; 2 Tim 1:11; 2:9; Titus 1:3).

C. PAUL'S OWN MINISTRY, A POSITIVE EXAMPLE (1:12-17)

[12]I thank Christ Jesus our Lord, who has given me strength, that he considered me faithful, appointing me to his service. [13]Even though I was once a blasphemer and a persecutor and a violent man, I was shown mercy because I acted in ignorance and unbelief. [14]The grace of our Lord was poured out on me abundantly, along with the faith and love that are in Christ Jesus.

[15]Here is a trustworthy saying that deserves full acceptance: Christ Jesus came into the world to save sinners — of whom I am the worst. [16]But for that very reason I was shown mercy so that in me, the worst of sinners, Christ Jesus might

display his unlimited patience as an example for those who would believe on him and receive eternal life. ¹⁷Now to the King eternal, immortal, invisible, the only God, be honor and glory for ever and ever. Amen.

1:12 I thank Christ Jesus our Lord, who has given me strength, that he considered me faithful, appointing me to his service.

Paul now expands on the personal reference of the last phrase of verse 11, expressing his gratitude to Jesus who empowered him ("given strength," ἐνδύναμαι, *endynamai*), deeming him trustworthy ("faithful," πιστός, *pistos*) and "appointing [him] to his service" ("ministry," διακονία, *diakonia*).

1:13 Even though I was once a blasphemer and a persecutor and a violent man,

Paul notes that God could well have looked at his former life and denied him such a privilege. After all he was "once a blasphemer" (having denied what God had done and said in Jesus) and "a persecutor" (Acts 22:4, 7; 26:11) and a "violent man" (one who acted as an insolent bully, a thoroughly objectionable fellow with outrageous disregard of other men's rights, cf. Acts 9:1, 2; 22:4, 5, 19, 20; 26:10, 11; Gal 1:13).

I was shown mercy because I acted in ignorance and unbelief.

But God had shown him mercy. Paul sees the reason for this mercy in the fact that he "acted in ignorance and unbelief," not that he merits the mercy, but that he was not acting in defiance. Here Paul is not minimizing the significance of his sin, but rather indicating something of its nature. His sin was not one that was "presumptuous" or "defiant" (Num 15:22-31).

1:14 The grace of our Lord was poured out on me abundantly, along with the faith and love that are in Christ Jesus.

While many would question the authorship of this book, the theology of this passage is thoroughly Pauline. Grace had been "poured out abundantly" upon Paul; that grace then stimulated his own faith and love. God's actions are always prior to man's. It is noteworthy that faith and love are located "in Christ Jesus."

1:15 Here is a trustworthy saying that deserves full acceptance:

In verse 15 Paul elaborates upon the grace God had shown him in Christ Jesus. This passage is the first of five sections in the Pastoral Epistles that contain the term "trustworthy saying" (1 Tim 1:15; 3:1; 4:9; Titus 3:8; 2 Tim 2:11).[13] Two of the passages contain the additional affirmation that the saying "deserves full acceptance" (this verse and 1 Tim 4:9).[14] Three issues arise when the formula appears: 1) Does the formula follow or precede the trustworthy saying? Here the formula obviously precedes the saying; in 4:9 it follows the saying; scholars debate the order in 3:1. 2) What portion of the verse or verses in question contain the trustworthy saying? 3) Just what is the meaning of the formula?[15]

Christ Jesus came into the world to save sinners

The saying which appears here — "Christ Jesus came into the world to save sinners" — emphasizes both the incarnation and the redemptive work of Christ; Christ came and he came to save. The origin of the saying has been much debated. It

---

[13]For a full discussion of the "faithful sayings," see George W. Knight III, *The Faithful Sayings of the Pastoral Letters* (Kampen, 1968; reprinted Grand Rapids, 1979).

[14]The phrase "full acceptance" could also be rendered "accepted by all." Fee rightly argues that context would suggest the emphasis is being placed on the saying's being "worthy of universal acceptance." Fee, p. 53.

[15]For a further discussion of these questions see Thomas D. Lea and Hayne P. Griffin, *1, 2 Timothy, Titus*, The New American Commentary (Nashville: Broadman Press, 1992), p. 75. Ellis has argued that this formula may be traced to Qumran and to Paul's experience with Qumran converts while imprisoned in Caesarea. E.E. Ellis, "Traditions in the Pastoral Epistles," *Early Jewish and Christian Exegesis: in Memory of William Hugh Brownlee*, ed. C. Stephens and W.F. Stinespring (Atlanta: Scholars Press, 1987), pp. 239-242. Fee feels that the source of the formulae in the PE is probably Paul's own common formula, "faithful is God" (1 Cor 1:9; 10:13; 2 Cor 1:18). Fee, p. 52.

seems likely that Paul is simply citing something that these Christians have frequently heard preached and perhaps have themselves recited or sung.

— of whom I am the worst.
The simple mention of the word "sinners" causes Paul once again to reflect upon his own life. The term "worst" is literally "first" (πρῶτος, *prōtos*). The term refers not to the sequence of Paul's sin or conversion but to its magnitude. This may well seem to be an exaggeration to the reader, but for Paul it is no exaggeration (1 Cor 15:9, 10; Gal 1:13; Eph 3:8). As Lea and Griffin put it, "[Paul] never got beyond a response of wonder and gratitude to God's act of saving him 'warts and all.' We must never move beyond the excitement and joy our conversion generates in us."[16]

1:16 But for that very reason I was shown mercy so that in me, the worst of sinners, Christ Jesus might display his unlimited patience as an example for those who would believe on him and receive eternal life.

In v. 16 Paul repeats the fact that he "was shown mercy" (v. 13) and his evaluation of his own sinfulness as "worst of sinners" (v. 15), but this time he gives reason that God had "shown mercy" on terrible sinner Paul. Christ Jesus was clearly demonstrating "his unlimited patience" (literally "the all longsuffering," τὴν ἅπασαν μακροθυμίαν, *tēn hapasan makrothymian*) to Paul which serves as an "example" of that patience for all believers. Paul is contending that, if God can be patient with him and show mercy to him, any believer should have confidence that he too can be forgiven and "receive eternal life."

1:17 Now to the King eternal, immortal, invisible, the only God, be honor and glory for ever and ever. Amen.

The fact that God has shown mercy on him and that same mercy is available to all "those who would believe in him"

---

[16]Lea and Griffin, p. 82.

leads Paul to break into a doxology. Such a reflection on the grace of God is not unusual in Paul's letters (cf. Rom 1:25; 9:5; 11:36; Gal 1:5; Eph 3:21; Phil 4:20; 1 Tim 6:17).

He begins by designating God as "the King eternal." This phrase (ὁ βασιλεὺς τῶν αἰώνων, *ho basileus tōn aiōnōn*) may mean either "eternal king" (NASB, NIV) or "king of the ages" (RSV, NEB, NRSV). Perhaps one should not be too concerned about the difference since the king over all ages differs little from the eternal king.

Paul continues by describing God as "immortal" (literally "incorruptible"), "invisible" (cf. Rom 1:20; Col 1:15), and "the only God" (cf. this theme throughout the OT, especially Deut 6:4). On account of God's nature all "honor and glory" are due him "for ever and ever." The "amen," common as the sign of assent to a prayer or proclamation in the synagogue and in the early church, serves as the conclusion of this doxology (cf. Rom 1:25; 9:5; 11:36; 16:27; Gal 3:21; Eph 3:21; Phil 4:20; 1 Tim 6:17).

The doxology concludes the digression on Paul's ministry and God's grace begun at v. 12. Paul is now ready to return to instructions for Timothy regarding the false teachers and his ministry.

D. THE NEGATIVE EXAMPLE OF HYMENAEUS AND ALEXANDER (1:18–20)

[18]Timothy, my son, I give you this instruction in keeping with the prophecies once made about you, so that by following them you may fight the good fight, [19]holding on to faith and a good conscience. Some have rejected these and so have shipwrecked their faith. [20]Among them are Hymenaeus and Alexander, whom I have handed over to Satan to be taught not to blaspheme.

1:18 Timothy, my son, I give you this instruction
Vv. 18–20 return to the discussion of vv. 3–7. This is even

clearer in Greek than in English. The word translated "instruction" (παραγγελία, *parangelia*) in v. 18 also appeared in vv. 3 and 5 where it was translated "command" in the NIV. The material in this section is not mere repetition. Paul is concerned that Timothy endure whatever hardship may come his way and thus fulfill his ministry. Paul uses examples of two failed ministers and their ministries to drive home his message.

in keeping with the prophecies once made about you,

Paul's instructions to Timothy are not merely his whim; they are "in keeping with the prophecies once made" about him. Paul will later refer to Timothy's "spiritual gift" (likely his ministry, 4:14) which was accompanied by a "prophetic message" from the elders and by the laying on of hands.[17] It seems likely that Timothy's Spirit-bestowed gift was his ministry, something recognized through some prophecy when Timothy was originally designated to assist Paul in his missionary work. This is consistent with the Spirit's designation of Barnabas and Saul in Acts 13:1-3.

so that by following them you may fight the good fight,

By means of these prophecies Timothy is to "fight the good fight."[18] The battle against Satan and heterodoxy is a genuine one. Paul's description of the "fight" (στρατεία, *strateia*) is a term filled with the military imagery of strategy, tactics, and preparation for an all-out battle.

1:19 holding on to faith and a good conscience. Some have rejected these and so have shipwrecked their faith.

In fighting the good fight Timothy must hold on to or keep faith and a good conscience — two of the three qualities that accompanied Paul's charge in v. 5.[19] "Conscience" (συνείδησις,

---

[17] Paul will also talk about his laying hands on Timothy in 2 Tim 1:6.

[18] Cf. Paul's declaration in 2 Tim 4:7 that he has "fought the good fight" (ἀγῶνα, *agōna*). See also 2 Cor 10:3-5.

[19] In v. 5, Paul says "the command is love, which comes from a pure heart, a good conscience and a sincere heart."

syneidēsis) becomes the compass of one's life. Rejecting or repudiating it results in spiritual shipwreck. Although conscience can be mistaught or defiled, one who refuses to be sensitive to his conscience will lose his faith. In 1 Timothy Paul places special emphasis on both "good conscience" and "sound doctrine." One should note Paul's change in meta-phor from the soldier ("fight the good fight") to the sailor ("shipwrecked their faith").[20]

1:20 Among them are Hymenaeus and Alexander,

Hymenaeus and Alexander, along with certain others, provide Paul with examples of those who have rejected conscience and made shipwreck of their faith. Hymenaeus will be mentioned again later with Philetus in 2 Tim 2:17. Other than these two brief references and his occurrence in the second-century apocryphal work *Acts of Paul and Thecla*, he is unknown. There are two other references to an Alexander who is connected to Ephesus: Acts 19:33-34 where a Jew by that name was hindered from speaking by a rowdy crowd and 2 Tim 4:14-15 where Paul warns Timothy about a metal worker bearing that name. Although many will link the Alexander of this passage with the Alexanders in one or both of the other texts, it is impossible to demonstrate that this is the case with any certainty. Fee is likely correct in suggesting that this Alexander may well be the one of 2 Tim 4:14-15.[21]

whom I have handed over to Satan to be taught not to blaspheme.

Paul states that he has handed these men "over to Satan" in order that they might be "taught not to blaspheme." The serious state of these men and the threat they offered to the church had led Paul to place an anathema on them. There has been much debate about the phrase and the parallel in 1 Cor 5:5 "hand this man over to Satan, so that the sinful

---

[20]Note Paul's rapid change of metaphors in 2 Tim 2:3-5 from soldier to athlete to farmer to illustrate his call for endurance.
[21]Fee, p. 296.

nature" (literally "that his body") "may be destroyed and his spirit saved on the day of the Lord." There are at least two primary interpretations for the phrase to "hand over to Satan": some would suggest that Paul was allowing Satan to inflict the evildoers with physical illness,[22] and others that the term is a semi-technical reference to disfellowshipping. The latter interpretation for this text and 1 Cor 5:5 seems most likely. Paul is turning the sinner back over to Satan's sphere of influence and removing offenders from the fellowship of believers.[23] The point of such action for Paul is always the redemption of the sinner. Here the discipline is clearly that they might learn "not to blaspheme." Discipline is to teach, not to punish. Here Paul hopes that turning the offenders over to the influence of Satan will teach them not to insult the Lord with their words and deeds.

---

[22]E.g., J.N.D. Kelly, *A Commentary on the Pastoral Epistles* (London: A & C Black, 1963), p. 59, who suggests that the reader "must infer that illness, paralysis, or some other physical disability was in the Apostle's mind."

[23]Paul can also speak of God's delivering (παραδίδωμι, *paradidōmi*) a sinner over to his sin (Rom 1:24, 26, 28).

1 TIMOTHY 2

III. DIRECTION FOR PUBLIC WORSHIP (2:1-15)

Following his charge to Timothy with regard to his faith and conscience and the warning with regard to false teachers, Paul moves to a series of specific instructions for what may be termed "church behavior." He first gives instructions for public prayer (2:1-7), then calls for a special role for men in that prayer (2:8), gives special admonition to the women (2:9-15), and concludes by giving qualifications for those who will serve in leadership in the church (3:1-13). In 3:14-15 Paul gives his overall purpose for the section which instructs believers as to how they are to conduct themselves within God's household or family.

In this larger section (2:1-3:15), Paul makes no direct reference to the false teachers. Some have seen these two chapters as an early church manual designed to set a local congregation in order. Often those who hold such a view see little connection between chapters 3 and 4 and the rest of the epistle, in particular to Paul's charge to Timothy in chapter 1. Such a view misses the significance of the "then" or "therefore" (οὖν, *oun*) of 2:1, the fact that prayers are to be offered "for everyone" and not just for Jews (2:1; cf. 1:7), the soiled hands and angry hearts of false teachers which one might expect from the rest of the epistle (2:8), the turmoil within the worship assembly which false teachers might encourage on the part of the women of the congregation (2:11-12), and the plausibility of some of those false teachers serving in positions of leadership (3:1-13).

A. PRAYERS BY ALL FOR ALL (2:1-7)

¹I urge, then, first of all, that requests, prayers, intercession and thanksgiving be made for everyone — ²for kings and all those in authority, that we may live peaceful and quiet lives in all godliness and holiness. ³This is good, and pleases God our Savior, ⁴who wants all men to be saved and to come to a knowledge of the truth. ⁵For there is one God and one mediator between God and men, the man Christ Jesus, ⁶who gave himself as a ransom for all men — the testimony given in its proper time. ⁷And for this purpose I was appointed a herald and an apostle — I am telling the truth, I am not lying — and a teacher of the true faith to the Gentiles.

2:1 I urge, then, first of all,

The phrase "first of all" does not introduce the first item in a list of issues to be discussed. It rather indicates that prayer for all kinds of people is of primary importance to Paul.

that requests, prayers, intercession and thanksgiving

In this verse Paul uses four words for prayer. The first word "requests" (δέησις, *deēsis*) indicates an entreaty for a specific need. The term "prayers" (προσευχή, *proseuchē*) is the more general word for prayer. "Intercession" (ἔντευξις, *enteuxis*) is the only term in the list which does not appear elsewhere in Paul. The term may convey the idea of one coming to a king with an appeal for his favor. It is used in Heb 7:25 of Christ's prayers for believers. The fourth word is "thanksgiving" (εὐχαριστία, *eucharistia*). While the first three words indicate various aspects of requests made to God, this word refers to gratitude toward God. As is the case in other Pauline lists of synonyms, these synonyms are given not because Paul expects his readers to perceive sharp distinctions among the words; rather the list is given to emphasize the importance of the topic.

be made for everyone —

The Ephesian believers are to pray "for everyone" (πάντων ἀνθρώπων, *pantōn anthrōpōn*), literally "all human beings." While the false teachers may have been concerned for an elite group, Paul bids the Ephesians to reach out to all.

2:2 for kings and all those in authority, that we may live peaceful and quiet lives

"Everyone" includes especially "kings and all those in authority." Prayers for civil authorities have a practical purpose designated by "that" (ἵνα, *hina*). Paul's desire is that Christians may lead lives that are "peaceful" (ἤρεμος, *ēremos*) and "quiet" (ἡσύχιος, *hēsychios*). The two words do not indicate that Paul expects Christians to live a life that is free from persecution or distress. False teachers are disrupting the churches and casting a bad light upon the church for those outside. A word from the same root, "quiet" (*hēsychios*), will appear later in 2:11 when Paul urges women in the assembly to "be silent" (*hēsychia*).

in all godliness and holiness.

Paul calls for these peaceful and quiet lives to be lived out "in all godliness and holiness." The term "godliness" (εὐσέβεια, *eusebeia*) along with the parallel verbal and adverbial forms represents a central idea in the Pastoral Epistles. The term has been rendered in various ways in the different English translations: "religion," "religious duty," "piety," and "godliness" (cf. Acts 3:12; Acts 10:7; 2 Pet 1:3, 6; 2:9; 3:11; 1 Tim 3:16; 4:7, 8; 5:4; 6:3, 5, 6, 11; 2 Tim 3:5; Titus 1:1). "Godliness" indicates a life that is lived with proper respect to deity. Fee suggests that Paul may use the false teachers' word to counteract their teaching.[1] Holiness (σεμνότης, *semnotēs*) also has various renderings: "respectful," "reverence," "dignity," "holiness," and "seriousness." While this word does not appear elsewhere in Paul, the cognate adjective (σεμνός, *semnos*) is used in the New Testament only in Paul to describe things that are "noble," "worthy of respect" (Phil 4:8; 1 Tim 3:8, 11; Titus 2:2, 7).

---

[1] Fee, p. 63.

2:3 This is good, and pleases God our Savior,

Paul gives the reason of the prayers for "all kinds of people." It is because "God wants all men" (ἄνθρωποι, *anthrōpoi*) "to be saved and to come to a knowledge of the truth." It is noteworthy that, while God is described as "our Savior," salvation is not just "our" salvation but rather that of "all men."

2:4 who wants all men to be saved

The fact that it is God's wish that all men be saved in no way implies that all *will* be saved nor does it suggest that God's will has in some way been frustrated. Here Paul's concern is the universal scope of the gospel. While "all men" may mean "all kinds of men," one is not forced to conclude that "God wants" all sorts of people to be saved embracing "Jew and Gentile, but not every person."[2]

Paul argues that God's universal concern is for the salvation of all men (πάντας ἀνθρώπους, *pantas anthrōpous*). "Men" here indicates persons of all genders. God's desire in no way obligates him to save all men.

and to come to a knowledge of the truth.

Salvation is closely connected to coming "to a knowledge of the truth." The term "truth" (ἀλήθεια, *alētheia*) appears frequently in 1 Timothy (2:7; 3:15; 4:3; 6:5; cf. 2 Tim 2:15; 3:8; Titus 1:1). It refers to the knowledge of and obedience to the gospel message. Spain suggests that the word "knowledge" (ἐπίγνωσις, *epignōsis*) is "almost a technical word in the Pastorals for conversion."[3]

2:5 For there is one God

Paul's affirmation of the desire of God for the salvation of all human beings is rooted in three facts concerning the nature of God the Father and Jesus Christ, his Son. First,

---

[2]Knight, p. 119.
[3]Carl Spain, *The Letters of Paul to Timothy and Titus*, The Living Word Commentary, vol 14 (Austin: R.B. Sweet, 1970), p. 41.

"there is one God." The significance of this statement can be seen in the emphasis on this doctrine in the Jewish faith (cf. Deut 6:4).

and one mediator between God and men, the man Christ Jesus,

The second fact is that there is "one mediator between God and men, the man Christ Jesus." Jesus' role as mediator (μεσίτης, *mesitēs*) between God and humankind is frequently linked to the idea of covenant (cf. Heb 8:6; 9:15; 12:24). Human beings and God are separated by sin and can be reconciled only by the act of the God-Man, Christ Jesus. Only he can serve as the go-between. Paul is again consistent in his use of ἄνθρωπος (*anthrōpos*, human being) for "man" rather than ἀνήρ (*anēr*, male person) in his description of "Christ Jesus."

2:6 who gave himself as a ransom for all men

Third, this Jesus "gave himself as a ransom for all men." Although the word for "ransom" (ἀντίλυτρον, *antilytron*) appears only here in the NT, a related word does appear in Mark 10:45. The concept of ransom is used outside the New Testament for the sum of money paid to set free captives taken in war or to liberate slaves from their masters. Christ's death is for Paul clearly the price paid to set mankind free from captivity to sin. Morris has suggested that the compound form used here (*antilutron*) may better be rendered "substitute-ransom."[4] The ransom was "for (ὑπέρ, *hyper*) all men," literally "in behalf of all." Notice that Paul declares that Jesus "gave himself," emphasizing the voluntary nature of his death.

— the testimony given in its proper time.

The dash before "the testimony given in its proper time" indicates the difficulty in translating the phrase and linking it to the immediate context. Literally the Greek can be translated

---

[4]Leon Morris, *The Apostolic Preaching of the Cross*, 3rd ed. (London, 1965), p. 51. Cf. F. Büschel, *TDNT*, IV:349.

"the witness for times of its/his own." Fee contends that the text implies that "in the 'history of salvation' the time for God's showing mercy to all people has now arrived, as witnessed in the death of Christ, which is 'for all.'"[5]

2:7 And for this purpose I was appointed a herald and an apostle

Paul emphasizes God's desire that all be saved by pointing to his own ministry. "For this purpose" points to "the testimony" of v. 6. Guthrie has suggested the following paraphrase: "To spread this testimony I was appointed *a preacher . . . and an apostle.*"[6] Paul clearly recognizes his ministry as a gift and an appointment from God. The emphatic "I" indicates Paul's wonder that one like himself would be given such a task. He begins by describing his task as that of "a herald." The word "herald" (κῆρυξ, *kēryx*) indicates one who publicly proclaims a message. He then moves to describe his work as that of "an apostle," that is, one sent on a mission.

— I am telling the truth, I am not lying

Easton and Harrison contend that Paul's strong assertion, "I am telling the truth, I am not lying," would be inappropriate if the book were really written to Timothy since he was well aware of Paul and had accepted his authority. The "semipublic" nature of the Pastoral Epistles and the need for Timothy to possess some authority to deal with church problems can, however, easily explain this assertion.

— and a teacher of the true faith to the Gentiles.

The third phrase used by Paul to describe his divinely appointed ministry is "a teacher of the true faith to the Gentiles." As Knight has noted, "The first and third terms that Paul applies to himself . . . seem to emphasize evangelism and exhortation on the one hand and instruction on the other. . . . In addition . . .

---

[5]Fee, p. 66.
[6]Donald Guthrie, *The Pastoral Epistles*, Tyndale New Testament Commentaries (Grand Rapids: Eerdmans, 1957).

Paul is Christ's authoritative eyewitness and spokesman. . . ."[7] The phrase "of the true faith" in the NIV is the rendering of a Greek phrase ἐν πίστει καὶ ἀληθείᾳ (*en pistei kai alētheia*) which more literally may be rendered "in faith and truth."

B. RESPECTIVE ROLES OF MEN AND WOMEN IN THE ASSEMBLY (2:8-15)

[8]I want men everywhere to lift up holy hands in prayer, without anger or disputing.

[9]I also want women to dress modestly, with decency and propriety, not with braided hair or gold or pearls or expensive clothes, [10]but with good deeds, appropriate for women who profess to worship.

[11]A woman should learn in quietness and full submission. [12]I do not permit a woman to teach or to have authority over a man; she must be silent. [13]For Adam was formed first, then Eve. [14]And Adam was not the one deceived; it was the woman who was deceived and became a sinner. [15]But women[a] will be saved[b] through childbearing — if they continue in faith, love and holiness with propriety.

[a]*15* Greek *she*   [b]*15* Or *restored*

2:8 I want men everywhere to lift up holy hands in prayer,

Paul now resumes his discussion of prayer. The work and authority he indicated in the last section give weight to "I want" (βούλομαι, *boulomai*) in this verse. "Men" here is the rendering of the Greek word ἀνήρ (*anēr*, male person) and not ἄνθρωπος (*anthrōpos*, human being). Attempts to argue that Paul is here giving general admonitions for both genders regarding prayer do not take into consideration Paul's consistent usage of these words both in this context and in the Pastoral Epistles in general (cf. *anthrōpos* in 1 Tim 2:1, 4, 5; 4:10; 5:24; 6:5, 9, 16; 2 Tim 2:2; 3:2, 8, 13, 17; Titus 2:11; 3:2, 8, 10 and *anēr* in 1 Tim 2:8, 12; 3:12; 5:9; Titus 1:6; 2:5) or his

---
[7]Knight, p. 127.

"also . . . women" (γυναῖκας, *gynaikas*) in the following verse. Paul is clearly distinguishing between *men* and *women*. Paul's instructions in v. 8 are addressed specifically to men. While *anēr* can mean "husband," that is unlikely in this verse.

"Everywhere" is literally "in every place" (ἐν παντὶ τόπῳ, *en panti topō*). Guthrie describes the phrase as "characteristically Pauline (cf. 1 Cor 1:2; 2 Cor 2:14; 1 Thess 1:8)."[8] Here, and at least in 1 Cor 1:2, it seems best to take the phrase as an indication of the place of public assembly for Christians (cf. Rom 16:3-5; Col 4:15). "Paul is probably referring to the various 'places' (house-churches) in which the Christians at Ephesus met."[9] This coincides with Paul's use of "lifting up holy hands" as the prayer posture for the men under consideration. While other prayer postures are seen in the biblical text, praying with uplifted hands was a normal posture for public prayer among Jews and Christians.[10] Fee paraphrases "everywhere" in this section as follows: "'Therefore,' Paul says, 'while we're on the subject, as the people gather to pray be sure it is for prayer and not in anger or disputing.'"[11] He goes on to say that "everywhere" means "in every place where believers gather in and around Ephesus (the house-churches)."[12] The most straightforward interpretation of this text would suggest that Paul is providing for male leadership in prayers in the public assembly.[13]

---

[8]Guthrie, p. 74. Cf. Everett Ferguson, "τοπος in 1 Timothy 2:8," *Restoration Quarterly* 33 (1991): 66-73; Thomas C. Geer, Jr., "Admonitions to Women in 1 Tim. 2:8-15." *Essays on Women in Earliest Christianity*, ed. Carroll D. Osburn (Joplin: College Press, 1993), p. 288, note 23; Thomas D. Lea and Hayne P. Griffin, *1, 2 Timothy, Titus*.

[9]Douglas Moo, "What Does It Mean Not to Teach or Have Authority Over Man? 1 Timothy 2:11-15." *Recovering Biblical Manhood & Womanhood: A Response to Evangelical Feminism*, ed. by John Piper and Wayne Grudem (Wheaton, IL: Crossway Books, 1991), p. 182.

[10]For a full list of postures in prayer, see William Hendriksen, *Thessalonians, Timothy, and Titus* (Grand Rapids: Baker, 1979), pp. 103-104.

[11]Fee, p. 71.

[12]Ibid.

[13]For an opposing view, see Fee, p. 71. This interpretation does provide some difficulty when one considers Paul's exhortation that women pray

without anger or disputing.

Paul's primary concern in the text is not the posture one assumes in prayer but the inner attitude and lifestyle of the one praying. "Holy hands" is a call for deeds that demonstrate the pure life. The closing words of this admonition, "without anger or disputing," refer to the kind of soiling hands may have. Both terms seem to point to particular sins of the false teachers. "Disputing" (διαλογισμός, *dialogismos*) means in general "thought," "opinion," or "reasoning." The term here refers to disputing with others.[14]

2:9 I also want women to dress modestly,

Paul's instructions to women clearly parallel those to men in v. 8. Despite recent attempts to suggest that "women" (γυναῖκας, *gynaikas*) should be translated "wives,"[15] there is nothing within the text that would suggest the need for such a change from the traditional "women." As Fee has noted, "Paul turns next to women (without the definite article, implying a broader context than merely wives)."[16] Similarly Knight says, "Just as Paul was asking not only husbands but men in general to pray, so also he is enjoining women in general, not just wives, to dress modestly and discreetly, and to behave in accord with their womanliness in relation to men."[17]

Geer has suggested that also (ὡσαύτως, *hōsautōs*) "*may* relate back to the concept of praying in v. 8. Just as he wants men to

---

veiled in 1 Cor 11:2-16. See Mark Black, "1 Cor 11:2-16 – A Reinvestigation," *Essays on Women in Earliest Christianity*, ed. Carroll D. Osburn (Joplin: College Press, 1993), pp. 191-218, for a possible reconciliation of the two texts.

[14]Knight, p. 130.

[15]Geer, pp. 289-290. Cf. N.J. Hommes, "Let Women Be Silent in Church...," *Calvin Theological Review* 4 (1969): 5-22; Douglas J. Moo, "1 Timothy 2:11-15: Meaning and Significance," *Trinity Journal* 1 (1980): 63-64.

[16]Fee, p. 71. The following authors also argue for "women" as the translation of *gunaikas*: Barrett, Dibelius and Conzelmann, Guthrie, Hendriksen, Kelly, Knight, Lea and Griffin, Lock, Simpson, and Spain.

[17]Knight, p. 133. Cf. Lea and Griffin's conclusion (p. 95): "The general tenor of the passage is more appropriate when applied to women in worship."

pray without arguments, Paul wants women to pray 'in modest clothing' . . . ."[18] Rather than seeing "also" as a call for a repetition of Paul's exhortation for men to pray now being offered to women, the simpler solution is to see "also" as indicating that Paul has a wish for the women as well as the men in terms of their behavior and demeanor in the worship assembly and times of public prayer.[19] Since "to pray" and "to dress" are linked syntactically by "also" and "I wish," it is reasonable to see the same general context for both admonitions — the worship assembly.

Paul's call for women to dress "modestly" is not an exhortation for clothing which is not sexually revealing. Nor is it simply an exhortation to avoid ostentation. It is rather a call not to be "dressing up." Fee has noted that, in both Hellenistic and Jewish circles, such extravagant dress on the part of women was often equated with "wantonness and wifely insubordination. . . . tantamount to marital unfaithfulness."[20] In addition such extravagant dress indicates a failure to recognize that the inner person is of more importance than wealth and what it has to offer. Paul is not here condemning dressing in good taste.

with decency and propriety, not with braided hair or gold or pearls or expensive clothes,

Literally Paul's admonition may be rendered "adorn themselves in adorning attire." He clarifies his instructions by adding "with decency and propriety." The first word indicates behaving in a way that would not bring shame, and the second indicates the use of good judgment in dress. "Braided hair, gold, pearls, and expensive clothes" indicate the specific kind of dress that Paul is forbidding.[21] Just as men need to be

---

[18]Geer, p. 290.

[19]This is indeed the understanding of the translators of the RSV, NASB, NIV, and NRSV.

[20]Fee, p. 71. Cf. Knight, p. 135; Moo, p. 182.

[21]Cf. 1 Pet 3:3; *The Testaments of the Twelve Patriarchs*, Reuben 5; Juvenal, *Satire*, 6. The same general problem is also being addressed in 1 Cor 11:2–16 where Christian women are adopting a style of dress (without the veil) and thereby proclaiming their independence from their husbands.

warned against anger and dispute when they stand to lead in public prayer, women need to be warned that their interest in clothing and apparel should not produce immodesty.

2:10 but with good deeds, appropriate for women who profess to worship.

Women who are believers are to adorn themselves with better things, namely "with good deeds, appropriate for women who profess to worship." Paul argues that the greatest asset a woman can possess is a devout and godly life. Such a life adorns and enhances. "Good deeds" is a phrase common in the Pastoral Epistles (1 Tim 3:1; 5:10, 26; 6:18; Titus 1:16; 2:7, 14; 3:1, 8, 14; 2 Tim 2:21; 3:17). The phrase "who profess to worship" has frequently been rendered "professing godliness." Although "worship," literally "godliness" (θεοσέβεια, *theosebeia*) occurs only here in the NT, its cognate (εὐσέβεια, *eusebeia*), also rendered "godliness," appears frequently in the Pastoral Epistles.[22]

2:11 A woman should learn in quietness

After his discussion of how women should adorn themselves when gathering, Paul moves to the part women are to play in those church meetings. The next few verses have been the subject of much discussion. Just what was Paul permitting and what was he forbidding in the Ephesian church? What of his teaching is applicable and binding upon the modern church?

The demeanor and behavior of women in the synagogue was never questioned. Women learned in silence. However, as the Christian faith spread so did what Kelly has called "a new spirit of emancipation . . . in the young Christian congregations."[23]

---

[22]1 Tim 2:2; 3:16; 4:7, 8; 6:3, 5, 6, 11; 2 Tim 3:5; Titus 1:1.
[23]J.N.D. Kelly, *The Pastoral Epistles*, Black's New Commentary (Peabody, MA: Hendrickson Publishers, 1960), p. 68.

While Paul does call for women to learn, a practice not encouraged in most of the world at his time, his primary emphasis falls on "in quietness and full submission." "In quietness" (ἐν ἡσυχίᾳ, *en hēsychia*) in v. 12 represents the rendering of a cognate to the adjective used in v. 2, "quiet lives" (ἡσύχιον βίον, *hēsychion bion*). The emphasis is not upon absolute silence as some would suggest but rather a quiet spirit, i.e., "in quietness." Paul is arguing against women "being 'up front,' talking foolishness,"[24] causing turmoil.

and full submission.

"In quietness" is further qualified by the phrase "in full submission" (ἐν πάσῃ ὑποταγῇ, *en pasē hypotagē*). Paul does not clarify to whom woman is to show her submission. One might assume that the Adam and Eve illustration which follows would indicate that Paul was addressing wives' submission to their husbands. Fee has noted that ". . . the implication of full ('in every conceivable way') probably has a larger front in view, which includes the conduct of the younger widows and their 'going about from house to house . . . saying things they ought not to' (5:13)."[25] Similarly Moo contends that ". . . the underlying issue in verse 11 is not just submission to the teaching of the church but the submission of women to their husbands and, perhaps, to the male leadership of the church. . . . The facts that verses 12-14 (and perhaps also 9-10) focus on the relationship of men to women incline us to think that the submission in view here is also this submission of women to male leadership."[26] Moo goes on to argue that the context points not just to husbands but to male leadership of the church in general. The call for "full submission" probably should simply be seen as a call for women to live within their God-ordained role. The key to understanding "submission" is not inferior value or worth but the recognition of one's role in a relationship.

---

[24]Fee, p. 72.
[25]Ibid.
[26]Moo, p. 183.

2:12 I do not permit a woman to teach

The phrase "full submission" serves as the link between Paul's call for women to "learn in quietness" and his call for them not "to teach or to have authority over a man."[27] Paul's use of "permit" rather than an imperative ("Women, do not teach") has been used by some to argue that Paul is giving a limited and temporary instruction.[28] As Moo has noted, "No doubt Paul viewed his own teaching as authoritative for the churches to whom he wrote. Paul's 'advice' to Timothy is the word of an apostle, accredited by God, and included in the inspired Scriptures."[29]

Paul's instruction that women were not "to teach" should be seen in the general context of the worship assembly.[30] Teaching in the Pastoral Epistles is generally to be seen in the "restricted sense of authoritative doctrinal instruction."[31]

or to have authority over a man;

The "or" (οὐδέ, *oude*) which links "to teach" and "to have authority over a man" can serve as a simple "and also," it can link opposites (e.g., Gentile or Jew, slave or free; Gal 3:28) or natural pairs or lengthy lists, or it can link two closely related terms where the second may define or clarify the first. The closest grammatical parallel is Acts 16:21 where infinitive phrases are linked by *oude*: "by advocating customs unlawful for us Romans to accept or practice." "Accept" and "practice" are closely related, and, in fact, the text may well be amplified, "they are advocating customs which are unlawful for us as Romans to accept and, therefore, practice." Similarly, the fact that Paul sandwiches the admonition not to teach between his call for full submission and the call not to have authority (not "to domineer") indicate that teaching and domineering are related. Such a link would permit the

---

[27]Cf. Moo, p. 184.
[28]Fee, p. 72.
[29]Moo, p. 185.
[30]See comments on 2:8, 9.
[31]Moo, p. 185.

following paraphrase: "I do not permit a woman to teach so as to exercise authority."[32] In the ancient world authority was inherent in the role of the teacher. Likewise, teaching today is considered the role of an authority.

The teaching that is prohibited for women is not universal. Timothy was taught by his mother and grandmother. Priscilla assisted and perhaps even took the lead in teaching Apollos. Older women are instructed to teach younger women (Titus 2:4-5). The following admonition to silence could not be seen as applicable to the Christian home or the marketplace; it must, therefore, as the earlier context would indicate, relate to the worship assembly and the Christian community.[33] Spencer has argued that the real problem is untrained women and that the very fact that women were to learn implies that they should eventually teach.[34] She has unfortunately failed to realize that the prohibition against teaching is not universal, and that one can learn without later functioning as public teacher.[35]

Recently Kroeger and Kroeger have done significant research into the nature and background of ancient Ephesus and have suggested an alternative interpretation to 1 Tim 2:11-15. While they have provided significant background data, their suggestion that the phrase "to have authority" (αὐθεντεῖν, *authentein*) should be rendered "to represent herself as originator of man" is, to say the least, far-fetched and has gained little support.[36] Significant research on the mean-

---

[32]For an opposing view see Moo, pp. 187-188, who sees separate activities being condemned here.

[33]Cf. Guthrie, pp. 76-77.

[34]Aida Besançon Spencer, *Beyond the Curse: Women Called to Ministry* (Nashville: Thomas Nelson, 1985), pp. 74-80. As Jack Cottrell has shown, however, the Greek word δέ (*de*) that connects verses 11 and 12 shows just the opposite of what Spencer claims ("1 Timothy 2:12 and the Role of Women," *Christian Standard*, Jan. 17, 1993, p. 5).

[35]Consider the admonition of James, "Not many of you should presume to be teachers" (3:1).

[36]Richard Clark Kroeger and Catherine Clark Kroeger, *I Suffer Not a Woman: Rethinking 1 Timothy 2:11-15 in the Light of Ancient Evidence* (Grand Rapids: Baker Book House, 1992), pp. 99-104.

ing of the word has been done by Knight. He has concluded that "Paul refers, then, with *authentein* to the exercise of a leadership role or function in the church (the contextual setting), and thus by specific application the office of *episkopos* [overseer]/*presbuteros* [elder], since the names of these offices . . . and the activities associated with them . . . indicate the exercise of authority."[37]

she must be silent.
Paul's injunction that "she must be silent" (εἶναι ἐν ἡσυχίᾳ, *einai en hēsychia*) must be seen in the light of his use of the cognate adjective earlier in v. 2 and the use of the same phrase (*en hēsychia*) connected to the imperative "learn" in v. 11 where it is rendered "in quietness." On all three ocassions the emphasis is not upon absolute silence, as some would suggest, but rather on the quiet spirit, i.e., "in quietness." The call for silence again points to Paul's restriction that a woman is not to teach in the assembly.[38]

2:13 For Adam was formed first, then Eve.
Paul uses the Adam and Eve story of Gen 2 and 3 to support his earlier admonitions. He bases his argument on the created order, something of the very nature of man and woman. Paul's argument here is very similar to the argument of Jesus regarding the permanence of marriage (Matt 19:4-6). As Knight has noted, Paul's concern in "for . . . then" goes beyond "mere chronology" but "what is entailed in this chronology."[39] Paul's concern is the headship of man and the recognition of divinely ordained roles. Paul's concern is not dominance but role. In this regard Eve serves as representative woman.

---

[37]Knight, p. 142. See also Leland Wilshire, "The TLG Computer and Further Reference to AUTHENTEŌ in 1 Timothy 2.12." *NTS* 34 (1988) pp. 120-134.
[38]*Ibid.*
[39]Knight, p. 143.

2:14 And Adam was not the one deceived; it was the woman who was deceived and became a sinner.

Paul's statement that "it was the woman who was deceived" is based on the deception of Eve by the serpent in Gen 3:13. He is not removing Adam from responsibility for the fall (Rom 5:12, 19; 1 Cor 15:22). In fact, Adam's sin would make him even more culpable. Paul undoubtedly has in mind the false teachers who serve as emissaries of Satan, are plaguing the Ephesian church, and are leading astray many women (4:1; 5:15). The phrase "became a sinner" is literally "has become in transgression," emphasizing a current status.

2:15 But women will be saved through childbearing — if they continue in faith, love and holiness with propriety.

This verse has perhaps caused as much ink to be spilled as any passage in the New Testament. After noting that "the woman was deceived" and fell into transgression, Paul provides the location of the remedy of the problem caused by the fall. He concludes that "*she* will be saved through childbearing — if *they* continue in faith, love and holiness with propriety." Paul makes a subtle shift from Eve to the women at Ephesus and women in general. Paul begins verse 15 with the singular verb "*she* will be saved." The NIV has accommodated their translation to Paul's change to a plural verb in the middle of the verse "if they continue" by beginning "women will be saved." This accommodation does carry the intent of Paul. As Fee has noted, "Obviously Paul is not talking about Eve's salvation but 'the woman' in Ephesus; hence the change back to the plural in the middle of verse 15."[40]

Paul's statement that she "will be saved through childbearing" has produced several alternative interpretations. One suggestion is that woman will be kept safe through childbirth. It is suggested that the false teachers advocated abstinence and that Paul is simply saying God will preserve Christian

---

[40]Fee, pp. 74–75.

women if they fulfill their God-ordained role.[41] Many Christian women have, however, died in childbirth. Such an understanding is also unlikely in view of Paul's use of "saved" (σώζω, *sōzō*) in the Pastoral Epistles (cf. 1:15-16; 2:4) and his use of another word to convey the idea of being "kept safe" (cf. 2 Tim 3:11; 4:8).

Another suggestion is that "childbearing" should be seen as equivalent to "child nurture." This suggestion would provide "children" as the subject of the next verb in the phrase "if they continue in faith, love and holiness with propriety." The difficulty with this interpretation is that woman's salvation is dependent upon works and then, even beyond that, the works of others, i.e., her children.

A third suggestion is woman will be saved even though she must bear children. This suggestion plays off of the curse upon Eve (Gen 3:16).

A fourth suggestion is that, although Eve did trangress, Christian women will be saved through the special childbirth, namely the birth of the Messiah through Mary, a woman. Although this view, originally popular among the Western Church Fathers, has recently gained some support,[42] the critique of Guthrie is still valid: "For if that were the author's intention he could hardly have chosen a more obscure or ambiguous way of saying it. That Paul would have left the words 'child-bearing' without further definition is highly improbable."[43] The use of the parallel verb form, "to have children" (τεκνογονέω, *teknogoneō*), in 5:14 would also mitigate against such an interpretation.

---

[41] See the margin notes in the NIV and TEV. Cf. Moffatt.

[42] C.J. Elliot, *Commentary on the Pastoral Epistles* (2nd ed.; Andover: Draper, 1897) p. 54; Geer, pp. 297-300; Lock, *The Pastoral Epistles*, p. 33; Knight, pp. 146-147; Thomas C. Oden, *First and Second Timothy and Titus* (Louisville: John Knox Press, 1989) pp. 100-102; Philip B. Payne, "Libertarian Women in Ephesus: A Response to Douglas J. Moo's Article, '1 Timothy 2.11-15: Meaning and Significance,'" *Trinity Journal* 1 (1981) pp. 169-197; Mark D. Roberts, "Women Shall Be Saved: A Closer Look at 1 Timothy 2:15," *The Reformed Journal* (1983) pp. 18-22.

[43] Guthrie, p. 78. Cf. Knight, p. 75.

The final interpretation may be termed "the majority view."[44] This view would hold that Christian women are not saved through teaching and asserting authority, but by attention to their traditional role. "Childbearing" serves as a figure of speech to illustrate Paul's argument that women need not behave as men but rather fulfill their divinely appointed role to find salvation. The figure may be termed either a metonymy[45] or a synecdoche.[46] Paul is not suggesting that women must have children to be saved. Childbearing represents Paul's teaching "that women prove the reality of their salvation when they become model wives and mothers whose good deeds include marriage and raising children (1 Tim 5:11, 14)."[47] 1 Tim 5:11 and 14 indicate that Paul clearly saw childbearing as a part of the role of women in his day. The text does not preclude that a woman can, within God's grace, remain single or that a married woman may work outside the home or that a married woman and her husband can decide not to have children. It is simply a call to realize that a woman's salvation is fulfilled within the role which she has been granted by God.

Paul could not leave the discussion without clarifying the fact that a saved person will demonstrate this relationship

---

[44]Paul W. Barnett, "Wives and Women's Ministry (1 Timothy 2:11-15)," *Evangelical Quarterly* 61 (1989) pp. 225-238; Robert Falconer, "1 Timothy 2:14, 15. Interpretive Notes," *Journal of Biblical Literature* 60 (1941) pp. 375-379; Fee, p. 75; Guthrie, p. 78; Hendriksen, p. 111; Kelly, p. 69; Lea and Griffin, pp. 102-103; Douglas Moo, "1 Timothy 2:11-15: Meaning and Significance," *Trinity Journal* (1980) pp. 71-73; Krijn A. Van der Jagt, "Women Are Saved Through Childbearing," *The Bible Translator* 39 (1988) pp. 201-208.

[45]A figure in which the name of one thing is used for another because the two are closely associated. For example we may say "the White House reported today that . . ." which really means the president and his staff have reported.

[46]A synecdoche is a figure in which a part is used for the whole or the whole for a part or a species is used for the genus. Cf. Lea and Griffin, p. 102.

[47]*Ibid.*, p. 102.

with God in terms of her lifestyle: "if they continue in faith, love and holiness with propriety." The change to a plural verb makes clear Paul's intent; he is discussing Christian women in general. The word "propriety" refers to her exercise of self-control.

1 TIMOTHY 3

IV. DIRECTIONS FOR CHURCH LEADERS (3:1-16)
A. QUALIFICATIONS OF OVERSEERS (3:1-7)

¹Here is a trustworthy saying: If anyone sets his heart on being an overseer,[a] he desires a noble task. ²Now the overseer must be above reproach, the husband of but one wife, temperate, self-controlled, respectable, hospitable, able to teach, ³not given to drunkenness, not violent but gentle, not quarrelsome, not a lover of money. ⁴He must manage his own family well and see that his children obey him with proper respect. ⁵(If anyone does not know how to manage his own family, how can he take care of God's church?) ⁶He must not be a recent convert, or he may become conceited and fall under the same judgment as the devil. ⁷He must also have a good reputation with outsiders, so that he will not fall into disgrace and into the devil's trap.

[a]*1* Traditionally *bishop*; also in verse 2

In the previous section, Paul has addressed some concerns related to what is occurring when the community gathers to worship. He now turns to the discussion of elders. There is without a doubt a problem with erring elders in the Ephesian church.

After his discussion of this group of leaders called "overseers" (ἐπίσκοποι, *episkopoi*) in vv. 1-7, Paul turns to "deacons" (διάκονοι, *diakonoi*) in vv. 8-13 with a brief excursus on "women" in v. 11.

At this juncture, it is significant to note that Timothy has not been left in Ephesus to appoint elders as Titus had on the island of Crete. Timothy is dealing with an established church with leaders already in place (cf. Acts 20). Paul's concern is the place these men may have in the false teaching which is presenting itself in Ephesus (5:17-22). Paul provides a sharp contrast between the characteristics of these men who serve as overseers or bishops and the false teachers who are present in Ephesus.

3:1 Here is a trustworthy saying:

This section begins with the second "trustworthy saying" of the Pastoral Epistles (1 Tim 1:15; 3:1; 4:9; Titus 3:8; 2 Tim 2:11). Paul is simply using the formula "here is a trustworthy saying" to reinforce the words that follow.

If anyone sets his heart on being an overseer, he desires a noble task.

The saying itself, "If anyone sets his heart on being an overseer, he desires a noble task," has unfortunately been misinterpreted and taken as Paul's requirement that a man must "go after the office." Paul is not here giving the first qualification for serving as an overseer. He is simply stating a proverb: "if a man seeks this work, it is a noble work he is seeking."

The expression "being an overseer" (ἐπισκοπή, *episcopē*) is closely related to the word for "overseer" (ἐπίσκοπος, *episcopos*), also translated "bishop." It is simply a synonym for "elder," used elsewhere in the NT (cf. Acts 20:17 and Acts 20:28; Titus 1:5-7). The verb from which this noun is derived indicates "looking after the needs of some person" (cf. James 1:27). It should be noted that the word "office" in the KJV ("This is a true saying, If a man desire the office of a bishop, he desireth a good work") has been supplied by the translators and does not represent a Greek word in the original. Paul sees the position in terms of a work or ministry.

3:2 Now the overseer must be above reproach,

Because the work of overseeing is such a "noble task," there are certain qualities which are a must for the overseer.

The word "must" (δεῖ, *dei*) indicates that the overseer is required to have these qualities; they are not optional, idealistic virtues.

These "qualifications" fall under the general rubric of the first qualification: he must be "above reproach" (ἀνεπίλημπτος, *anepilēmptos*). In the section which follows, Paul is simply clarifying what it means to be above reproach. Put another way, "*Above reproach* dominates the whole list."[1] It should be noted that the things Paul requires of overseers represent outward, observable behavior. He is, as noted earlier, making clear lines of distinction between the lives of the false teachers and those of the overseers within the church. Fee is likely correct when he says, "Paul is concerned not only that elders have Christian virtues (these are assumed) but that they reflect the highest ideals of the culture as well."[2] Paul will repeat this call for being above reproach in his discussion of widows (5:7) and in his plea for Timothy himself (6:14).

the husband of but one wife,

The overseer must be the "husband of but one wife" (literally "one woman's man"). Some have suggested that Paul is here prohibiting polygamy. Since polygamy was only infrequently practiced in the Greco-Roman world of the first century, it seems very unlikely that Paul would write to condemn a practice among overseers that would not be practiced even among Christians outside the leadership. Since Paul offers a similar call for widows who are to be enrolled (5:9) and polyandry (women having more than one husband) was not practiced in the Greco-Roman world of the first century, another solution must be sought.

Some (e.g., Tertullian) have suggested that Paul is prohibiting second marriages. If one sees this quality as further clarification of "above reproach," one wonders how marrying after losing a mate due to death could bring the overseer under

---

[1] Ronald A. Ward, *Commentary on 1 & 2 Timothy & Titus* (Waco: Word Books, Publisher, 1974) p. 54.
[2] Fee, pp. 78-79.

condemnation.

Another suggestion is that Paul was requiring overseers to have living mates. When one realizes that Paul uses a parallel phrase in the description of widows who are to be enrolled ("one man's woman" 5:9), it becomes clear that this cannot be Paul's intent.

The most likely interpretation involves seeing the phrase as a call for marital fidelity. Greeks and Romans accepted the option of men having sexual relations with women other than their wives. Sexual promiscuity would, of course, be forbidden for all Christians. Another wrinkle comes from the fact that divorce and remarriage was common. Paul is here requiring that an overseer be one about whom there would be no question in terms of his faithfulness to his wife. He must exemplify the teaching of Jesus that God's intent in marriage was one man and one woman for life. More than one woman cannot lay claim to this man who is to serve as overseer. His marital life must provide the example and pattern for the church to imitate. The character of a man who is married and divorced and remarried will not likely be "above reproach."

temperate, self-controlled,

The next quality is "temperate" (νηφάλιον, *nēphalion*; cf. 3:11; Titus 2:2). Although the word can refer "moderation in the use of alcohol," since Paul will turn to that topic in vv. 3 and 8, his concern here is "sober in the sense of clear-headed, self-controlled" (BAGD). The next word, "self-controlled" (σώφρων, *sōphrōn*), is a synonym often denoting being "prudent, thoughtful" (BAGD).

respectable, hospitable,

Next Paul says that the overseer must be "respectable" (κόσμιος, *kosmios*). This word carries with it the basic principle of "being orderly" but here bears the sense of "being virtuous and being held in respect."

The overseer is to be "hospitable" (φιλόξενος, *philoxenos*, literally "a lover of strangers"). Hospitality was a highly valued

Greek and Jewish virtue. It was absolutely necessary for the expansion of the gospel and necessary for the maintenance of the fellowship within the church as well as the image of the church from without.

able to teach,

The next phrase in English "able to teach" represents a single Greek word (διδακτικός, *didaktikos*). The word appears only here and in 2 Tim 2:24, indicating one who is an able teacher. This section focuses primarily on the outward qualities of the man who is to serve as overseer. Only here and in v. 5 does Paul give a glimpse of the function of the overseer. While the word translated "able to teach" does not appear in Titus 1:9, Paul does there spell out the need for this ability: to encourage others by sound doctrine and refute those who oppose it.[3] The need for leaders to be active teachers of God's word is seen in 1 Thess 5:12; 1 Tim 5:17; and Heb 13:7.

3:3 not given to drunkenness,

One wonders whether Paul is attempting to distinguish between the overseers and the false teachers with his call that they must not be "given to drunkenness." While the false teachers apparently called for asceticism (4:3), they may have at the same time been overindulgent about wine. Drunkenness was a very common vice in the Greco-Roman world. The word (πάροινος, *paroinos*) also appears in the parallel in Titus 1:7. Hendriksen has suggested the translation, "not (one who lingers) beside (his) wine."[4] A synonymous phrase (οἴνῳ πολλῷ προσέχοντας, *oinō pollō prosechontas*) in v. 8 is rendered by the NIV "not indulging in much wine."

not violent but gentle, not quarrelsome,

The prohibition of violence, "not violent," indicates that the overseer is not to be a pugnacious man. The basic mean-

---

[3]See the parallel idea in Eph 4:11: "pastor-teacher."
[4]Hendriksen, p. 124.

ing is "not given to blows." The false teachers are given to quarrels and strife (6:3-5; cf. 2 Tim 2:22-26; Titus 3:9). Those who serve as the leaders within the church must be different. Hendriksen has offered the following description of the quality Paul intends to prohibit: "He is thinking of a man who is ever ready with his fists, a bellicose person, a spitfire or fire-eater."[5]

In contrast to a tendency toward violence, the overseer must be "gentle" (ἐπιεικής, *epieikēs*). Possible translations include "yielding, kind, forbearing, and considerate." An elder is to be gentle even when he must correct those who oppose him (2 Tim 2:23-25).

A "quarrelsome" man is a fighter. The battle may be waged with words or with fists. Paul demands that the church leader cannot be contentious but must be peaceable.

not a lover of money.

Although the phrase "not a lover of money" may well hint at the fact that the overseer has responsibility for handling the congregational finances, the primary emphasis is not on that aspect of his work, but rather on the church's need for men who are not caught up in greed and avarice to serve as leaders. Interestingly, this quality is seen in nearly every list of qualities required by those who serve in a leadership role in the church (3:8; Titus 1:7. Cf. Acts 20:33; 1 Tim 6:5-10; 2 Tim 3:6-7).

3:4 He must manage his own family well

In v. 4 Paul suggests that the testing ground for the overseer in terms of leadership and caring abilities is the Christian home. This status as upstanding family man is not arbitrary. Leading a church is like leading a family, and church members frequently behave like children. The Greek words translated "manage well" (καλῶς προϊστάμενον, *kalōs proistamenon*) in the NIV were rendered "ruleth well" in the KJV. Unfortu-

---

[5]Hendriksen, p. 125.

nately "ruling" carries with it the idea of "cracking the whip" and "arbitrary decision making." Even the NIV's "manage well" fails to convey the basic sense of the phrase. The verb carries the basic meaning of "to lead" (literally "to stand in front"). The correlation of "manage" (προΐστημι, *proistēmi*) and "take care" (ἐπιμελέομαι, *epimeleomai*) in v. 5 suggest a leadership style characterized by loving care.

and see that his children obey him with proper respect.
The ability of an overseer to lead and direct a church are to be seen in the submission of his children (i.e., their respect for him and their recognition of his leadership). The English word "see that his children obey him" represents a Greek phrase (τέκνα ἔχοντα ἐν ὑποταγῇ, *tekna echonta en hypotagē*) which might literally be translated "having/keeping [his] children in subjection." The NIV takes the phrase which follows, "with proper respect" (μετὰ πάσης σεμνότητος, *meta pasēs semnotētos*), as modifiying "obey." It normally signifies "seriousness." Lea and Griffin have suggested that the phrase should be seen as modifying and clarifying the action of the father, i.e., "keeping his children in subjection with all seriousness."[6] This interpretation best fits the Greek construction. In Titus the concern about children who obey and show respect is the reputation this carries with outsiders (1:6). Knight has argued that, although "children" (*tekna*) can be used of adults, here they represent those who are under authority and, therefore, not of age.[7]

3:5 (If anyone does not know how to manage his own family, how can he take care of God's church?)
The elder who has not demonstrated the ability to lead his own family has not demonstrated that he can lead and care for a local church. The emphasis is not on his ability to dominate, but on his willingness to take care of the needs of the flock.

---

[6]Lea and Griffin, p. 112.
[7]Knight, p. 161.

3:6 He must not be a recent convert, or he may become conceited

The overseer also "must not be a recent convert," representing a Greek metaphor "not newly planted" (μὴ νεόφυτος, *mē neophytos*). The primary concern is not chronology (how long in years) but maturity (cf. 5:22). The real concern here is the danger of a swelled-head, becoming conceited. Since the false teachers are described as conceited, Fee ponders the possibility that some of them may have been recent converts.[8]

and fall under the same judgment as the devil.

This conceit can lead these men to fall under the same judgment as the devil. The "same judgment as the devil" means "the condemnation pronounced upon the devil" both in the death and resurrection of Jesus and in the final judgment to come.

3:7 He must also have a good reputation with outsiders, so that he will not fall into disgrace and into the devil's trap.

Finally Paul concludes by turning to the "reputation" of the elder "with outsiders." Outsiders may work side by side with a prospective overseer. His demeanor and lifestyle can easily be read by them. His reputation with the world affects the influence of the church for good in the world. One who lacks this favorable testimony from those outside the church "will fall into disgrace and into the devil's trap."

B. QUALIFICATIONS OF DEACONS AND WOMEN (3:8–13)

⁸Deacons, likewise, are to be men worthy of respect, sincere, not indulging in much wine, and not pursuing dishonest gain. ⁹They must keep hold of the deep truths of the faith with a clear conscience. ¹⁰They must first be tested; and then if there is nothing against them, let them serve as deacons.

---

[8]Fee, p. 83.

¹¹**In the same way, their wives**[a] **are to be women worthy of respect, not malicious talkers but temperate and trustworthy in everything.**

¹²**A deacon must be the husband of but one wife and must manage his children and his household well.** ¹³**Those who have served well gain an excellent standing and great assurance in their faith in Christ Jesus.**

[a]*11 Or way, deaconesses*

3:8 Deacons, likewise,

The term "deacons" (διάκονοι, *diakonoi*) can be rendered as "household servant," "servant" in a generic sense, "minister" or "deacon." Here, as in Phil 1:1, it is used of a particular work within a local congregation. These men serve in some special capacity, fulfilling a need in that church. Although the noun "deacon" is never used for the seven men appointed to serve in Acts 6:5-6, the verb in Acts 6:2 "to wait on tables" (διακονέω, *diakoneō*, literally "to minister" or "to serve") comes from the same root.

are to be men worthy of respect,

The qualifications for deacons are very similar to those required of overseers. As with the overseers in v. 2, the first term in the list of qualification for deacons provides the primary qualification for the work with the terms and phrases which follow clarifying. These men are to be "worthy of respect" (σεμνός, *semnós*). A cognate noun is used in 3:4 to describe the manner of the overseer in disciplining his children: "proper respect." If the ministry of men appointed to this task is to be anything like that required of the seven men of Acts 6, they must be well-received and well-respected by those within the church.

sincere, not indulging in much wine, and not pursuing dishonest gain.

The NIV translation of the second adjective "sincere" (μὲ δίλογος, *me dilogos*) unnecessarily obscures the basic meaning of the original. The literal meaning is "not two-worded" or "double-tongued." He must be a man of his word if he is to minister successfully. He cannot say one thing on one occasion or to one group and another thing on a different occasion or to a different audience.

The prohibition against "indulging in much wine" is parallel to the prohibition given to overseers in v. 3. In the same way the requirement that deacons were not to "pursue dishonest gain" parallels Paul's demand that an overseer was not to be "a lover of money" in v. 3. A deacon might well be faced with the temptation to use his position for personal gain. Perhaps even more at the heart of Paul's prohibition is that the love of money points to misplaced priorities and questionable integrity. Paul will use the same word in Titus 1:7 in the qualifications of an elder.

3:9 They must keep hold of the deep truths of the faith with a clear conscience.

From negative characteristics Paul turns to the positive: deacons must "keep hold of the deep truths of the faith with a clear conscience." The false teachers have turned away from a good conscience and "have suffered shipwreck in the faith" (1:5-6, 19-20). These men who serve must also show "a proper doctrinal and moral response to Christ's message."[9] "Deep truths" represents the favorite Pauline word "mystery." Paul here uses "the faith" in an objective manner, the substance of what is believed, a synonym for "the gospel." The "deep truths of the faith" are neither deep truths hard to understand nor secrets preserved only for the enlightened. They are rather truths of the gospel hidden until revealed by God in Jesus. "Conscience" is used frequently in the Pastoral Epistles (1 Tim 1:5, 19; 4:2; 2 Tim 1:3; Titus 1:15). It represents the inner guide to life. The deacon must be a man who demonstates a continual struggle to live a life characterized by obedience to the gospel message.

---

[9]Lea and Griffin, p. 117.

3:10 They must first be tested; and then if there is nothing against them, let them serve as deacons.

Deacons must be men of proven worth. They must "be tested" (from δοκιμάζω, *dokimazō*). "Unknown" men are not to be appointed to fulfill this task. The testing, a word used for the testing of a metal to determine its purity, should make it clear that "there is nothing against" these men. The phrase there is nothing against them (ἀνέγκλητοι, *anenklētoi*) is used of elders in Titus 1:6 where it is rendered by the NIV "blameless" and is a synonym for the word used of overseers in 3:2 rendered "above reproach." Only after this has been established are these men to be appointed and to serve as deacons.

3:11 In the same way, their wives

At this point, Paul makes a transition in the topic under discussion. This sentence (v. 11) has proven to be a real puzzle for those studying 1 Timothy. Who are the "women" (γυναῖκας, *gynaikas*) of this verse? Are they "wives" as the NIV has suggested in the text? Or should one favor the margin reading of the NIV "deaconesses"? The Greek word "woman" (γυνή, *gynē*) can be rendered either "woman" or "wife" depending upon the context.

The problem is complicated by the fact that "deacons" are addressed on both sides of the discussion of these "women." Also the structure of v. 11 is parallel to v. 8 and therefore dependent upon the "must" of v. 2. It looks as if Paul is giving qualifications for a ministry like that of overseer and deacon. If Paul had in mind the wives of deacons, he could have clarified the matter by simply adding the Greek word for "their" (αὐτῶν, *autōn*). It should be noted that the word "their" in the text of the NIV has been supplied by the translators and is not present in the Greek text. The issue is complicated even further because in Paul's time there is no word in Greek for "deaconess."

Several alternatives have been offered for understanding who these "women" were. First, some have suggested that these women represent the wives of the deacons because they reflect on the character and ministry of their husbands. In favor of this suggestion is the omission of any qualification regarding marital status found in qualifications for overseers, deacons and older women who were to be enrolled. This can easily be explained if they are deacons' wives.

Others, troubled by the idea that Paul would give qualities required for deacons' wives and not those of elders, have suggested that these are qualities required for the wives of both sets of church leaders. A primary problem with this interpretation is, of course, the placement of the qualifications.

A third suggestion is that these women represent deaconesses or women deacons. The difficulty with this interpretation is threefold: First, Paul begins v. 11 with "in the same way" (ὡσαύτως, *hōsautōs*) indicating a distinct group (cf. v. 8 and deacons as distinct from overseers). He is, therefore, apparently dealing with a new group of people or workers. Second, if these women are serving as *deacons*, why not make one set of qualifications that would apply to men and women? Third, why place this list in the middle of the qualifications of deacons? A fourth alternative is to see these women serving in some form of ministry assisting the deacons.[10] One problem with this interpretation is the omission of any requirement regarding marital status and fidelity when this requirement is so prominent in the other groups.

When all of the data is considered, options one and four seem to be most viable. Although he does not formerly propose it, Knight seems to suggest a fifth option which amounts to a combination of the first and fourth. He suggests that Paul is proposing "the deacons' wives as their assistants rather than women in general."[11] How ever one takes this passage, it is clear that the church throughout the ages has had women

---

[10]Lewis offers an interesting twist by suggesting that the "women" of 1 Tim 3:11 are indeed assistants to the deacons but adds the qualifier "unmarried." While Lewis's suggestions are interesting they are not convincing. Robert M. Lewis, "The 'Women' of 1 Timothy 3:1," 136 *Bibliotheca Sacra* (April–June 1979), 167–175.

[11]Knight, p. 171.

who serve in special capacities or ministries. Paul is simply calling these women to bear the characteristics one would expect of women to whom others look.

are to be women worthy of respect, not malicious talkers but temperate and trustworthy in everything.

The qualifications for these "women" are virtually synonymous with those of the deacons. Both groups are to be "worthy of respect." Not malicious talkers (μὴ διαβόλους, *mē diabolous*) is parallel to "sincere" (*me dilogos*). Temperate (νηφαλίους, *nēphalious*) — a word which Knight suggests is compressed and encompasses "temperate use of alcoholic beverages, sober, clear-headed, self-controlled"[12] — may well include everything from "not given to drunkenness" to "not violent but gentle" to "not quarrelsome" to "not a lover of money."

3:12 A deacon must be the husband of but one wife and must manage his children and his household well.

Here Paul returns to the discussion of the "deacon." As with the overseer, the deacon must be a family man whose family members are shining examples. In vv. 2 and 4 identical terms are used to describe the overseer (see above for a discussion of these terms).

3:13 Those who have served well gain an excellent standing and great assurance in their faith in Christ Jesus.

The promise offered to those who serve well as deacons may not be quite what humans seek: not financial wealth or even promotion to overseer. Rather Paul promises "excellent standing and great assurance." "Excellent standing" (βαθμὸν καλόν, *bathmon kalon*) is literally a "good step" and undoubtedly refers to standing before God. "Great assurance" (πολλὴν παρρησίαν, *pollēn parrēsian*) likely refers to the courage and confidence to stand before God and speak. Both of these blessings are to be seen as located "in their faith in Christ Jesus."

---

[12]Knight, p. 172.

C. PAUL'S PURPOSE IN WRITING AND THE BASIS FOR THESE DIRECTIONS (3:14-16)

¹⁴**Although I hope to come to you soon, I am writing you these instructions so that,** ¹⁵**if I am delayed, you will know how people ought to conduct themselves in God's household, which is the church of the living God, the pillar and foundation of the truth.** ¹⁶**Beyond all question, the mystery of godliness is great:**
> **He[a] appeared in a body,[b]**
> **was vindicated by the Spirit,**
> **was seen by angels,**
> **was preached among the nations,**
> **was believed on in the world,**
> **was taken up in glory.**

[a]*16 Some manuscripts God*   [b]*16 Or in the flesh*

3:14 Although I hope to come to you soon, I am writing you these instructions so that,

In this section Paul pauses briefly to put into perspective his admonitions. Although Paul is anticipating a visit to Timothy in Ephesus, he takes the precaution, in case he faces delays, of writing this letter to set in order the church. His concern is behavior within the Christian community, behavior which shows itself in worship (chapter 2) and in leadership (chapter 3).

3:15 if I am delayed, you will know how people ought to conduct themselves in God's household,

Paul begins with behavior or conduct "in God's household" (οἶκος, *oikos*). In this paragraph Paul uses three phrases to describe the church. He first uses the family metaphor — "God's household." This metaphor will play a prominent role in 1 Timothy (1:2, 18; 3:4-5, 15; 4:6; 5:1-2, 14-16; 6:2).

which is the church of the living God, the pillar and foundation of the truth.

Next this family is "the church of the living God." The word "church" (ἐκκλησία, *ekklēsia*) means "group" or "assembly";

this time that group belongs to "the living God." The phrase "living God" will appear again in 4:10. A God who is alive provides a dire contrast with the gods of the Gentiles. Finally the church is seen as "the pillar" (στῦλος, *stylos*) and "foundation" (ἑδραίωμα, *hedraiōma*) of the truth. The truth is in no danger of collapse as long as the church fulfills her task. She is the pillar or "column" and the foundation or "base" to support "the truth" against the false teachers.

3:16 Beyond all question, the mystery of godliness is great:

With the mention of the truth, Paul is moved to proclaim the greatness of "the mystery of godliness." Paul returns to the mystery (μυστήριον, *mystērion*), a subject he has already discussed in v. 9 where the plural form of the word is rendered "deep truths." Here again Paul is referring to God's redemptive work in Jesus which was not known in times past but has now been revealed in him. "Godliness" (εὐσέβεια, *eusebeia*; see the discussion of this term at 2:2) is "the duty that man owes God, piety, godliness, religion" (BAGD).

The six lines which follow represent what appears to be a fragment from an early Christian hymn. It bears many of the qualities one would expect in such a fragment. (1) The statement begins with an introductory relative pronoun, "who" (ὅς, *hos*, rendered "He" by the NIV) which has no clear antecedent. (2) The six lines are very much alike in form — an aorist passive third person singular verb generally followed by a phrase rendered "in," "by," "among," or "on." (3) The material is arranged in verses, with three pairs of couplets.

He appeared in a body,
was vindicated by the Spirit,

Christ was made known by the Father. This one who has always existed but was formerly unknown "appeared in a body" (literally "in flesh"). Christ is made known through the incarnation.

The vindication of Christ occurs in or "by the Spirit." The Spirit is for Paul the one who vindicates Jesus in his resurrection: "the Spirit of him who raised Jesus from the dead is living in you, he who raised Christ from the dead will also give life to your mortal bodies through his Spirit, who lives in you" (Rom 8:11). While it is possible to understand "spirit" (πνεῦμα, *pneuma*) as "the human spirit" of Jesus, this is unlikely.[13]

was seen by angels,
was preached among the nations,

The resurrected Christ "was seen by angels." All other NT references to "was seen" which are connected to Jesus refer to his post-resurrection appearances to human beings. Apparently angels are seen here as the recipients of his appearances to indicate the cosmic nature of his work.

In the fourth line, the hymn proclaims that Christ "was preached among the nations" (or "Gentiles"). Emphasis falls upon the universal nature of the gospel. The word translated "preached" (κηρύσσω, *kēryssō*) suggests the "heralding" of a message.

was believed on in the world,
was taken up in glory.

The fifth line declares the result of the fourth. This proclamation leads to faith on the part of many hearers "in the world."

The hymn closes with an apparent allusion to the ascension: He was "taken up in glory." The final verse provides a fitting conclusion which is typical of the NT passages identified as possible hymn fragments. The humiliated Messiah triumphs in glory.

---

[13]Knight, pp. 184-185.

1 TIMOTHY 4

V. SPECIAL INSTRUCTIONS FOR TIMOTHY (4:1-16)

Paul begins by elaborating on the nature of the errors in Ephesus (4:1-5) and then giving Timothy instructions for opposing those errors (4:6-16). Paul had earlier warned of the "myths and endless genealogies," the "meaningless talk," and the abuse of the law by the false teachers (1:3-7). He now moves to give some specific examples of the false teaching.

A. THE APOSTASY TIMOTHY WAS TO FACE (4:1-5)

[1] The Spirit clearly says that in later times some will abandon the faith and follow deceiving spirits and things taught by demons. [2] Such teachings come through hypocritical liars, whose consciences have been seared as with a hot iron. [3] They forbid people to marry and order them to abstain from certain foods, which God created to be received with thanksgiving by those who believe and who know the truth. [4] For everything God created is good, and nothing is to be rejected if it is received with thanksgiving, [5] because it is consecrated by the word of God and prayer.

4:1 The Spirit clearly says that in later times

For Jews the advent of the Messiah would usher in the last days. It was as if history was moving forward to the coming of the Messiah and then taking a 90° turn. Christians clearly saw themselves as living "in later times" (Acts 2:16, 17; cf. 2 Thess

2:3-4; 2 Tim 3:1). It is impossible to determine with certainty what prophecy Paul had in mind which referred to followers abandoning "the faith" and following "deceiving spirits and things taught by demons." Suggestions include warnings of apostasy from Jesus (Matt 13:21; 24:10, 11; Mark 4:17; Luke 8:12) and Paul's own warning to the elders in Acts 20:28-31. For Paul the Spirit has spoken clearly, perhaps in a combination of settings that point to the inevitability of heresy and falling away.

some will abandon the faith and follow deceiving spirits and things taught by demons.

In the phrase "will abandon the faith" (ἀποστήσονται τῆς πίστεως, *apostēsontai tēs pisteōs*), "faith" is used in an objective sense (see 3:9) and "will abandon" could be translated "will fall away" or "will apostasize." This apostasy occurs because people are following "deceiving spirits and things taught by demons." Paul sees Satan and his allies behind the false teachers and their teaching. The word translated "follow" also appears in 3:8 where it is translated "indulging in," in 4:13 where it is translated "devote," and in 6:3 where it is translated "agree."

4:2 Such teachings come through hypocritical liars, whose consciences have been seared as with a hot iron.

The demons use "hypocritical liars" (ψευδολόγοι, *pseudologoi*, literally "false words") as the human agents to accomplish their task. These false teachers are described as having their "consciences seared as with a hot iron." Two options are available for understanding this searing "with a hot iron." The more traditional interpretation is to see the false teachers as those who have so resisted and stood against the dictates of conscience that they no longer feel its pangs when they sin. Fee has suggested that one might also understand the text in terms of the false teachers bearing the brand of Satan on their consciences, indicating that they belong to him.[1] The

---

[1]Fee, p. 98. See also Robertson, Lock, and Kelly.

former interpretation seems to match the sense of Paul in Rom 1:18, 28-32 and does provide an inner reason for the hypocrisy and lies.[2]

4:3 They forbid people to marry

At this point Paul specifies something of the nature of the false teaching plaguing the church at Ephesus. The exact nature and origin of the heresy at Ephesus has produced considerable debate (see the Introduction). Although not bearing all of the characteristics of later Gnosticism, the false teachers do seem to disparage the physical and bear some resemblance to Neoplatonism. The heresy also has clear Jewish elements including a special emphasis on the law (e.g., 1 Tim 1:6-9), a characteristic one would not expect to find in the later Gnostic teachers. It would appear that Hendriksen's assessment of the basic premise of the false teachers is correct: "Anything physical or sensuous is contaminating."[3] The heresy probably arose as a syncretistic effort on the part of Jewish Christians to proclaim a gospel that would hold on to their Jewish upbringing and at the same time speak in terms of the pagan culture and philosophical milieu in which they lived. Little more can be concluded with certainty.

Paul mentions two particular ascetic doctrines which characterized the teachings propounded by the false teachers. These two doctrines lure many into the predicted apostasy (cf. the heretical asceticism of Col 2:20ff).

The sentence structure at the beginning of v. 3 represents a figure of speech known as a zeugma.[4] Literally the Greek could be translated: "They forbid people to marry and to abstain from certain foods." One needs to supply "order them" to complete the thought.

---

[2]Cf. Knight, p. 188.

[3]Hendriksen, p. 146.

[4]A zeugma is a specialized ellipsis where one verb controls two objects or infinitives, but the supplied verb fits only one object or infinitive. The reader or listener must supply a different and sometimes opposite verb to complete the sense of the sentence.

First, some false teachers forbade marriage. Apparently they felt that abstinence from marriage led to some higher spiritual plane.[5]

and order them to abstain from certain foods, which God created to be received with thanksgiving by those who believe and who know the truth.

Second, the false teachers demanded abstinence from certain foods. This error likely reflects the distinction between clean and unclean foods in the Mosaic law. The same false teaching was apparently present at Colosse (Col 2:16-23). Paul's answer to this heresy was to see the foods as created by God and to contend that they are wholesome when "received with thanksgiving by those who believe and who know the truth."

It should be noted that Paul is not suggesting that abstinence from marriage was unspiritual; in fact, in 1 Cor 7:7-8 and 26-27, he calls Christians who are currently single to remain so. Likewise, the eating or not eating of food will neither in and of itself commend or condemn one before God (1 Cor 8:8-9; Rom 14). Paul's concern is the demand of these false teachers and the claim that their regulations both save and make one holier.

4:4 For everything God created is good, and nothing is to be rejected if it is received with thanksgiving,

Paul declares that "everything God created is good." He likely has in mind Gen 1:11-13, 20-23, 24-25 where the text proclaims after the creation of all the substances used for food: "And God saw that it was good." Nothing need be rejected as long as it is eaten "with thanksgiving."

---

[5]In 1 Cor 7:1-9, Paul counters a similar heresy that saw sex and marriage as undesirable for the truly spiritual. The forbidding of marriage in a non-Christian, Greco-Roman cultural setting need not mean that sexual intercourse was also forbidden. Thus men went off to the prostitutes but avoided marriage bonds. The forbidding of marriage appears to be an element not derived from the false teachers' Jewish background.

4:5 because it is consecrated by the word of God and prayer. In v. 5 Paul combines "the word of God" and "prayer." The "word of God" can point back to the Genesis proclamation by God that all food is "good." God's pronouncement has then "consecrated" it. Lea and Griffin argue against this interpretation because Paul uses the present tense verb, "it is being consecrated," (ἁγιάζεται, *hagiazetai*) rather than the "more appropriate" perfect tense.[6] They suggest that "the word of God" may refer to the gospel message; thus when the Christians at Ephesus responded to the gospel they had learned that there are now no food laws. "The gospel had brought them to a proper understanding of food, and they acknowledged by prayer that it was the gift of God."[7] The word translated "consecrated" signifies that the food has been set apart. While neither interpretation of "the word of God" above produces a theological problem, the suggestion of Lea and Griffin does seem to fit the context and the syntax.

B. THE DISCIPLINE OF A GOOD MINISTER (4:6-16)

⁶If you point these things out to the brothers, you will be a good minister of Christ Jesus, brought up in the truths of the faith and of the good teaching that you have followed. ⁷Have nothing to do with godless myths and old wives' tales; rather, train yourself to be godly. ⁸For physical training is of some value, but godliness has value for all things, holding promise for both the present life and the life to come.

⁹This is a trustworthy saying that deserves full acceptance ¹⁰(and for this we labor and strive), that we have put our hope in the living God, who is the Savior of all men, and especially of those who believe.

¹¹Command and teach these things. ¹²Don't let anyone look down on you because you are young, but set an example

---

[6]Lea and Griffin, p. 131.
[7]*Ibid.*, p. 132. Cf. Guthrie, p. 94.

for the believers in speech, in life, in love, in faith and in purity. ¹³Until I come, devote yourself to the public reading of Scripture, to preaching and to teaching. ¹⁴Do not neglect your gift, which was given you through a prophetic message when the body of elders laid their hands on you.

¹⁵Be diligent in these matters; give yourself wholly to them, so that everyone may see your progress. ¹⁶Watch your life and doctrine closely. Persevere in them, because if you do, you will save both yourself and your hearers.

In this section Paul gives Timothy some instructions for dealing with the false teachers, for developing his own godliness, for setting the proper example for the church, and for persevering in his ministry of preaching and teaching the Scriptures.

4:6 If you point these things out to the brothers, you will be a good minister of Christ Jesus,

Paul's call for Timothy to "point these things out to the brothers" is a call for a gentle approach to the Christians at Ephesus. Guthrie has noted that the word translated "point" (ὑποτίθημι, *hypotithēmi*, literally "to place under") "means no more than 'suggest.'"[8] Making clear the nature of the false teaching is required if Timothy is to be "a good minister." The Greek word behind "minister" (διάκονος, *diakonos*) is the same word translated "deacon" in 3:8. Here it is used in the same sense as in Col 1:23 (cf. 1 Cor 3:5; 2 Cor 3:6; 6:4; 1 Thess 3:2; 2 Tim 4:5).

brought up in the truths of the faith and of the good teaching that you have followed.

The minister must be "brought up" or "nourished in" "the truths of the faith and of the good teaching" which Timothy has already been following. The phrase "the truths of the faith" represents a Greek phrase which could more literally be

---

[8]Guthrie, p. 94.

rendered "the words of faith." It represents the substance of doctrine in which Christians like Timothy have put their trust. The "good teaching," which may refer either to the gospel or to the proper use of Scripture, lies in contrast to the false teaching which the church was facing. The word "followed" (from παρακολουθέω, *parakoloutheō*), which also appears in Luke 1:3 and 2 Tim 3:10, indicates close investigation. As Guthrie has noted, "The best refutation of error is a positive presentation of truth."[9]

4:7 Have nothing to do with godless myths and old wives' tales;

The NIV leaves a word (δέ, *de*), "but," untranslated, a word which sets up the contrast between the healthy teaching to which Timothy subscribes and the teaching propounded by the heretics, their "godless myths and old wives' tales." These teachings are deemed "myths" (μῦθοι, *mythoi*, see discussion of the word at 1:4) and are characterized as "godless" or profane signifying opposition to the sacred. Paul also connects them with "old wives' tales," "a sarcastic expression often used in philosophical polemic comparing one's opponents' position to the tales perpetuated by the older women of those cultures as they would sit around weaving and the like."[10] Timothy is to "have nothing to do" with this foolish false teaching which is not grounded in the truth.

rather, train yourself to be godly.

Instead, Timothy is to "train" himself (a favorite Pauline metaphor taken from athletic exercise, cf. 1 Cor 9:24-27) in godliness (εὐσέβεια, *eusebeia*; see discussion of 2:2). While the heretics might have been subjecting their bodies to an ill-conceived discipline of asceticism, Timothy must exercise discipline in godliness, living one's life with God at the heart.

---

[9]Guthrie, p. 95.
[10]Fee, p. 105.

4:8 For physical training is of some value, but godliness has value for all things, holding promise for both the present life and the life to come.

Kelly terms the next phrase by Paul as "what, by its jingle, sounds like a proverbial tag": "For physical training is of some value, but godliness has value for all things." He suggests that the original apothegm was directed by Stoics and Cynics toward those involved in excessive training.[11] In the present context, "physical training" (γυμνασία, *gymnasia*) is not under discussion. Paul is helping Timothy to see that, while an athlete will accomplish some good through all his discipline, the discipline required for "godliness" has far wider reaching consequences. It has "value for all things" or perhaps better "is of benefit in every way," "holding promise for both the present life and the life to come." Life should likely be seen as eternal life which has already begun for the believer. This life is a "present" reality and offers hope in the age "to come."

4:9 This is a trustworthy saying that deserves full acceptance

This is the third "trustworthy saying" formula in 1 Timothy (1:15; 3:1). This time Paul adds "that deserves full acceptance" as he did in 1:15. The real problem this time is knowing what composes the "trustworthy saying." Four options have been suggested: (1) Paul may be referring back to all of v. 8. If this is the case the trustworthy saying is "physical training is of some value, but godliness has value for all things."[12] (2) The trustworthy saying may be the last part of v. 8: "godliness has value for all things, holding promise for both the present life and the life to come."[13] (3) Paul may have in mind what follows immediately in v. 10: "(and for this we labor and strive), that we have put our hope in the living God, who is the Savior of all men, and especially of those who believe."[14] (4) The final alternative, seeing the trustworthy saying as the second

---

[11]Kelly, pp. 99–100.
[12]Hendriksen, p. 152; Knight, pp. 201–202; cf. Barrett.
[13]NAB; Kelly, p. 101; Fee, p. 105; cf. Ward and White.
[14]NEB.

half of v. 10, is suggested by the arrangement of the NIV text: "we have put our hope in the living God, who is the Savior of all men."[15] The two alternatives which seem best to fit the language and syntax, and from which one should likely choose, are (1) and (2).

4:10 (and for this we labor and strive),

The "this" for which Paul says he and other believers "labor and strive"[16] likely refers neither to "life" nor to "godliness" in the previous verse, but rather the whole concept of discipline in godly living which results in life. The word rendered "that" (ὅτι, *hoti*) by the NIV in v. 10 should be rendered "because." The real reason that Paul and others labor (κοπιάω, *kopiaō*, "make strenuous effort") and strive (ἀγωνίζομαι, *agōnizomai*, "struggle like an athlete in competition") is the nature of the God in whom they have put their hope.

that we have put our hope in the living God, who is the Savior of all men, and especially of those who believe.

He is "living" (cf. 3:15), and He is "the Savior of all men." The phrase "the Savior of all men" has caused concern by some who want to see a kind of universalism on the part of Paul. God's wish for all men is their salvation; he has paid the price for that salvation in Jesus. He can, therefore, rightly be called the Savior of all men (cf. "a ransom for the sins of all," 2:6). The word "especially" introduces the assurance of salvation which belongs to those who have put their trust in the work of God in Jesus.

4:11 Command and teach these things.

Paul's instruction for Timothy in 4:11-16 is perseverance both in what he had been teaching, in the exercise of his gift,

---

[15]Guthrie, p. 96.

[16]The KJV has instead "and suffer reproach" following the textual variation ὀνειδιζόμεθα (*oneidizometha*) rather than ἀγωνιζόμεθα (*agōnizometha*). The reading of the NIV is to be favored both on grounds of weightier MS support and the better fit in the context.

and in progression in the godly life. Timothy was instructed to "command and teach these things." The word "command" indicates the authority with which he is to do his teaching. Timothy must speak authoritatively.

4:12 Don't let anyone look down on you because you are young,

Due to his age and perhaps other reasons, Timothy seems to display some timidity. Paul's instructions that Timothy was not to "let anyone look down on" him because he was "young" have led many to assume that Timothy was a mere youngster, a teenager, or perhaps a young man in his twenties. The word "young" (νεότης, *neotēs*) could be used to indicate any age up to forty.[17] If Timothy joined Paul's missionary travels in A.D. 49-50 and 1 Timothy is being written A.D. 62-63, it would be reasonable to assume that he was thirty to thirty-five years old.[18] It is important to remember that age is relative. The elders at Ephesus, as well as many members there, could very well look at Timothy as a young man. He might, after all, be the age of some of their children.

but set an example for the believers in speech, in life, in love, in faith and in purity.

As apostolic representative, Timothy must gain the respect of those to whom he ministers. The virtues Timothy is to model will offset the handicap of his youth. There are five areas in which Timothy is to demonstate the virtuous life. All of these virtues show a contrast between the behavior of Timothy and that of the false teachers. First, "in speech" refers to the everyday talk of Timothy. He is not be be argumentative but rather is to be known for his wise words. Second, "in life" (ἀναστροφῇ, *anastrophē*; better "in conduct")

---

[17]Irenaeus, *Against Heresies* 2.22.5. Cf. Lea and Griffin, p. 138, note 107; Knight, p. 205; Hendriksen, p. 157; Kelly, pp. 103-104.

[18]Fee, p. 69. Hendriksen, p. 157, suggests an even older Timothy — somewhere between thirty-five and thirty-nine.

represents a call for the proper lifesytle. The third and fourth, "in love" and "in faith" represent two of the basic Christian virtues included in every such list. The fifth area for virtuous living is "in purity" or "in chastity," perhaps given as a contrast to the false humility and asceticism of the false teachers.

4:13 Until I come, devote yourself to the public reading of Scripture, to preaching and to teaching.

From his discussion of Timothy's personal behavior, Paul now turns to Timothy's ministry. "Until I come" indicates Paul's conviction that he will soon be with Timothy at Ephesus. Timothy is to "devote" himself to "the public reading of Scripture, to preaching and to teaching." Paul is not attempting here to give a pattern for Christian worship. He makes no mention of prayers, singing, or the Lord's Supper. He does indicate three areas in which Timothy exercises leadership.

The reading of Scripture in the public assembly was a prominent feature of both synagogue worship and the worship of the early church. Since believers did not have the advantage of having personal copies of the Old Testament and many could not read, the public reading of Scripture provided them with an opportunity to hear God speak. "Preaching" (παράκλησις, *paraklēsis*) indicates "exhortation" or "comfort." It here implies the presentation of a message of relevance to Timothy's audience derived from the biblical text that was read (cf. Acts 13:15; Rom 15:4; Heb 12:5 for the common connection between reading and exhortation). "Teaching" (διδασκαλία, *didaskalia*) implies the intellectual instruction in Christian doctrine either within or without the assembly.

4:14 Do not neglect your gift,

The imperative, "do not neglect your gift," is natural since that gift enables Timothy to fulfill his ministry (cf. 2 Tim 1:6). The word "gift" (χάρισμα, *charisma*) is used to designate "a gift freely and graciously given." The word is often used by

Paul of "spiritual gifts" like tongues, prophecy, and knowledge (1 Cor 12, 13, 14). The gift is "in Timothy" (although translated "your" in the NIV, literally "in you"). It here is Timothy's calling, the gift of ministry as a preacher and teacher of the word of God.[19]

which was given you through a prophetic message when the body of elders laid their hands on you.

The "gift" of ministry (see 1:18) was given to Timothy "through a prophetic message." The word "through" in the NIV repesents a Greek word (μετά, *meta*) better translated "with." The gift comes from God and is accompanied both by a "prophetic message" and by the "laying on of hands" of "the body of elders." The "prophetic message" indicates the Spirit's role likely here in the predicting of the kind of ministry Timothy would have. The "laying on of hands" symbolizes the recognition or ordination of a person for a work by a group of local elders (cf. Acts 13:2,3). These two phrases likely refer to what happened at Lystra on Paul's second missionary tour when Timothy became a co-worker and fellow missionary. Both prophetic message and the laying on of hands by the presbytery provide public testimonies to Timothy's ministry. Timothy cannot become careless about this gift.

4:15 Be diligent in these matters; give yourself wholly to them,

In vv.15-16 Paul summarizes his concerns for Timothy and his ministry from the previous section. He offers Timothy four imperatives. First, he is to "be diligent in these matters." The verb can mean either "to give one's mind to" or "to practice."[20] The second imperative is "give yourself wholly to them." This verb indicates that Timothy is to be absorbed in them.[21]

---

[19]Fee, p. 108.
[20]*Ibid.*, p. 109.
[21]Hendriksen, p. 160.

so that everyone may see your progress.

The result of this practice and devotion will be a clear recognition of Timothy's progress. "Progress" or advancement to deeper truths may well have been one of the slogans of the false teachers at Ephesus (2 Tim 2:16; 3:9).[22] Their speculative nonsense is to be contrasted with Timothy's faithful progress as a minister of the gospel.

4:16 Watch your life and doctrine closely. Persevere in them, because if you do, you will save both yourself and your hearers.

Paul spells out what he means by "these matters" (v. 15) in v. 16. With the third imperative, Paul says that Timothy is to "watch closely" first his life (see Paul's call for Timothy to be an example for believers, 4:12) and second his doctrine or teaching. In the final imperative, Paul calls Timothy to "persevere" (ἐπίμενε, *epimene*) both in the godly life and in godly teaching. In so doing Timothy "will save both" himself and his hearers. Salvation does involve perseverance. If Timothy perseveres in modeling and teaching the gospel, the church at Ephesus will also persevere.

---

[22]Fee, p. 109.

1 TIMOTHY 5

VI. RELATIONSHIPS WITHIN THE CHRISTIAN COMMUNITY (5:1-6:2)

In this section Paul gives Timothy instructions for dealing with special groups within the Christian community: first groups by age, then widows, then elders, and finally slaves. The lifestyle demonstrated in these relationships is to be influenced by Christian values. It must also win the approval and respect of the pagan population.

A. THE MINISTER AND THE CHURCH (5:1-2)

¹Do not rebuke an older man harshly, but exhort him as if he were your father. Treat younger men as brothers, ²older women as mothers, and younger women as sisters, with absolute purity.

Paul is well aware of Timothy's youthfulness. Since the church is a family, Paul instructs Timothy how he is to respond to those within that family.

5:1 Do not rebuke an older man harshly, but exhort him as if he were your father.

The respect for one's elders was very much a part of the world of the Ancient Near East. Timothy was to deal with older men in a way that was not harsh. The word "rebuke" (ἐπιπλήσσω, *epiplēssō*) appears only here in the NT. It signifies a verbal rebuff. Paul was not saying that Timothy was to avoid correcting older men when they were found to be in error. He is to "exhort" (παρακαλέω, *parakaleō*, a word translated "urge" in 1:3 and 2:1, and "preach" in 4:13 and 6:2) them "as he would his own father."

Treat younger men as brothers,
The verb "treat" has been supplied by the NIV translators. In reality the verb "exhort" is to be understood with each of the next three groups: "younger men," "older women," and "younger women."

5:2 older women as mothers, and younger women as sisters, with absolute purity.
"Younger men" are to be exhorted "as brothers," "older women as mothers, and younger women as sisters." To the latter group Paul adds "with absolute purity." Although some[1] would see the phrase as descriptive of Timothy's relationship with all four groups, it is more reasonable to see it in terms of his relationship with "younger women."[2] Younger women could pose a special problem for Timothy, and indeed they continue to do so for any young minister. The word "purity" (ἁγνεία, *hagneia*) can be used in a general sense (4:12), but here it is likely used with the more specific meaning "chastity" in the sense of sexual purity. The church at Ephesus may well have been experiencing some problem with lack of purity on the part of some younger women (1 Tim 5:1; 2 Tim 3:6-7).

B. THE CARE OF WIDOWS (5:3-16)

This section serves as a normal transition of subject from Paul's instructions to exhort "older women as mothers." In the culture of the time widows were often forgotten. This was not so among Jews, and it was not to be the case among

---

[1]E.g., Spain, p. 83.
[2]So, Fee, p. 112; Guthrie, p. 100; Hendriksen, pp. 166-167; Kelly, p. 110; Knight, pp. 214-215; Lea and Griffin, p. 145.

Christians. The key word in this larger section about the church's responsibility to widows is "honor" (τιμα, *tima*) rendered by the NIV "give proper recognition." The word carries with it both the idea of respect and that of material support.

1. Family Responsibilities (5:3-8)

³Give proper recognition to those widows who are really in need. ⁴But if a widow has children or grandchildren, these should learn first of all to put their religion into practice by caring for their own family and so repaying their parents and grandparents, for this is pleasing to God. ⁵The widow who is really in need and left all alone puts her hope in God and continues night and day to pray and to ask God for help. ⁶But the widow who lives for pleasure is dead even while she lives. ⁷Give the people these instructions, too, so that no one may be open to blame. ⁸If anyone does not provide for his relatives, and especially for his immediate family, he has denied the faith and is worse than an unbeliever.

5:3 Give proper recognition to those widows who are really in need.

The English phrase "who are really in need" in the NIV represents a single Greek word (ὄντως, *ontōs*) which means "really." The point is not "widows in need" but "widows indeed."[3] Paul is using the word to indicate widows who have no one to look after their needs. The qualification is intended to designate a widow who is *left alone*, who has material needs which are not being met. V. 16 indicates that the phrase "give proper recognition" (τιμᾶ, *tima*) or "honor" means more than giving respect. It clearly involves helping them.

5:4 But if a widow has children or grandchildren, these should learn first of all to put their religion into practice by

---

[3] Cf. NASB.

caring for their own family and so repaying their parents and grandparents, for this is pleasing to God.

This verse gives the first qualification of those who are not "widows indeed." If they have "children or grandchildren," they do have those who should meet their needs. Caring for a needy widowed mother or grandmother is a first step in "putting their religion into practice" (εὐσεβεῖν, *eusebein*, literally "practicing godliness"). It is repayment for services rendered and "is pleasing to God."

5:5 The widow who is really in need and left all alone puts her hope in God and continues night and day to pray and to ask God for help.

The real widow has been "left alone," indicating that with the death of her husband she has no family to care for her. Such a widow must, however, demonstrate some spiritual qualities. She must "put her hope in God." She must have a prayer life that can be described as "night and day" (note the Jewish reckoning of time — sunset to sunset) indicating that she lives a life characterized by prayer.

5:6 But the widow who lives for pleasure is dead even while she lives.

The true widow does not "live for pleasure," a verb found in James 5:5 and used of general self-indulgence. A woman who *does* live for pleasure needs to be seen as dead spiritually "even while she lives."

5:7 Give the people these instructions, too, so that no one may be open to blame.

Timothy is to "give these instructions" (i.e., vv. 5–6) probably to the widows.[4] Paul wants them not to "be open to blame," a phrase Paul used in 3:2 to introduce the qualifications of overseers.

---

[4]Fee, p. 171.

5:8 If anyone does not provide for his relatives, and especially for his immediate family, he has denied the faith and is worse than an unbeliever.

Now Paul moves to the instructions Timothy is to share with the families of the widows. One who does not provide for his relatives and especially those "under his own roof,"[5] i.e., his immediate family, "has denied" the essence of the Christian faith. He is "worse than an unbeliever." Unbelievers or pagans in the contemporary world would acknowledge the responsibility of children to parents. As Guthrie has noted, "It was unthinkable that Christian morality should lag behind general pagan standards."[6]

2. Widows to Be Enrolled (5:9-10)

⁹**No widow may be put on the list of widows unless she is over sixty, has been faithful to her husband,ᵃ ¹⁰and is well known for her good deeds, such as bringing up children, showing hospitality, washing the feet of the saints, helping those in trouble and devoting herself to all kinds of good deeds.**

ᵃ9 Or *has had but one husband*

5:9 No widow may be put on the list of widows

There has been considerable debate about who the widows were who were to be put on the list and just how they were to function with the church. Some have suggested that the Greek word translated "put on the list" (καταλεγέσθω, *katalegesthō*) carries the more general meaning "to count." Most, however, would see a more technical use of the word to indicate enrolling of these widows on some official list. The real question is the nature of the list and the function of the ladies on the list. (1) Some would see the enlisted widows as simply a

---

[5]Fee, p. 118.
[6]Guthrie, p. 101.

roll of widows who receive regular compensation from the church. The list would simply be a compilation of the "widows indeed" discussed above.[7] (2) Since specific qualifications similar to those for overseers and deacons are given for these widows, many have suggested "an order of widows" given specific duties with the church.[8] These duties are thought to have included spiritual and charitable works for which the widows received compensation. (3) Lea and Griffin prefer to see the development of "an order" of widows as later evolution.[9] They would agree with Guthrie that it is "preferable . . . to suppose that special duties in the Church were reserved for some of the old widows receiving aid, and some official recognition of this fact was given."[10] Guthrie's assessment seems reasonable. The fact that a widow was not "on the list" did not mean that she would not receive any assistance from the church.

unless she is over sixty,

Paul gives three basic requirements for a widow to be "put on the list." First, she must be not less than sixty years of age. This does not imply that a thirty-year-old widow with children still under her care would not receive aid. Women under sixty would generally be expected to work and ultimately to remarry. Lea and Griffin are likely right in suggesting that Paul has here singled out the younger widows "who were apparently a source of great difficulty for the Ephesian church (5:15)."[11]

has been faithful to her husband,

Second, a widow who is to be placed on the list must have "been faithful to her husband." This phrase represent a Greek phrase that might literally be translated "one man's woman." The parallel "one woman's man" was used in the qualifications

---

[7]Yet another alternative is to see these widows as deaconesses. See the discussion of deaconesses at 3:11.
[8]Bernard, pp. 80–81; Hendriksen, pp. 172–174.
[9]Lea and Griffin, p. 149.
[10]Guthrie, p. 102.
[11]Lea and Griffin, p. 149.

for overseers and deacons (3:2, 12; Titus 1:6). Although some have assumed that Paul is forbidding second marriages,[12] it is more reasonable to see it as a call for a woman who has demonstrated marital fidelity. No more than one man can lay claim to her.

5:10 and is well known for her good deeds, such as bringing up children, showing hospitality, washing the feet of the saints, helping those in trouble and devoting herself to all kinds of good deeds.

The third requirement involves a list of good deeds this widow is to have done, likely before the death of her husband. She must have "brought up children." The emphasis here is not the ability to have children but rather child-rearing, a significant part of the role of women in the first century. She should show "hospitality, washing the feet of the saints." These widows should show service to the traveling Christians. Washing feet was a necessary part of showing that hospitality. "Helping those in trouble" indicates that these widows have rendered relief to persecuted Christians. Paul concludes with an all-encompassing summary statement: "and devoting herself to all kinds of good deeds." She must have a reputation for doing good deeds.

3. Younger Widows (5:11-15)

[11]As for younger widows, do not put them on such a list. For when their sensual desires overcome their dedication to Christ, they want to marry. [12]Thus they bring judgment on themselves, because they have broken their first pledge. [13]Besides, they get into the habit of being idle and going about from house to house. And not only do they become idlers, but also gossips and busybodies, saying things they ought not to. [14]So I counsel younger widows to marry, to

---

[12]E.g., Kelly, pp. 115-116.

have children, to manage their homes and to give the enemy no opportunity for slander. ¹⁵Some have in fact already turned away to follow Satan.

5:11 As for younger widows, do not put them on such a list.

In this section Paul explains his reasons for excluding "younger widows" from the "list." The exclusion of these younger widows from the list would in no way exclude them from receiving necessary assistance. They are likely to be excluded from being regular recipients and from serving in some form of special ministry.

For when their sensual desires overcome their dedication to Christ, they want to marry.

Paul first suggests that these women would be overcome in "sensual desires." While it is true that many of these women would remarry, one should not see vv. 11-12 as a suggestion that the desire of these younger women to remarry was tantamount to abandoning the faith. The solution to this problem involves the interpretation one brings to v. 12.

5:12 Thus they bring judgment on themselves, because they have broken their first pledge.

This verse may literally be translated, "having judgment because they have set aside their first faith." Fee has suggested three alternative interpretations for the key word in the verse: (1) The word rendered "pledge" (πίστις, *pistis*) may indicate a pledge to widowhood, which the widow would break when she remarried. (2) The pledge may have to do with her "faithfulness" to her first husband and her abandoning the ideal of being married only once (v. 9). (3) The word "pledge" should be translated literally as "faith," indicating her abandonment of her faith in Christ when she remarries.[13] Lea and Griffin have suggested that this pledge is broken when the widows do not marry a believer and thus abandon their faith

---

[13]Fee, pp. 121-122.

in Christ.[14] Although this position has the advantage of taking *pistis*, the word here rendered "pledge," in the way it is used elsewhere in the Pastoral Epistles, there is nothing within the text to suggest such a marriage. When connected to the verb here translated "broken" (ἀθετέω, *atheteō*), *pistis* should likely be rendered "pledge."[15] It would seem that the primary problem with enrolling younger widows was not remarriage because Paul will later suggest that they should remarry (5:14), rather the tendency to "sensual desires." The mention of a broken first pledge should be taken as the widow's promise to serve Christ as a widow.

5:13 Besides, they get into the habit of being idle and going about from house to house. And not only do they become idlers, but also gossips and busybodies, saying things they ought not to.

Second, the behavior of these younger women might disgrace the cause of Christ. The financial support of the church might lead these widows to learn idleness as they would flit about "from house to house," sharing gossip wherever they went and being "busybodies," (περίεργοι, *periergoi*)[16] meddling in the affairs of others. The word "idle" (ἀργαί, *argai*) appears in Titus 1:12 as "lazy," in James 2:20 as "useless," and in Matt 20:3 as "with nothing to do." The NIV translation renders a Greek word (φλύαροι, *phluaroi*) "gossips" which is in reality a much richer word, meaning one who talks foolishly or makes false accusations.

5:14 So I counsel younger widows to marry, to have children, to manage their homes

The verb "to have children" is the same one used in 2:15

---

[14]Lea and Griffin, p. 151.

[15]Knight, p. 226.

[16]Kelly, p. 118, has suggested that the word περίεργοι (*periergoi*) should be rendered so as to indicate that these women were practicing the occult as in Acts 19:19. It is more likely that the word is used in the sense of "busybodies" as in 2 Thess 3:11.

where Paul said that "women will be saved through childbearing." The use of the word here does indicate that Paul clearly saw "childbearing" as a part of the role of women. The verb "to manage their homes" (οἰκοδεσποτεῖν, *oikodespotein*) appears only here in the NT and signifies taking charge of the matters of the home.

and to give the enemy no opportunity for slander.
Paul's concern is that these younger widows behave in such a manner as "to give the enemy no opportunity for slander." The enemy here may be either any non-Christian enemy or Satan. Although the context here is not conclusive,[17] v. 16 points to Satan as the adversary. The word "opportunity" represents the Greek word ἀφορμήν (*aphormēn*) which can literally be translated "the starting-point or base of operations for an expedition."[18]

5:15 Some have in fact already turned away to follow Satan.
Paul's concern is urgent because some have already turned away to follow Satan. Some likely indicates some of the younger widows.

4. Women and Widows (5:16)

[16]If any woman who is a believer has widows in her family, she should help them and not let the church be burdened with them, so that the church can help those widows who are really in need.

In v. 16 Paul returns to the subject of the responsibility of family members to care for widows. The difficulty with v. 16 is that the shorter and better attested reading is a bit problematic: "any woman who is a believer." On the other hand, the longer reading seems to fit better what one would expect

---

[17]Knight, p. 229.
[18]*Ibid.*

here from Paul, "any man or woman who is a believer." Fee has suggested that "the problem behind vv. 4 and 8 was a specific case of a younger widow of means rejecting the care of a widowed mother and/or grandmother."[19] While one need not see the "any woman who is a believer" as a widow, there may well have been a problem with women of means failing to care for widows within their households.

C. ELDERS (5:17-25)

[17]The elders who direct the affairs of the church well are worthy of double honor, especially those whose work is preaching and teaching. [18]For the Scripture says, "Do not muzzle the ox while it is treading out the grain,"[a] and "The worker deserves his wages."[b] [19]Do not entertain an accusation against an elder unless it is brought by two or three witnesses. [20]Those who sin are to be rebuked publicly, so that the others may take warning.

[21]I charge you, in the sight of God and Christ Jesus and the elect angels, to keep these instructions without partiality, and to do nothing out of favoritism.

[22]Do not be hasty in the laying on of hands, and do not share in the sins of others. Keep yourself pure.

[23]Stop drinking only water, and use a little wine because of your stomach and your frequent illnesses.

[24]The sins of some men are obvious, reaching the place of judgment ahead of them; the sins of others trail behind them. [25]In the same way, good deeds are obvious, and even those that are not cannot be hidden.

[a]*18* Deut. 25:4   [b]*18* Luke 10:7

5:17 The elders who direct the affairs of the church well

Like the concern for widows at the beginning of 5:11-15, Paul expresses concern that elders be cared for. One wonders

---
[19]Fee, p. 124.

why Paul did not discuss caring for the needs of elders in chapter 3. The answer may rest in the fact that Paul is now dealing with correcting church problems, here erring elders. Likewise the use of "honor" (τιμή, *timē*) in this verse provides a clear link to the use of the verb form "give proper respect" (τιμάω, *timaō*), in v. 3, concerning widows.

The elders of v. 17 represent Paul's use of a synonym for the overseers of 3:1-7. The Greek phrase (καλῶς προεστῶτες, *kalōs proestōtes*) rendered in the NIV "direct the affairs of the church well" is translated "rule well" by the KJV. Neither translation carries the intent of the original, which might more literally be translated "lead well."[20]

are worthy of double honor,

At least five options have been suggested for the meaning of the phrase "worthy of double honor": (1) such elders are to be properly honored and properly paid; (2) they should receive "honor" (not pay) first because they serve as elders and second because they serve "well"; (3) they should receive "double" the stipend of "widows indeed"; (4) they should receive more pay, although not necessarily double, than the widows; or (5) they should receive more honor, not pay, than widows (5:3) and masters (6:1). It seems best to see the "double honor" as respect that includes remuneration. The emphasis on compensation is clear from the discussion earlier of honor to true widows and from Paul's illustrations in v. 18.

especially those whose work is preaching and teaching.

The word "especially" may indicate a subgroup of "elders whose work is preaching and teaching," or Knight has suggested that it may be used to delineate what it means to lead "well."[21] If one takes the first option, Paul has in mind those who spend perhaps all their time "preaching and teaching." This would indicate "full-time elders." The second option sug-

---

[20]See the discussion of προΐστημι (*proistēmi*) in 1 Tim 3:4 where it is rendered "manage."
[21]Knight, p. 232.

gests that the work (κοπιάω, *kopiaō*, a word indicating "hard work")[22] of all elders involves preaching (literally "in word") and teaching. The first option may explain the need for compensation.

5:18 For the Scripture says, "Do not muzzle the ox while it is treading out the grain," and "The worker deserves his wages."

In this verse Paul supports his call for support of these elders who lead well with two quotations. The first quotation is from Deut 25:4 and is also used by Paul in 1 Cor 9:9 for the support of those in ministry. The second quotation appears in Luke 10:7 (cf. Matt 10:10). The question here is whether the formula "for the Scripture says" is to be taken only with the first quotation which is clearly an OT quote or with both. If it is to be taken with both quotations, then Paul would be referring to a statement of Jesus as "Scripture." Fee argues that the second quotation is simply a proverb cited both by Jesus and by Paul.[23] Knight makes a very convincing argument for Paul's citing Jesus, perhaps even from Luke's Gospel since Luke traveled with Paul.[24] Both citations illustrate Paul's point that these men who labor in the church should receive financial support in the work they perform for the church.

5:19 Do not entertain an accusation against an elder unless it is brought by two or three witnesses.

In vv. 19-20 Paul takes up a second item in regard to elders — correcting an elder who is in sin. Paul provides Timothy with two basic guidelines: (1) do not accept any charges against an elder which are not certain; (2) when an elder is found to be guilty he must be reprimanded in public. The call for "an accusation" to be supported by "two or three witnesses" follows the OT procedure for verifying a sin or crime (Deut 19:15). Paul is here simply calling for Timothy to

---

[22]Cf. 1 Tim 4:10.
[23]Fee, p. 129.
[24]Knight, p. 234.

protect the reputation of an elder as one should anyone (2 Cor 13:1). It is very easy for elders, or for that matter anyone in a leadership position, to be the recipient of unfair and untrue accusations.

5:20 Those who sin are to be rebuked publicly, so that the others may take warning.

The second item may well be the reason for this entire section.[25] "Those who sin" (literally "those who are sinning") "are to be rebuked publicly." Paul's instructions may seem harsh and unfair but likely assume that Timothy has already followed the admonition of 5:1 "not [to] rebuke an older man harshly, but exhort him as if he were your father." The instructions are to be carried out for those who persist in sin. The point of the rebuke is "that the others may take warning" (literally "have fear").

5:21 I charge you, in the sight of God and Christ Jesus and the elect angels, to keep these instructions without partiality, and to do nothing out of favoritism.

Here Paul indicates the solemn nature of the charge he has given to Timothy in correcting elders who sin. The charge is an oath of sorts taken before the heavenly tribunal — "in the sight of God and Christ Jesus and the elect angels." Timothy must carry out the task "without partiality" or "favoritism." "Partiality" (πρόκριμα, *prokrima*) involves prejudging a case while "favoritism" (πρόσκλισις, *prosklisis*) indicates the inclination to side with one party against another.

5:22 Do not be hasty in the laying on of hands,

In this verse Paul moves from the public rebuke of an elder who sins to the appointment of men who will serve as elders and perhaps also deacons. Paul warns Timothy against making a hasty appointment of those who were to serve in leadership capacities within the church (cf. Acts 13:3). The

---

[25]Fee, p. 130.

"laying on of hands" is used of the appointment of those who are to serve in ministry (see discussion at 4:14; cf. 2 Tim 1:6).

and do not share in the sins of others. Keep yourself pure.

"Do not share in the sins of others" can mean either (1) do not assist in the appointment of men who bear the kind of sins described earlier in the letter because, if one does, he shares in their sins[26] or (2) do not become partners in the sins of others, i.e., do not be like those you are correcting.[27] The first alternative seems best to fit the immediate context.

5:23 Stop drinking only water, and use a little wine because of your stomach and your frequent illnesses.

Timothy may well have been in danger of taking Paul's advice to keep himself pure and the earlier admonition that overseers and deacons not abuse wine as support for his practice of drinking only water. The other explanation of Paul's instruction to use a little wine (οἶνος, *oinos*) might be the possibility that Timothy had bought into the ascetic tendencies of the false teachers. Paul does not specify the nature of Timothy's frequent illnesses; however, some have thought that Timothy's being told to use a little wine because of his stomach might indicate that drinking only water was affecting his stomach. In the ancient world wine was often seen as having medicinal value. While one cannot say with certainty what initiated the need for these instructions, it seems likely that Timothy was taking very seriously his obligations to be pure and to set a good example to the detriment of his health.

5:24 The sins of some men are obvious, reaching the place of judgment ahead of them; the sins of others trail behind them.

After his brief digression with personal advice for Timothy, Paul returns to the matter of sins of elders. He first notes that

---

[26]Knight, p. 239; Hendriksen, p. 185; Lea and Griffin, p. 158.
[27]Fee, p. 132.

"the sins of some" are so clear they cannot be missed. Their sins race ahead and reach "the place of the judgment ahead of them." On the other hand, there are others whose sins are not as evident. Only later on do their sins become clear.

5:25 In the same way, good deeds are obvious, and even those that are not cannot be hidden.

The same thing can be said with regard to "good deeds." For some they are "obvious." For others they may not be so clear, but for these as well they will eventually come to the forefront.

1 TIMOTHY 6

D. SLAVES (6:1-2)

¹All who are under the yoke of slavery should consider their masters worthy of full respect, so that God's name and our teaching may not be slandered. ²Those who have believing masters are not to show less respect for them because they are brothers. Instead, they are to serve them even better, because those who benefit from their service are believers, and dear to them. These are the things you are to teach and urge on them.

6:1 All who are under the yoke of slavery

Paul continues his discussion of relationships within the church by turning to slaves. The section may be related to the previous sections on widows and elders because of its common use of the word "honor" or "respect" (τιμή, *timē*).

Slavery in the first century was considerably different from what most Americans imagine. It had little to do with race. Most people came into slavery because of economic situations, because of war, or because they were born into slavery. The manumission of slaves was fairly common. For many slaves slavery to a good master was to be preferred to being freed. Being a poor freed man was often a terrible fate.

Slaves made up a fairly large number in early churches (1 Cor 7:21-24; Col 3:22-25; Eph 6:5-8; 1 Pet 2:18-25; Titus 2:9-10). But why the special attention to slaves here? Fee has suggested, ". . . perhaps problems have arisen among some Christian slaves and their attitudes toward Christian masters similar to those among younger widows. . . . [Perhaps] an over-realized eschatology or an elitist spirituality caused them to disdain the old relationships that belong to the [old] age. . . ."[1]

The fact that Paul mentions "believing masters" in v. 2 makes it possible to assume that he is referring to those who are pagans in v. 1. It is, however, more likely that v. 1 gives general instructions that would apply to all those "who are under the yoke of slavery" (literally "slaves under yoke").[2] Paul's redundant use of "slaves under yoke" may be given to emphasize the oppressive nature of slavery.

should consider their masters worthy of full respect, so that God's name and our teaching may not be slandered.

Even though the institution of slavery was dehumanizing, Paul insisted that Christian slaves show "full respect" to their masters. The purpose of Paul's concern for this respect was that "God's name," i.e., the Christian cause, and the message which he and Timothy had been teaching might "not be slandered."

Many have expressed concern that Paul could tolerate the existence of this oppressive institution. As Hendriksen has said, "[Paul] aimed to destroy slavery without waging war to do so!"[3] A primary concern for Paul was that the gospel might not be treated with disrespect.

6:2 Those who have believing masters are not to show less respect for them because they are brothers.

V. 2 begins with a word "but" (δέ, *de*) not translated by the NIV. Although this word may indicate a contrast between v. 1 (pagan masters) and v. 2 (Christian masters),[4] it is more likely that Paul moves in v. 2 to give instructions to slaves with

---

[1] Fee, p. 137.
[2] So Fee, p. 137; and Kelly, p. 131. Lea and Griffin, p. 163, favor seeing v. 1 as a reference to pagan masters and v. 2 as a reference to Christian masters.
[3] Hendriksen, p. 192.
[4] Lea and Griffin, p. 163.

"believing masters" because they might be tempted to take advantage of their unique relationship and, in so doing, bring disrespect on the cause of Christ. The term "believers" (πιστοί, *pistoi*, literally "faithful") is used as an equivalent to the adjective "Christian." These slaves are called "not to show less respect" (καταφρονέω, *kataphroneō*, literally "think down on") to their masters who are brothers.

Instead, they are to serve them even better, because those who benefit from their service are believers, and dear to them.

Rather they are "to serve them even better." The phrase "even better" (μᾶλλον, *mallon*) should likely be rendered "all the more so" since the point is not "even better service," but rather showing "all the more" *respect*. Christian masters who enjoy the benefit of their service are, after all, "believers" and "dear" (ἀγαπητοί, *agapētoi*, literally "loved"). Paul's concern is that Christian slaves behave toward their pagan or Christian masters in a way that will not bring disrespect to God or his gospel.

These are the things you are to teach and urge on them.

Again (cf. 3:14; 4:6, 11; 5:7, 21) Paul instructs Timothy to "teach and urge" (or "exhort") these things. "These things" may refer only to the section which immediately precedes this one (5:3–6:2) or, since this section is very much a concluding one, may point back all the way to 2:1.

VII. FINAL EXHORTATIONS (6:3-21)

Much of the material in this section hearkens back to chapter 1. Paul's dominant concerns are the false teachers and Timothy's role as minister.

A. AN INDICTMENT OF FALSE TEACHERS (6:3-5)

³If anyone teaches false doctrines and does not agree to the sound instruction of our Lord Jesus Christ and to godly

teaching, ⁴he is conceited and understands nothing. He has an unhealthy interest in controversies and quarrels about words that result in envy, strife, malicious talk, evil suspicions ⁵and constant friction between men of corrupt mind, who have been robbed of the truth and who think that godliness is a means to financial gain.

6:3 If anyone teaches false doctrines and does not agree to the sound instruction of our Lord Jesus Christ and to godly teaching,

In contrast to the "these things" of v. 2 which Timothy was to teach, Paul now turns to those who teach "false doctrines" (see 1:3 where the same word occurs, literally "who teach differently") of the heretics. Paul describes this teaching which differs from the gospel as not agreeing with "the sound instruction of our Lord Jesus Christ" or with "godly teaching." The word "sound" literally is "healthy" (cf. 1:10). The word "instruction" (λόγοις, *logois*) is literally "words." These "healthy words" come from Jesus (notice the full title for Jesus, "our Lord Jesus Christ") but need not indicate that Timothy is reading from one of the Gospels. The "false" teaching is also not in agreement with "godly teaching" (literally "teaching according to godliness").[5] It does not demonstrate a life of reverence to God.

6:4 he is conceited and understands nothing. He has an unhealthy interest in controversies and quarrels about words that result in envy, strife, malicious talk, evil suspicions

Paul describes these false teachers as "conceited" (literally "having been blinded") and "understanding nothing." These people saw themselves as a spiritual elite who possessed special knowledge. They were in reality caught up in their own self-importance and lacked real understanding (1:7; Titus 1:15–16).

---

[5]On "godliness" (εὐσέβεια, *eusebeia*) see 2:2; 3:16; 4:7, 8.

They have "unhealthy interest in controversies and quarrels about words." Paul here contrasts the desired healthy or sound teaching with an unhealthy or "morbid craving" (BAGD) for "controversies" (described elsewhere in the Pastoral Epistles as "foolish" and/or "ignorant")[6] and "quarrels about words" ("word-battles").

6:5 and constant friction between men of corrupt mind,

Paul then spells out the *result* of the attitude and action of the false teachers: "envy" or "jealousy"; "strife" or "discord" (usually linked to envy); "malicious talk" or "slander" (βλασφημίαι, *blasphēmiai*); "evil suspicions" or "conjectures"; and "constant friction" or "thorough or mutual irritation"[7] which results "between men of corrupt [or 'ruined'] mind."

who have been robbed of the truth

At this point Paul explains why these people go the direction they do. First they "have been robbed of the truth." The perfect tense here for "have been robbed" indicates that these men were robbed of "the truth" in the past and are now reaping the consequence of that event. Knight has suggested that the one doing the action conveyed by the passive verb, "have been robbed," should be seen as "'the god of this world,' [who] has brought about this condition."[8]

and who think that godliness is a means to financial gain.

Second, these men "think that godliness is a means to financial gain." Since Paul warns against the quest for money governing a church leader's life (3:3, 8; Titus 1:7, 11) and argues that he himself does not minister in order to gain financially (1 Thess 2:5), it is apparent that some have been using ministry or church leadership simply as a way to get ahead financially. These false teachers are dangerous, and the

---

[6]Cf. Titus 3:9; 2 Tim 2:23.
[7]Knight, pp. 251-252.
[8]*Ibid.*, p. 252.

church must be warned against them and their teaching by Timothy.

B. GODLINESS, CONTENTMENT, AND MONEY (6:6-10)

⁶**But godliness with contentment is great gain. ⁷For we brought nothing into the world, and we can take nothing out of it. ⁸But if we have food and clothing, we will be content with that. ⁹People who want to get rich fall into temptation and a trap and into many foolish and harmful desires that plunge men into ruin and destruction. ¹⁰For the love of money is a root of all kinds of evil. Some people, eager for money, have wandered from the faith and pierced themselves with many griefs.**

6:6 But godliness with contentment is great gain.
Paul picks up the word "godliness" (εὐσέβεια, *eusebeia*) from vv. 3 and 5 where he has indicated that it is clearly missing in the teaching and life of the false teachers. Godliness (*eusebeia*) is the whole religious bent to life. It does provide "great gain," but not the kind the false teachers were seeking. It should not be seen as a way to get rich. It provides great gain only when accompanied "with contentment" (αὐτάρκεια, *autarkeia*). "Contentment" was a significant term among Stoic and Cynic philosophers. For them it meant "self-sufficiency," the ability to grit one's teeth and bear whatever fate delivered. Paul, however, does not use the word like the Stoics. As Fee has noted, he "'turned the tables' on the Stoics by declaring that genuine *autarkeia* is not self-sufficiency but *Christ*-sufficiency . . . (Phil 4:13)."[9]

6:7 For we brought nothing into the world, and we can take nothing out of it.
"Contentment" must accompany "godliness" because "we

---
[9]Fee, p. 143.

brought nothing into the world, and we can take nothing out of it." That is, material things are inconsequential in the grander scheme of things.

6:8 But if we have food and clothing, we will be content with that.

If one has the basic necessities of life, "food and clothing," in them he can find contentment, the opposite of the greedy attitude of the false teachers. Lea and Griffin have suggested that food and clothing should be seen as a synecdoche in which a part of life's necessities is used for the whole.[10] According to Spain, the two words are themselves broader than the English translations would suggest. "Food" (διασ-τροφή, *diastrophē*) is used for something to eat and also for a job that would enable one to buy that food; similarly, "clothing" (σκέπασμα, *skepasma*) is used for lodging as well as something to wear.[11] Jesus himself called disciples to be free from the anxiety over food and clothing and to rest in God by seeking first his kingdom (Matt 6:25-34).

6:9 People who want to get rich fall into temptation and a trap and into many foolish and harmful desires that plunge men into ruin and destruction.

Those who are obsessed with the desire "to get rich" and the love of money are certain to "fall into temptation and a trap and into many foolish and harmful desires that plunge men into ruin and destruction." Fee has suggested that one should here see a downward spiral for the one caught up in the pursuit of material possessions. "Temptation" (πειρασμός, *peirasmos*) can mean either a "test" or an "enticement to sin." Here it is clearly the latter. That "enticement" becomes a "trap." The word "trap" (παγίς, *pagis*) is a snare used to catch a bird or wild animal (3:7; 2 Tim 2:26). The trap then is "many desires" or "lusts" which can be characterized as "foolish and

---

[10]Lea and Griffin, pp. 168-169.
[11]Spain, p. 98.

harmful" — "foolish" because wealth has nothing to do with true godliness and "harmful" because these "desires . . . plunge men into ruin and destruction."[12]

6:10 For the love of money is a root of all kinds of evil.

Paul substantiates the point in v. 9 with a proverb: "the love of money is the[13] root of all kinds of evil." Various translations of v. 10 have been abused by those who wish to contend that all sins are rooted in "the love of money." While almost any kind of evil can be linked to avarice, not every specific instance of evil can be linked to greed. The NIV has corrected this misunderstanding by indicating that it is the "root of all kinds of evil." Knight has demonstrated that this is the proper understanding when one takes into consideration the immediate context: "[Paul] does not assert that 'all' desires result in 'many desires' . . . He does not assert that 'all' desires result from 'the will to be rich' but that 'many' do."[14]

Some people, eager for money, have wandered from the faith and pierced themselves with many griefs.

Those who are "eager for" (ὀρεγόμενοι, *oregomenoi*, literally, "strive for" or "reach for" BAGD) "money have wandered from the faith." Paul is here again using the word faith as a synonym for "gospel." In wandering "from the faith," they "pierced" (literally, "impaled") "themselves with many griefs." As Fee has put it, ". . . they had come to love money, and it did them in."[15]

---

[12]Fee, pp. 144-145.

[13]Although the NIV has "a root of all kinds of evil" the translation should be "the root of all kinds of evil." The definite article ("the") is not present in Greek simply because in Greek a predicate nominative is usually anarthrous (without an article). For the opposing argument see Knight, p. 257 and Kelly, p. 138. It is legitimate and right to take the word "all" (πάντων, *pantōn*) to mean "all kinds of."

[14]Knight, p. 258.

[15]Fee, p. 146.

C. A CHARGE TO TIMOTHY (6:11-16)

¹¹But you, man of God, flee from all this, and pursue righteousness, godliness, faith, love, endurance and gentleness. ¹²Fight the good fight of the faith. Take hold of the eternal life to which you were called when you made your good confession in the presence of many witnesses. ¹³In the sight of God, who gives life to everything, and of Christ Jesus, who while testifying before Pontius Pilate made the good confession, I charge you ¹⁴to keep this command without spot or blame until the appearing of our Lord Jesus Christ, ¹⁵which God will bring about in his own time — God, the blessed and only Ruler, the King of kings and Lord of lords, ¹⁶who alone is immortal and who lives in unapproachable light, whom no one has seen or can see. To him be honor and might forever. Amen.

6:11 But you, man of God, flee from all this,
Again Paul moves from discussing the false teachers to an exhortation directed to Timothy himself. Timothy is called to keep his spiritual life in order, to remember his own spiritual pilgrimage, and to reflect on Christ's own confession. Paul's reflection upon that confession leads him to praise God in the doxology that ends this section.

Paul addresses Timothy as "man of God." In so doing he draws a sharp contrast between Timothy and the "sick" doctrine and greed of the false teachers. Although the NIV supplies the word "all," the Greek simply says flee "these things." The things to which Paul is referring should be seen as representing not just the greed of the previous section, but rather everything in his final indictment of the false teachers (6:2b-10).

and pursue righteousness, godliness, faith, love, endurance and gentleness.
Timothy must "pursue" those qualities which should

characterize a "man of God."[16] First he must seek "righteousness" or "upright conduct"; then "godliness," that reverential attitude and lifestyle missing from the false teachers (cf. 3:16; 4:7-8; 6:5-6); then "faith" or "trust"[17] and "love," two of the virtues that frequently appear together in lists like this one in the Pastoral Epistles (1 Tim 1:5; 2:15; 4:11; 2 Tim 2:22; Titus 2:2); next "endurance," another important Christian virtue in Paul (cf. Gal 5:23); and finally "gentleness" (πραϋπαθία, *praupathia*), a word that appears only here in the NT.[18]

6:12 Fight the good fight of the faith.

Paul continues his exhortation to Timothy with a call to "fight the good fight of the faith." Both the verb "fight" (ἀγωνίζομαι, *agōnizomai*)[19] and the noun "fight" (ἀγών, *agōn*)[20] are athletic metaphors carrying the idea of a struggle or a contest. The command here is a present imperative indicating that Paul is calling for Timothy to "keep on fighting" the good fight. Paul will repeat the imperative almost verbatim in 2 Tim 4:7. There Paul's emphasis is clearly on his desire for Timothy to be willing to suffer for the gospel. Notice that the struggle for the "faith" (i.e., the gospel) is to be regarded as "good" because the cause is noble.

Take hold of the eternal life to which you were called when you made your good confession in the presence of many witnesses.

With the third imperative, Paul calls Timothy to "take hold

---

[16]It should be noted at this point that the word "man" in this context is ἄνθρωπος (*anthrōpos*), which primarily means "human being," and not ἀνήρ (*anēr*), which exclusively means "male person."

[17]While the word "faith" (πίστις, *pistis*) may indicate either "trust" or "faithfulness," the context here and usage in similar lists elsewhere in Paul would point to "trust." Cf. Knight, pp. 261-262.

[18]For the use of a close synonym, πραΰτης (*prautēs*), in Paul see 1 Cor 4:21; 2 Cor 10:1; Gal 5:23; 6:1; Eph 4:2; Col 3:12; Titus 3:2; 2 Tim 2:25.

[19]Cf. Luke 13:24; John 18:26; 1 Cor 9:25; Col 1:29; 4:12; 1 Tim 4:10; 2 Tim 4:7.

[20]Cf. Phil 1:30; Col 2:1; 1 Thess 2:2; 2 Tim 4:7; Heb 12:1.

of the eternal life to which [he was] called." "Take hold of" is used here and in 6:19 in the figurative sense "to make one's own" (BAGD). As Fee has argued this "imperative . . . extends the metaphor [of the athletic contest] to focus on the prize."[21] Paul uses the phrase "eternal life" to refer to both the present and the future aspect of salvation. It is this life to which Timothy was called, and to some degree is experiencing now. Yet it is beyond. Timothy was called to the "eternal life when [he] made [his] good confession in the presence of many witnesses." Although some have argued that Timothy's "good confession" refers to his "ordination to ministry," the pursuit of "eternal life" fits better with Timothy's confession of Jesus at his baptism.

6:13 In the sight of God, who gives life to everything, and of Christ Jesus, who while testifying before Pontius Pilate made the good confession, I charge you

Paul's description of the ones before whom he charges Timothy — "God" and "Christ Jesus" — are particularly appropriate. God is the one who "gives life to" or "preserves life for" everything, an especially appropriate concept for Paul's call to steadfastness. Christ Jesus testified "before Pontius Pilate" and "made the good confession"; his example is appropriate for Paul's call for Timothy to "take hold of the eternal life" to which he was called when he had made his good confession.

6:14 to keep this command without spot or blame until the appearing of our Lord Jesus Christ,

Paul calls Timothy to take an oath before God and Christ Jesus that he will "keep a commandment," whatever that commandment may be. The commandment has been interpreted in various ways: (1) the exhortations of vv. 11-12; (2) some charge he received at his baptism; (3) a commandment received at his "ordination"; (4) the whole of the Christian

---

[21]Fee, p. 150.

faith; or (5) the commandment for Timothy to persevere in his own faith and ministry in 4:16.[22] The call to "keep" this charge "without spot or blame until the appearing of our Lord Jesus Christ" would suggest that the commandment might well represent the commitment Timothy made at his baptism. This would fit the context of the "good confession" if it indeed refers to Timothy's confession of Jesus as Messiah at his baptism.

6:15 which God will bring about in his own time —

The emphasis on persevering is made even plainer by the addition of "until the appearing of our Lord Jesus Christ." This "appearing," the second coming, "God will bring about in his own time." The second coming rests in God's sovereign control. It will occur on his timetable, "in his own time."

God, the blessed and only Ruler, the King of kings and Lord of lords,

In a manner which is typically Pauline, the mention of "the appearing of Jesus" and God's control of that event move Paul to a doxology. Paul uses the word "blessed" (μακάριος, *makarios*) of God only in the Pastoral Epistles (cf. 1:11; Titus 2:13). The word "Ruler" is also applied to God in the apocrypha (2 Macc 12:15; Ecclus 46:5) and is used to indicate princely dignity. The descriptions "King of kings" and "Lord of lords" are used twice in the book of Revelation of Christ (17:14; 19:16). There are also parallels in the OT (Deut 10:17; Ps 86:3; Dan 4:34, LXX) and in the apocrypha (2 Macc 13:4). The usage of these descriptions for God by Jews and Christians are clearly designed to indicate "a conscious rebuttal of the claims of earthly potentates."[23]

6:16 who alone is immortal and who lives in unapproachable

---

[22]Fee, p. 151. Fee favors the final option which he sees as a kind of summary of the basic thrust of the whole letter.
[23]Kelly, p. 146.

light, whom no one has seen or can see.
Paul's declaration that God is "immortal" is parallel to the previous doxology in 1:17. The description "who lives in unapproachable light, whom no one has seen or can see" probably is a conscious reflection on Ps 104:2. The image of God as a blinding light which no one could see is common in the OT (Exod 24:15-17; 34:29-35; 1 Kings 8:11). The picture of God as light is especially important in Johannine literature (John 1:7-9; 3:19-21; 1 John 1:5-7; cf. John 1:18; 6:46). Paul in Col 1:12 can refer to Christians as "saints in the kingdom of light."

To him be honor and might forever. Amen.
Paul ends the doxology in a customary way: "To him be honor and might forever. Amen." God's role as supreme Ruler places him above all rivals.

D. INSTRUCTIONS FOR THE RICH (6:17-19)

[17]Command those who are rich in this present world not to be arrogant nor to put their hope in wealth, which is so uncertain, but to put their hope in God, who richly provides us with everything for our enjoyment. [18]Command them to do good, to be rich in good deeds, and to be generous and willing to share. [19]In this way they will lay up treasure for themselves as a firm foundation for the coming age, so that they may take hold of the life that is truly life.

After the doxology Paul returns to a topic closely associated with his warning in v. 9 addressed to "people who want to get rich." Some scholars have argued that this discussion does not belong at this place in the epistle. Vv. 17-19 may well be an afterthought to Paul's earlier discussion. In this section he is, after offering a word of praise to God in the doxology, seeking to finish that earlier discussion (vv. 9-10) by providing some positive advice to those who are already rich.

6:17 Command those who are rich in this present world not to be arrogant

Timothy is to speak authoritatively (i.e., to "command," παράγγελλε, *parangelle*; cf. 1:3, 5; 4:11; 5:7) to "those who are rich in this present world." Guthrie describes Paul's instructions to the rich regarding their rightful approach to wealth as "strikingly moderate."[24] The rich face two dilemmas: the temptation "to be arrogant" and the temptation "to put their hope in wealth." To be arrogant is literally "to think proud thoughts" and indicates that the rich may begin to think that they are of greater worth than those around them.

nor to put their hope in wealth, which is so uncertain,

"To put their hope in" represents the perfect tense of the Greek verb ἐλπίζω (*elpizō*) used to emphasize both the placement of their hope and the abiding consequence of that action. Paul uses two phrases to describe the "wealth" of the rich: the riches are "in this present world," indicating that there are other riches that need to be considered, namely those "for the coming age" (v. 19); and they are "so uncertain" in contrast with hope which is to be found "in God."

but to put their hope in God, who richly provides us with everything for our enjoyment.

Paul offers four admonitions for the rich: (1) they are to "put their hope in God," who is dependable; (2) they are "to do good"; (3) they are "to be rich in good deeds"; and (4) they are "to be generous and willing to share." Although Paul says that God "richly provides us with everything for our enjoyment," one should not understand "enjoyment" as self-indulgence (5:6-10). Everything, in context especially the wealth of the rich, is from God.

6:18 Command them to do good, to be rich in good deeds, and to be generous and willing to share.

Although "to do good" and "to be rich in good deeds"

---

[24]Guthrie, p. 117.

function as synonyms, the second phrase — "to be rich (πλουτεῖν, *ploutein*) in good deeds" — provides a word play on the phrase "the rich" (τοῖς πλουσίοις, *tois plousiois*) with which Paul began v. 17. Paul argues that true riches are to be found in giving.

6:19 In this way they will lay up treasure for themselves as a firm foundation for the coming age, so that they may take hold of the life that is truly life.

This verse is very much like the words of Jesus (Luke 12:32-33; 18:22; cf. Matt 6:19-21; 19:23-24). Although material wealth is of "this present world" and "uncertain," some eternal good can be accomplished through its generous use (the meaning of "in this way"). The final clause, "so that they may take hold of the life that is truly life," clarifies the nature of real treasure and wealth, the "eternal life," which Paul had instructed Timothy take hold of in v. 12. Again the language of Paul is reminiscent of the sayings of Jesus (Luke 12:15, 21).

E. PAUL'S FINAL CHARGE TO TIMOTHY (6:20-21)

20Timothy, guard what has been entrusted to your care. Turn away from godless chatter and the opposing ideas of what is falsely called knowledge, 21which some have professed and in so doing have wandered from the faith.

Grace be with you.

6:20 Timothy, guard what has been entrusted to your care.

Fee has noted that this letter is a bit unusual in that it has no final greeting or benediction. "To the very end this letter is characteristically 'all business,' and except for some new language, this final charge merely summarizes that business."[25]

Paul's final appeal to his young colleague has a personal note as he calls him by name, using the Greek vocative,

---

[25]Fee, p. 160.

before giving the final two charges. First, Timothy is to "guard what has been entrusted" to his care. The verb "guard" (φύλαξον, *phylaxon*) is literally "keep the deposit," "reflecting the highest kind of sacred obligation in ancient society, . . . being entrusted with some treasured possession for safe-keeping while another is away."[26] Paul concludes this letter by placing Timothy under such a trust, as he had done already in 1:18, and will do in 2 Tim 1:14. The trust given to Timothy may be the gospel or it may refer to the letter as a whole — the tasks of standing against the false teachers, maintaining a pure life, and faithfully proclaiming the truth.[27] This does fit the rest of the verse where Timothy is called to avoid "godless chatter" and "falsely called knowledge."

Turn away from godless chatter and the opposing ideas of what is falsely called knowledge,

In his final charge, Paul instructs to resist the false teachers. He is to "turn away from godless chatter" (cf. 1:16; 4:7). He is also to avoid "the opposing ideas of what is falsely called knowledge." The description of "the opposing ideas" as "falsely called knowledge" has led some to suggest that the author cannot be Paul because he is battling Gnosticism (from the Greek word γνῶσις [*gnōsis*], "knowledge"), a heresy which will come to full flower at a time later than Paul. Fee has accurately assessed this conclusion: ". . . that is to make far too much of this language, the essential matters for a Gnostic heresy . . . are simply not found in 1 Timothy. Paul has previously had trouble with those who opposed his gospel in the name of wisdom and *gnōsis* (1 Cor 1:10–4:21; 8:1–13, . . . a semi-technical term for philosophy)."[28] The relationship between the heresy in 1 Timothy and the similar one seen a few years earlier at Colosse (Col 2:1–10) is sufficient to explain Paul's use of the term.

---

[26]Fee, p. 160.
[27]*Ibid.*, p. 161.
[28]*Ibid.*

6:21 which some have professed and in so doing have wandered from the faith.
Grace be with you.
These false teachers and their followers have unfortunately "wandered from the faith" (from ἀστοχέω, *astocheō*, "miss the mark with regard to the faith," BAGD).

Paul concludes the letter with a rather abrupt benediction: "Grace be with you." Paul's use of the plural "you" is a clear indication that he intends the letter to be read by the church at Ephesus. Perhaps Fee is correct in assessing this abrupt conclusion, which is very similar to the one in Galatians, as being a result of "the distress of the situation in both these churches" which call for an "all business" approach.[29]

The final "amen" of the KJV is not in the earlier manuscripts of the book and was likely added to provide an appropriate conclusion to the book when it was read aloud.

---

[29]Fee, p. 161.

THE BOOK OF
TITUS

INTRODUCTION

PLACE OF ORIGIN AND DATE

At the time of writing Titus, Paul was in or on his way to Nicopolis where he planned to spend the winter (3:12). Titus had been left at Crete to complete the work which he and Paul had begun (1:5). The only other reference to Crete in the New Testament occurs when Paul spent time at the harbor of Fair Havens (Acts 27:8). Because of the brevity of that stay, it is unlikely that Paul engaged in evangelistic work at that time. While it is possible that Paul completed evangelistic work in Crete during some of the gaps in Acts (cf. the details in 2 Cor 11:23-29 which are not narrated in Acts), it seems probable that Titus — like 1 Timothy — occurred after Paul's release from the "house arrest" of Acts 28:30 but before the later arrest assumed by 2 Timothy.

While Robinson argues for a date of A.D. 57 for Titus with Paul writing the work on his way to Jerusalem, thus finding a place for the book within the chronology of Acts, few scholars find this suggestion plausible. Those who hold that Titus is pseudonymous date the book in the second century (see on The Place of Origin and Date of 1 Timothy). Those who hold to Pauline authorship date the book before 2 Timothy and in the same time period as 1 Timothy, the mid 60s.

DESTINATION AND AUDIENCE

In contrast to the work at Ephesus where Timothy was working with an established church, Titus' task was to grow a church in a climate that was less than desirable. Timothy's task was to maintain a healthy eldership, but Titus was called upon to appoint elders for a young church.

Titus himself is not mentioned in the book of Acts. He was a Gentile and became Paul's test case for circumcision, securing for Gentiles a gospel separate from the law (Gal 2:1, 3). In all likelihood he was one of Paul's converts (Titus 1:4). He was probably a co-worker with Paul from the early years of Paul's ministry and, as such, was trusted with some very difficult situations (2 Cor 2:3-4, 13; 7:6-16; 8:16-24). After Titus and Paul had evangelized the island of Crete, Titus had been left to set things in order in the churches. He was soon to be replaced by Artemas and to join Paul in Nicopolis (Titus 3:12).

As Titus ministered to the church in Crete, he confronted hostile environs. This small island in the Mediterranean Sea was, at best, an outpost. Its inhabitants were known for their lying, gluttony, and laziness (Titus 1:12, 13).

THE CONTRIBUTION OF TITUS

Titus is very much like 1 Timothy. Only two passages (2:11-14; 3:3-7) have no corresponding material in 1 Timothy. Fee has noted that "Titus has often been viewed as a miniature 1 Timothy and, except for 2:11-14 and 3:3-7, has been treated with benign neglect."[1] There are, however, some striking differences between Titus and 1 Timothy. First the church at Crete had only recently been established while the church at Ephesus had been in existence for some time. As Fee has noted, even the lack of urgency in terms of Paul's instructions to the young evangelist and in terms of the false teachers may indicate that he is preparing the evangelist and the church for what they may face rather than what they are already facing.[2]

---

[1]Fee, *1, 2 Timothy, Titus*, p. 11.
[2]*Ibid.*, pp. 11-12.

The dominant theme in Titus is good works (1:8, 16; 2:7, 14; 3:1, 8, 14). These good works will provide this young church and its minister with a means of affecting outsiders (2:5, 7, 8, 10, 11; 3:1, 8).

OUTLINE

I. SALUTATION — 1:1-4
II. APPOINTING ELDERS — 1:5-16
   A. Qualifications of Elders — 1:5-9
   B. Elders' Responsibilities Toward False Teachers — 1:10-16
III. INSTRUCTIONS FOR VARIOUS GROUPS — 2:1-15
   A. Behavior and Sound Doctrine — 2:1
   B. Instructions for Older Men — 2:2
   C. Instructions for Older and Younger Women — 2:3-5
   D. Instructions for Younger Men — 2:6-8
   E. Instructions for Slaves — 2:9-10
   F. The Theological Basis for the Christian Life — 2:11-15
IV. STANDARDS FOR CHRISTIAN BEHAVIOR — 3:1-11
   A. Respect for Government Authorities — 3:1
   B. Respect for All — 3:2
   C. The Theological Basis for Living with Non-Christians — 3:3-8
   D. Final Warnings Concerning False Teachers and the Divisive — 3:9-11
V. PERSONAL DIRECTIONS AND CLOSING SALUTATIONS — 3:12-15

TITUS 1

I. SALUTATION (1:1-4)

¹Paul, a servant of God and an apostle of Jesus Christ for the faith of God's elect and the knowledge of the truth that leads to godliness — ²a faith and knowledge resting on the hope of eternal life, which God, who does not lie, promised before the beginning of time, ³and at his appointed season he brought his word to light through the preaching entrusted to me by the command of God our Savior,

⁴To Titus, my true son in our common faith:
Grace and peace from God the Father and Christ Jesus our Savior.

The salutation to Titus differs from the salutations in 1 and 2 Timothy at some significant points. In Titus, Paul offers an elaborate discourse on his apostleship (vv. 1-3). Only Romans has a similar elaboration. These verses are comprised of one long, complex sentence emphasizing the purpose of Paul's apostleship. The reason for this elaboration does not seem to be that people are questioning his authority (cf. 2 Cor). Rather the concern is to encourage relatively new Christians in their faith as a safeguard against false teaching. This elaboration may, therefore, be no more than a verification of the message they have accepted.

1:1 Paul, a servant of God and an apostle of Jesus Christ

Paul begins by describing himself as a servant (δοῦλος, *doulos*, literally "a slave") of God. Usually Paul describes himself as "a slave of Christ Jesus." The variation here simply indicates the high christology of Paul. Here, as in most of his letters, Paul indicates that he is "an apostle of Jesus Christ" to signify his apostolic authority.

for the faith of God's elect

While Paul normally identifies his apostleship by giving its source (e.g., "by the will of God"), here he moves to its purpose. His apostleship is first "for the faith of God's elect." Although the word translated "for" (κατά, *kata*) frequently means "according to," when the KJV translates it thus in this verse, it has probably missed Paul's intended sense. The basic meaning in this context is "with a view to"; thus the NIV rendering is correct. Paul's apostleship was given him by God so that the "elect" of God might be brought to faith (here to be understood as "trust"). The phrase "God's elect" is used in the NT only by Paul (cf. Rom 8:33; Col 3:12; 2 Tim 2:10). As Lea and Griffin have noted the concept of the elect "produces a certain intellectual tension, particularly with regard to 'free will' or personal activity in one's salvation."[1] The term "elect" is always used by Paul of those who have accepted the gospel message and emphasizes their security before God.

and the knowledge of the truth that leads to godliness —

Paul's apostleship is also concerned with the "knowledge of the truth" (cf. 1 Tim 2:4; 2 Tim 2:25; 3:7). Paul's discussion later in the book of false teachers indicates that some have a defective grasp of "the truth," i.e., the gospel message. The truth is concerned with "godliness" (εὐσέβεια, *eusebeia*, see discussion on 1 Tim 2:2 and 3:16). The visible manifestation of the truth in the lives of the elect is godly, reverential behavior.

1:2 a faith and knowledge resting on the hope of eternal life,

The NIV translators have seen the next phrase "on the hope of eternal life" as modifying both "faith" and "knowledge" and have thus repeated them in v. 2. Kelly, however,

---

[1]Lea and Griffin, p. 265.

has argued that the phrase should be translated "*in* the hope of eternal life" and be seen as modifying Paul's claim as an apostle of Jesus Christ in v. 1.[2] It is probably most reasonable to follow Hendriksen's suggestion (a kind of both/and approach) and to understand that Paul intends for Titus to see "*all* that has been said so far — his service and apostleship in the interest of the faith of God's elect and their acknowledgement of the truth which accords with godliness — rests on the hope of life everlasting. . . ."[3] In a somewhat similar fashion, Knight suggests that this phrase speaks of a hope which Paul as apostle shares with the elect as he carries out his ministry.[4]

which God, who does not lie, promised before the beginning of time,

The word "hope" (ἐλπίς, *elpis*) is used in the normal NT sense of "earnest expectation" or "anxious awaiting." That hope is sure because "God does not lie." He promised that life "before the beginning of time" (literally "before the time of the ages").

1:3 and at his appointed season he brought his word to light through the preaching entrusted to me by the command of God our Savior,

At his own just-the-right time, "his appointed season,"[5] he made clear "his word" (used in the Pastoral Epistles as a synonym for "the gospel message"; Titus 1:9; 2:5; 2 Tim 2:9, 15; 4:2). That message was delivered through Paul's preaching. Paul emphasizes that his preaching was not a matter of his

---

[2]Kelly, p. 227.
[3]Hendriksen, p. 340. See Hendriksen, pp. 340-341, note 188, for a fuller discussion of the two options.
[4]Knight, p. 284.
[5]This verse serves as an excellent illustration of the difference between the two Greek words for time: "before the beginning of time" (χρόνος, *chronos*, "the duration of time") and "at his appointed season" (καιρός, *kairos*, "suitable opportunity").

choosing, but a sacred trust given by God's command. The phrase "by the command of God our Savior" is exactly paralleled in 1 Tim 1:1.

1:4 To Titus, my true son in our common faith:
Paul addresses Titus as his "true" or "legitimate" son, a phrase that also finds an exact parallel in 1 Tim 1:2. That legitimacy is still Paul's focus with the added descriptive phrase "in our common faith."

Grace and peace from God the Father and Christ Jesus our Savior.
Paul concludes the salutation with his normal greeting, "grace and peace."

The grace and peace which he desires for Titus come "from God the Father and Christ Jesus our Savior." Paul's use of "God our Savior" in v. 3 indicates that God is the originator of salvation. With the phrase "Christ Jesus our Savior" in v. 4 he identifies the same function for *Jesus,* again reflecting his high christology.

II. APPOINTING ELDERS (1:5-16)

In v. 5 Paul moves immediately to the subject at hand without his typical thanksgiving. "This letter, like 1 Timothy, is all 'business,' not a personal communication to Titus (cf. the very different 2 Timothy)."[6] Unlike 1 Timothy the "business" is not primarily false teachers and their heretical teachings, rather it is a threat from a "circumcision group" (1:10) and Paul's concern that elders be appointed who will be able to resist and refute the false teachers.

Paul begins with the matter of setting the church in order by getting elders appointed (vv. 5-9) and then moves to discuss their response to the false teachers (vv. 10-16). The first paragraph, on the surface, looks very much like 1 Tim 3:1-7.

---
[6]Fee, p. 171.

In both texts Paul lists fifteen characteristics or qualifications for overseers or elders; in fact five of the qualifications are identical and five or six others correspond rather closely in the two lists. See the chart below which details some of these similarities. There are, however, some striking differences. (1) Titus is to appoint elders in new works. (2) Although overseers are to be able teachers in 1 Timothy, in Titus 1:9 Paul spells out even clearer the duty of these men: they are to "encourage others by sound doctrine and refute" false teachers who oppose the truth. (3) Fee has noted that the whole list in Titus has a more orderly arrangement.[7]

A. QUALIFICATIONS OF ELDERS (1:5-9)

⁵The reason I left you in Crete was that you might straighten out what was left unfinished and appoint[a] elders in every town, as I directed you. ⁶An elder must be blameless, the husband of but one wife, a man whose children believe and are not open to the charge of being wild and disobedient. ⁷Since an overseer[b] is entrusted with God's work, he must be blameless — not overbearing, not quick-tempered, not given to drunkenness, not violent, not pursuing dishonest gain. ⁸Rather he must be hospitable, one who loves what is good, who is self-controlled, upright, holy and disciplined. ⁹He must hold firmly to the trustworthy message as it has been taught, so that he can encourage others by sound doctrine and refute those who oppose it.

[a]5 Or *ordain* [b]7 Traditionally *bishop*

1:5 The reason I left you in Crete

Paul had "left" Titus (the implication is that Paul had been with Titus on Crete) to "straighten out what was left unfinished and appoint elders in every town," as Paul had "directed" him. The events mentioned here do not fit the context of

---

[7]Fee, p. 172.

Paul's first visit to Crete on his way to Rome (Acts 27:8). A visit after Paul's release from the Roman imprisonment at the end of Acts should be assumed (see the Introduction).

was that you might straighten out what was left unfinished and appoint elders in every town, as I directed you.

The phrase "straighten out" need not imply that major problems existed. Rather the primary task was to do some things that had not yet been accomplished. The things "left unfinished" are clarified by Paul's instructions to "appoint elders in every town." The fact that Titus had already been directed by Paul to do so may well indicate that the message was as much for the church as for Titus. The word appoint (καταστήσῃς, *katastēsēs*) need not mean that Titus was to do all the picking. It may rather indicate a task more like that of the apostles in Acts 6:7 after the congregation has selected men bearing the required qualities. Paul has given the qualifications for elders both for the benefit of Titus, who may well lead the process, and also for the churches on Crete.

1:6 An elder must be blameless,

In Titus Paul begins the qualification list differently than in 1 Timothy. Instead of beginning "an elder must be" as he did with the overseer in 1 Tim 3:2 and as the NIV renders Titus 1:6, the sentence actually begins "if any man is." Paul does move to "an overseer must be" in v. 7. This difference is really of little consequence in terms of Paul's intent. Paul begins by saying that an elder is to be "blameless" (ἀνέγκλητος, *anenklētos*), a synonym to the word used in 1 Tim 3:2, "above reproach" (ἀνεπίλημπτος, *anepilēmptos*).[8] "Blameless," like "above reproach" in 1 Timothy, serves as the primary qualification by which other qualifications must be understood.

The qualification lists for overseers/bishops in Titus 1 and 1 Timothy 3 have much in common. The chart opposite provides a means of comparing those qualifications.

---

[8]Paul does use the same word "blameless" of deacons in 1 Tim 3:10.

English Word or Phrase in Titus 1	Greek Word or Phrase in Titus 1	Literal Translation	English Word or Phrase in 1 Timothy 3	Greek Word or Phrase in 1 Timothy 3
blameless	anenklētos	"beyond reproach, blameless"	above reproach v. 2	anepilēmpton
the husband of but one wife	mias gunaikos anēr	"one woman's man"	the husband of but one wife v. 2	mias gunaikos andra
a man whose children believe and are not open to the charge of being wild and disobedient	tekna echōn pista, mē en katēgoria asōtias ē anupotaka	"having believing (faithful) children, not under accusation of living recklessly or *being* out of step	manage his own family well and see that his children obey him with proper respect v. 4	tou idiou oikou kalōs proistamenon, tekna echonta en hupotagē, meta pasēs semnotētos
not overbearing	mē authadē	"not self-willed"		
not quick-tempered	mē orgilon	"not furious, quick tempered"		
not given to drunkenness	mē paroinon	not *remaining long* beside *his* wine	not given to drunkenness v. 3	mē paroinon
not violent	mē plēktēn	"not a striker"	not violent but gentle v. 3	mē plēktēn, alla epieikē
not pursuing dishonest gain	mē aischrokerdē	"not greedy for shameful gain"	not a lover of money v. 3	aphilarguron
hospitable	philoxenon	"lover of strangers"	hospitable v. 2	philoxenon
one who loves what is good	philagathon	"lover of good"		
self-controlled	sōphrona	"showing good sense"	self-controlled v. 2	sōphrona
upright	dikaion	"righteous, just"		
holy	hosion	"devout, pious"		
disciplined	enkratē	"under control, self-controlled"		
hold firmly to the trustworthy message	antechomenon tou kata tēn didachēn pistou logou	"holding firm the teaching of the faithful (reliable) word"	able to teach v. 2	didaktikon
			temperate v. 2	nēphalion
			respectable v. 2	kosmion
			not quarrelsome v. 3	amachon
			not be a recent convert v. 6	mē neophuton
			good reputation with outsiders v. 7	marturian kalēn echein apo tōn exōthen

the husband of but one wife, a man whose children believe

In Titus Paul begins by giving two items regarding the elders' home life which are necessary if he is to be "blameless." First, he must be "the husband of but one wife" (see the discussion of the phrase at 1 Tim 3:2). Second he must have "children who believe" and who "are not open to the charge of being wild and disobedient." There has been much debate as to the meaning of "whose children believe" (τέκνα ἔχων πιστά, *tekna echōn pista*).

(1) Is Paul simply using the term "believe" to indicate that the children are Christians (cf. 1 Tim 6:2 where the word is used in this way of masters)? In favor of such a choice are the renderings of many English translations. Spain argues in favor of such an interpretation: "It seems safe to conclude that children who are old enough to conduct themselves in [the] . . . manner [described in the immediate context] are also old enough to obey the gospel and embrace the Christian faith, with its moral demands."[9]

(2) Or is he using the word to indicate the children's "loyalty" to their father? In favor of this option is the fact that Paul continues by saying that these children are not to be "open to the charge of being wild and disobedient." For this reason, Knight has argued for "submissive" or "obedient."[10]

(3) Or is he demanding that they be "faithful" Christians? While there is nothing in the immediate context that rules out the other interpretations, there is much to be said for this final option.[11] It encompasses the qualities required by the first two options, and it is consistent with usage elsewhere in the Pastoral Epistles (e.g., 1 Tim 1:12). In all likelihood, few in the first century would have made distinctions between options (1) and (3). "They should . . . share their father's faith in Christ."[12] "If [the children] remained pagans, it would throw into question the father's ability to lead others to

---

[9]Spain, p. 170.
[10]Knight, pp. 289-290.
[11]Fee, p. 184.
[12]Kelly, p. 231.

faith."[13] The issue goes beyond children being "faithful" as long as they are under their father's roof. It is, however, not designed by Paul to be so firm that congregations cannot make decisions regarding men who have some faithful children and some who are not.

and are not open to the charge of being wild and disobedient.
The children are not to be "open to the charge of being wild" (ἀσωτίας, *asōtias*, literally "unable to save" and therefore "loose living")[14] and "disobedient" (ἀνυπότακτα, *anypotakta*, literally "out of step or order").[15] The father of rebellious children will not be "blameless" within or without the church.

The point of the first two qualifications is rather clear. Elders are expected to have Christian households. They are expected to be faithful husbands, whose faithfulness to their wives is never questioned. They are expected to have served as good fathers. Guthrie is correct: "As in 1 Timothy, the home is regarded as the training ground for Christian leaders."[16]

1:7 Since an overseer is entrusted with God's work, he must be blameless —
In this verse Paul repeats the call for an elder to be blameless. There are, however, two significant developments. First, Paul changes from elder (πρεσβύτερος, *presbyteros*) in v. 5 to overseer (ἐπίσκοπος, *episkopos*) in v. 7. The terms are simply synonymous designations for the same work of spiritual leadership within the church.[17] Second, in this verse Paul gives the

---

[13]D.E. Hiebert, *Titus*, Evangelical Bible Commentary (Grand Rapids: Zondervan, 1978), p. 430.

[14]Cf. Eph 5:18; 1 Pet 4:4. The adverbial form of the root (ἀσώτως, *asōtōs*) is used of the prodigal son in Luke 15:13.

[15]This term is used in the LXX (1 Sam 10:27) to describe Eli's sons. It will be used later in the next paragraph (Titus 1:10) of the false teachers who are "rebellious."

[16]Guthrie, p. 185.

[17]At this point Fee makes an assertion which he does not prove: "It also seems likely that not all elders are *episkopoi*, and therefore the words are interchangeable only in a limited sense. . . . [However,] an overseer is probably a generic term, as in verse 6." Fee, p. 174.

reason that an elder or overseer "must be blameless" (in the sense of v. 6, a man whose marital life is above reproach and a good father): "Since an overseer is entrusted with God's work" (θεοῦ οἰκονόμον, *theou oikonomon*, literally "entrusted as God's steward" or "entrusted as the caretaker of God's house").

Having repeated the call for this leader to be blameless, Paul gives a list of adjectives much as he did in 1 Tim 3:2-3. This time he uses five adjectives to describe the vices which should not characterize the elder followed by six virtues which should characterize his life.

not overbearing, not quick-tempered,

The first two vices — "not overbearing" (μὴ αὐθάδη, *mē authadē*, literally "not self-willed") and "not quick-tempered" (μὴ ὀργίλον, *mē orgilon*) — should be taken as a pair. Fee says that it is appropriate for "not overbearing" to head the list because "God's household manager must be a servant, not stubbornly self-willed, since it is God's household, not his own."[18] Likewise, an ill temper will render him ineffective, since he must patiently deal with brothers and sisters in the church.

not given to drunkenness, not violent, not pursuing dishonest gain.

The next two vices which must be avoided also make up a pair — "not given to drunkenness" and "not violent" (see discussion of 1 Tim 3:3 for these two terms). The final vice prohibited is "pursuing dishonest gain" (μὴ αἰσχροκεδῆ, *mē aischrokedē*). The same prohibition is used in the qualifications of deacons (1 Tim 3:8). False teachers are said to exhibit this characteristic (v. 11). A parallel phrase, "not a lover of money," is used of overseers in 1 Tim 3:3.

1:8 Rather he must be hospitable, one who loves what is good, who is self-controlled, upright, holy and disciplined.

In v. 8 Paul moves to the positive attributes required of those who are to be appointed as elders. An overseer "must

---

[18]Fee, p. 174.

be hospitable" (see discussion of this word in 1 Tim 3:2), "one who loves what is good" (φιλάγαθον, *philagathon*, a characteristic which frequently appears in inscriptions to people of noble character), "self-controlled" (see discussion of this word, a favorite in the Pastoral Epistles, in 1 Tim 3:2; cf. Titus 2:2, 5), "upright" and "holy" (δίκαιον, *dikaion*; and ὅσιον, *hosion*; words frequently linked in Scripture to indicate one who fulfills duty to others and duty to God respectively), and finally "disciplined" (ἐγκρατῆ, *enkratē*, a term very much like "self-controlled" earlier in the list; cf. Gal 5:23 where this quality is listed as a "fruit of the Spirit").

1:9 He must hold firmly to the trustworthy message as it has been taught, so that he can encourage others by sound doctrine and refute those who oppose it.

This verse provides an element of the qualifications that is distinctive to Titus. Although Timothy was told that overseers were to be "able teachers" (1 Tim 3:2) and that deacons were to be "devoted to the gospel" (1 Tim 3:9), only in Titus is the reason for being a good teacher and for being devoted to the gospel spelled out in terms of the function of the elder. "He must hold firmly to the trustworthy message as it has been taught" for two reasons: first, "so that he can encourage others by sound doctrine" and second, so that he can "refute those who oppose it" (ἀντιλέγοντας, *antilegontas*, literally, "objectors"). The word translated "encourage" (παρακαλεῖν, *parakalein*) could perhaps better be translated "exhort" in this context (cf. 1 Tim 4:1; 5:1; 6:2). For a discussion of sound ("healthy") doctrine ("teaching") see the discussion of the phrase in 1 Tim 1:10. Paul also uses the term "refute" or "convict" in 1 Tim 5:20 and will use it again in 2 Tim 3:16; 4:2. This final sentence serves as the perfect transition to the next section which deals with the response of Titus and the elders to false teachers.

B. ELDERS' RESPONSIBILITIES TOWARD FALSE TEACHERS (1:10-16)

[10]For there are many rebellious people, mere talkers and deceivers, especially those of the circumcision group. [11]They must be silenced, because they are ruining whole households by teaching things they ought not to teach — and that for the sake of dishonest gain. [12]Even one of their own prophets has said, "Cretans are always liars, evil brutes, lazy gluttons." [13]This testimony is true. Therefore, rebuke them sharply, so that they will be sound in the faith [14]and will pay no attention to Jewish myths or to the commands of those who reject the truth. [15]To the pure, all things are pure, but to those who are corrupted and do not believe, nothing is pure. In fact, both their minds and consciences are corrupted. [16]They claim to know God, but by their actions they deny him. They are detestable, disobedient and unfit for doing anything good.

Worthy elders must be appointed because "there are many rebellious people." Someone must silence these false teachers. Paul argues that part of the difficulty these men will face is the cultural background of the Cretan converts.

1:10 For there are many rebellious people, mere talkers and deceivers,

The word "rebellious" was used in v. 6 when Paul explained the characteristics that were necessary of a prospective elder's children. There the word was translated "disobedient." It carries with it a sense of insubordination which results in their rejection of "the truth" (v. 14). They are described as "mere talkers," a word used in 1 Tim 1:6 of the false teachers at Ephesus; there it is rendered "meaningless talk." These false teachers, like those at Ephesus, are deceiving and misleading other believers (cf. 1 Tim 4:2; 2 Tim 3:13).

especially those of the circumcision group.
Unlike the description of the false teachers at Ephesus, Paul identifies these people as "those of the circumcision group," this time representing a Jewish threat that is different from the one Paul encountered earlier at Galatia (Gal 2:7-9, 12). The word "especially" can either indicate that most but not all of the false teachers Paul is discussing are from this group, or it can function as a "that is" or as an "in particular." Whichever rendering one chooses, Paul's point is that Jewishness is a dominant characteristic of these false teachers.[19] Paul's references to "Jewish myths" (v. 14) and to quarrels "about the law" (3:9) make this clear. It would seem that the threat is no longer requiring circumcision of Gentile believers, but rather other issues that grow out of a Jewish syncretistic interpretation.

Although there may have been significant differences between the situations at Ephesus and Crete, the false teaching here has much in common with the one seen in 1 Tim 1:3-11. See the chart below for some of the more striking similarities.

Description of False Teachers in Titus	Greek Words Used in Titus 1:10-16	Description of False Teachers in 1 Timothy	Greek Words Used in 1 Tim 1:3-11
mere talkers (v. 10)	*mataiologoi*	meaningless talk (v. 6)	*mataiologian*
teaching things they ought not (v. 11)	*didaskontes ha mē dei*	to teach false doctrines (v. 4)	*heterodidaskalein*
always liars (v. 12)	*aei pseustai*	liars (v. 10)	*pseustais*
sound in faith (v. 13)	*hugiainōsin en tē pistei*	contrary to the sound doctrine (v. 10)	*heteron tē hugainousē didaskalia*
Jewish myths (v. 14)	*Ioudaikois muthois*	myths (v. 4)	*muthois*
to the pure, all things are pure (v. 15)	*kathara tois katharois*	a pure heart (v. 5)	*katharas kardias*
consciences (v. 15)	*suneidēsis*	conscience (v. 5)	*suneidēseōs*

1:11 They must be silenced, because they are ruining whole households
These false teachers "must be silenced" (ἐπιστομίζειν, *epis-*

---

[19]See Knight, p. 297, for a discussion of this point.

tomizein, literally, "it is necessary to stop their mouths," a word which means to put a muzzle on an animal's mouth[20]). Their teaching is dangerous "because they are ruining [literally 'overturning'] whole households" (cf. 1 Tim 3:5, 15; 2 Tim 3:6-9). Knight has suggested that the heresy in Crete, like the one at Ephesus, was prohibiting marriage and demanding the practice of certain other purity rules which would have devastating effects on families.[21] Fee, however, is likely correct when he argues that the language does not suggest the dividing of families, but rather that the church is facing the defection of certain *whole* families.[22]

by teaching things they ought not to teach — and that for the sake of dishonest gain.

These false teachers are "teaching things they ought not to teach" (cf. 1 Tim 1:6-7; 6:3-4). They are motivated by greed or "dishonest gain" (cf. the false teachers at Ephesus, 1 Tim 6:5-10; and Paul's instructions that elders not be of this disposition, 1 Tim 3:3; Titus 1:7).

1:12 Even one of their own prophets has said,

Paul cites the well-known reputation of the Cretans as an explanation of the direction of the false teachers. Epimenides (ca. 600 B.C.) had provided an epigram that illustrated Paul's point. It should be noted that Epimenides was himself from Crete making the statement a self-contradiction — all Cretans are liars; Epimenides is a Cretan; he must, therefore, be a liar; which means that all Cretans are not liars; which means that he might be telling the truth; and so on. In addressing Epimenides as "one of their own prophets," Paul was doing no more than recognizing the Cretan claim that he was a prophet. Plato recognized the tradition that Epimenides had predicted the Persian War ten years before it occurred.[23] According to

---

[20] Kelly, p. 234.
[21] Knight, pp. 297-298.
[22] Fee, p. 178.
[23] Plato, *Laws*, I, p. 642.

Diogenes Laertius, he advised the Athenians to sacrifice "to the appropriate god," leading to the construction of "the altar to the unknown god" which Paul saw in Athens (Acts 17:23).

"Cretans are always liars, evil brutes, lazy gluttons."

The reputation of the Cretans is clear from Epimenides' quote: "Cretans are always liars, evil brutes, lazy gluttons." Their reputation as liars is seen in their claim to have the tomb of Zeus, who as a god could not die. To "behave like a Cretan" came to be synonymous with "being a liar."[24] In addition to lying, they were characterized as "evil brutes" (i.e., they would do anything to get ahead) and as lazy gluttons (i.e., greedy hedonists).

1:13 This testimony is true. Therefore, rebuke them sharply, so that they will be sound in the faith

Paul concludes that the "testimony is true" and that Titus must "rebuke them sharply" ("correct them rigorously"[25]). His concern is that these recent converts might "be sound in the faith" (see discussion at 1 Tim 1:10).

1:14 and will pay no attention to Jewish myths or to the commands of those who reject the truth.

In contrast to the soundness in the faith which Paul desires for the church on Crete, he moves in vv. 14-16 to describe the unsound teaching of the false teachers. They "pay attention to Jewish myths" (cf. 1 Tim 1:4; 4:7).[26] The Christians at Crete are to "pay no attention to the commands" of these men. Fee notes the similarity of the language here to the "commands" or Pharisaic regulations which Jesus opposed (Mark 7:7; Matt 15:9) and the ascetic rules at Colosse which Paul opposed (Col 2:22). As elsewhere in the Pastoral Epistles

---

[24]See Hendriksen, p. 353, for various references in Greek literature to the nature of the Cretans.

[25]Fee, p. 180.

[26]Although Paul does not mention here the "genealogies" of 1 Tim 1:4, the error being taught seems to be very similar.

those making these commands are described as "those who reject the truth," i.e., the gospel and salvation by grace.

1:15 To the pure, all things are pure,

Apparently the commands to which Paul objects are related to food laws and issues of ritual purity. Paul begins with a positive statement — "to the pure, all things are pure" — which is very much like what he says in Rom 14:20 when addressing a different topic (cf. Luke 11:38-41). The things which some deem unclean are pure; nothing is unclean of itself (cf. 1 Tim 4:4, "For everything God created is good, and nothing is to be rejected if it is received with thanksgiving").

but to those who are corrupted and do not believe, nothing is pure. In fact, both their minds and consciences are corrupted.

"To those who are corrupted" (i.e., they buy into the false teaching and misunderstand the nature of the gospel) "and do not believe" (i.e., do not put their trust in the saving work of Christ but rather in ritual) "nothing is pure." Such a stance means that "both their minds and consciences are corrupted." They have lost the capacity to think for themselves and to distinguish between good and evil (cf. 1 Tim 4:2; 6:5; 2 Tim 3:8).

1:16 They claim to know God,

Some see the "claim" of the false teachers at Crete to "know God" as a clear indication of "a higher, more esoteric knowledge of God"[27] and, therefore, of Gnosticism at the time the epistle was written. Fee is correct in assessing that the data could simply be seen as supporting "the special boast of Jews . . . putting themselves forward as those who can lead others to God."[28]

but by their actions they deny him. They are detestable, disobedient and unfit for doing anything good.

The very "actions" of those who "claim to know God" indi-

---

[27]Kelly, p. 237.
[28]Fee, p. 182.

cate that they do not know him. In fact with their "actions they deny him." The exact nature of the actions Paul has in mind is uncertain. It likely refers to all of the characteristics Paul has indicated: their ascetic practices and rules, their divisiveness, their greed, and their rebellion and insubordination. Paul describes them as "detestable" (or "abominable"), "disobedient" (note that they demand obedience to "commands" but are "disobedient" to God) and "unfit for doing anything good" (what God wants by way of good works they will never do).

TITUS 2

III. INSTRUCTIONS FOR VARIOUS GROUPS (2:1-15)

The current section is similar to 1 Tim 5:1-2, where people are grouped by sex and age. This time, however, Paul does not give instructions as to how the minister is to relate to each group. Instead he gives instructions as to the attitudes and behaviors of the members of each group. Paul is very much concerned about how Christians will be viewed by pagans "so that in every way they will make the teaching about God our Savior attractive" (2:10).

A. BEHAVIOR AND SOUND DOCTRINE (2:1)

¹You must teach what is in accord with sound doctrine.

The sentence begins with an adversative conjunction not translated by the NIV followed by an emphatic pronoun (σὺ δέ, *su de*, "but *you*"). After being given instructions about men to be appointed as elders and their responsibility of dealing with false teaching, Titus is now given instructions about what he is to teach. The word translated "teach" (λάλει, *lalei*) is literally "speak." It may well be deemed a milder term than the imperatives of 1 Timothy ("exhort, charge, teach"). Titus is to make sure that his teaching accords with "sound doctrine" ("healthy teaching"; see discussion of the phrase in 1 Tim 1:10).

B. INSTRUCTIONS FOR OLDER MEN (2:2)

²Teach the older men to be temperate, worthy of respect, self-controlled, and sound in faith, in love and in endurance.

Paul begins his instructions to the various groups in Titus with older men just as he did in 1 Tim 5:1.[1] It is primarily, if not exclusively, from this group of men that elders/overseers were selected. As Fee has noted, it is not then surprising that the qualities that these "older men" are to have parallel the qualifications for elders/overseers and deacons. Older men are to be "temperate" (νηφαλίους, nēphalious; cf. 1 Tim 3:2), "worthy of respect" (σεμνούς, semnous; cf. 1 Tim 3:8), and "self-controlled" (σώφρονας, sōphronas; cf. 1:8; 2:5; 1 Tim 3:2).

Older men are to be "sound" (or "healthy") in a triad of Christian virtues — "in faith, in love and in endurance." These three virtues are also linked in 1 Tim 6:11-12; 2 Tim 3:10; and 1 Thess 1:3.

C. INSTRUCTIONS FOR OLDER AND YOUNGER WOMEN (2:3-5)

³Likewise, teach the older women to be reverent in the way they live, not to be slanderers or addicted to much wine, but to teach what is good. ⁴Then they can train the younger women to love their husbands and children, ⁵to be self-controlled and pure, to be busy at home, to be kind, and to be subject to their husbands, so that no one will malign the word of God.

2:3 Likewise, teach the older women to be reverent in the way they live,

---

[1]According to Philo, *On Creation*, p. 105, Hippocrates used the phrase "older men" to designate the sixth of the seven age groups, comprised of those 50-56. Philo himself used the phrase to refer to a man over sixty in *On Special Laws*, pp. 2, 33. Fee, p. 185.

Paul uses the word "likewise," a favorite expression in the Pastoral Epistles to indicate a closeness of comparison, to introduce his instructions to "older women." They are to be taught to be reverent in the way they live (literally "with a demeanor which suits the sacred").

not to be slanderers or addicted to much wine,

Guthrie has suggested that the next two terms — "not to be slanderers or addicted to much wine" — "again vividly portray the Cretan environment."[2] Similar prohibitions were used earlier in giving the qualifications of deacons: the first (μὴ διαβόλους, *mē diabolous*) in 1 Tim 3:11 and the second (μὴ οἴνῳ πολλῷ δεδουλωμένας, *mē oinō pollō dedoulōmenas*) in 1 Tim 3:8. With the second prohibition Paul uses a much stronger participle than he uses with deacons. As Guthrie has noted, "Evidently in Crete the liability to these excesses was more severe than in Ephesus, especially among women, the verb (δουλόω, *douloō*) used here signifies 'bondage' (RSV 'slaves to drink'), a much stronger expression than the corresponding phrase in 1 Timothy."[3]

but to teach what is good.

Paul now calls "older women" "to teach what is good" (καλοδιδασκάλους, *kalodidaskalous*, a word that appears only here in the NT). This does not envisage the formal instruction of men. Such teaching is forbidden in 1 Tim 2:12, and there is no reason why Paul should take a different line at Crete than in Ephesus. Kelly holds that this is "rather the advice and encouragement they can give privately, by word and example."[4]

2:4 Then they can train the younger women to love their husbands and children,

The call for older women to teach what is good provides for Paul's transition to "younger women" in vv. 4-5. Paul gives

---
[2]Guthrie, p. 192.
[3]*Ibid.*
[4]Kelly, p. 240.

instructions to the younger women, but he does so by way of "the older women." The word translated "train" (σωφρονίζωσιν, *sōphronizōsin*) is from the same root as the word translated "self-controlled" in v. 2 and literally means "to bring someone to his or her senses." Fee suggests a rendering of something like "'wise them up' as to their responsibilities as wives."[5] Paul gives seven qualities that younger women are to learn. The first two qualities are expressed by two Greek words (φιλάνδρους, *philandrous*; φιλοτέκνους, *philoteknous*) which seem to comprise a single quality in English: "to love their husbands and children." These two qualities appear frequently in passages that discuss the characteristics of the good wife in antiquity. Guthrie has suggested that these requirements may well pinpoint a special weakness in the character of Cretans.[6]

2:5 to be self-controlled and pure, to be busy at home, to be kind,

These younger women are also "to be self-controlled" (σώφρονας, *sōphronas*; a term used of "older men" in v. 5; cf. 1:8; 1 Tim 3:2) and "pure" (i.e., "morally pure, chaste"; cf. 1 Tim 5:22). The next two characteristics can form a pair: "to be busy at home" (οἰκουργούς, *oikourgous*, literally "home workers") and "to be kind" (ἀγαθάς, *agathas*; literally "good *women*," perhaps in the sense of not being irritable); or they may be taken together with the second being understood as a simple adjective, producing "good workers at home" or "fulfilling their household duties well."[7] Since all of the virtues to this point have consisted of single adjectives or nouns, it is likely that one should understand Paul as giving two qualities for "younger women" at this juncture. "Busy at home" should be understood "diligent homemakers" with a wide range of activities included (cf. the worthy wife of Prov 31:10-31).

---

[5]Fee, p. 187.
[6]Guthrie, p. 193.
[7]This is apparently the understanding of the UBS Greek text. Cf. M. Dibelius and H. Conzelmann, *The Pastoral Epistles*, trans. P. Buttolph and A. Yarbro (Philadelphia: Fortress Press, 1972), p. 141.

and to be subject to their husbands,

The younger women are also "to be subject to their husbands" (cf. Col 3:8; Eph 5:21-23; 1 Pet 3:1). The original literally says they are "to be subject to their *own* husbands." The NIV has apparently taken the word "own" (ἰδίοις, *idiois*) as unnecessary. The word "own" does indicate that Paul has in mind submission to "husbands" and not men in general. The word translated "to be subject" (ὑποτασσομένας, *hypotassomenas*) is a perfect middle participle in Greek which, as Knight has noted, indicates that Paul has in mind an act which is both continual and voluntary.[8] For Paul the idea of submission and, at the same time, equality is not problematic. One has to do with role and the other value. Subjection does not imply inferiority.

so that no one will malign the word of God.

Paul concludes with the reason for the training that the younger women are to receive: "so that no one will malign the word of God." "The word of God" is here "God's message," "the gospel" (cf. Phil 1:14; 2 Tim 2:9). For the world to "malign" or "blaspheme" the message or God's name on account of the actions of a believer is unthinkable (cf. Rom 2:24; 1 Tim 6:2; Titus 2:10).

D. INSTRUCTIONS FOR YOUNGER MEN (2:6-8)

⁶Similarly, encourage the young men to be self-controlled. ⁷In everything set them an example by doing what is good. In your teaching show integrity, seriousness ⁸and soundness of speech that cannot be condemned, so that those who oppose you may be ashamed because they have nothing bad to say about us.

---

[8]Knight, pp. 308-309.

2:6 Similarly, encourage the young men to be self-controlled.

Titus is to teach the "younger men" both by words and by his "example." Paul again begins his admonition to a new group with "similarly" (ὡσαύτως, *hōsautōs*, "likewise" in v. 3). He is to "encourage" them "to be self-controlled" (σωφρονεῖν, *sōphronein*, "to keep their heads"[9]) a concept indicating self-mastery, sensibleness, and clear thinking met earlier in Titus (vv. 2, 4, 5) with regard to "older men" and "younger women." One wonders, given the frequency of this word and its cognates in Titus, if self-control was not a particularly ominous problem on Crete.

2:7 In everything set them an example by doing what is good.

The prepositional phrase "in everything" (περὶ πάντα, *peri panta*) can be taken either with v. 6 ("to be self-controlled in everything") or with v. 7 ("set an example in everything"). In the context, it seems more likely that the phrase should be taken with v. 6 indicating the sphere of self-control for "younger men."[10] Titus is to "set an example" of self-control for these men. Again the NIV chooses not to translate a Greek word in the original (σεαυτόν, *seauton*) which would produce the following more emphatic translation: "set an example for them *yourself*." Titus' example should be seen "in his good deeds" (a literal translation of the Greek phrase rendered "by doing what is good" in the NIV).

In your teaching show integrity, seriousness

In v. 7 Paul moves from Titus' "example" to his "teaching." His teaching must "show integrity" (literally "incorrupt"), "seriousness" (cf. 1 Tim 2:2; 3:4; denoting "a high moral tone and serious manner"[11]), and "soundness of speech" (λόγον ὑγιῆ, *logon hygiē*).

---

[9]Fee, p. 188.
[10]Cf. Fee, p. 188; Lea and Griffin, p. 304. Knight, p. 311, deems the arguments favoring each rendering too close to call.
[11]Kelly, p. 242.

2:8 and soundness of speech that cannot be condemned, so that those who oppose you may be ashamed because they have nothing bad to say about us.

The "soundness of speech" which Titus is to use does not refer to sound doctrine or teaching, but rather to a sound or "healthy" (cf. 1 Tim 1:10; and Titus 1:9, 13, 2:1, 2) manner of speech. The phrase that follows validates this interpretation: "that cannot be condemned" (i.e., "is beyond reproach"). Paul tells Titus that teaching in the manner he has prescribed will guarantee that "those who oppose" (literally "the one who opposes") him will "be ashamed because they have nothing bad to say about us." Paul seems to be saying that Titus' conduct should be such that the opponents of Titus, Paul, and the truth will either (a) be disgraced or (b) be shamed into repentance. Paul indicates that Titus and his teaching reflect on Paul and his associates ("about us").

One can here see similarities between the way Paul deals with "younger women" through "older women" (vv. 4-5) and the way he here deals with "younger men" through Titus.

E. INSTRUCTIONS FOR SLAVES (2:9-10)

⁹Teach slaves to be subject to their masters in everything, to try to please them, not to talk back to them, ¹⁰and not to steal from them, but to show that they can be fully trusted, so that in every way they will make the teaching about God our Savior attractive.

The move to instructions for slaves[12] from other instructions based on sex and age seems a bit strange to the modern reader.

2:9 Teach slaves to be subject to their masters in everything,
The instructions are clearly linked by the word "teach"

---

[12]See the discussion of slavery in 1 Tim 6:1-2.

(παρακαλεῖ, parakalei, rendered "encourage" in v. 6). The instructions given to "slaves" have much in common with the instructions earlier to "younger women" (vv. 4-5).

Guthrie has suggested that Paul's change from "obey" in instructions given to slaves in Ephesus (Eph 6:5) and Colosse (Col 3:22) to "be subject" (ὑποτάσσω, *hypotassō*) in Titus may well suggest a "greater tendency on part of Christian slaves in Crete to abuse new-found emancipation in Christ."[13] Again the verb "to be subject" is present middle (this time an infinitive; cf. v. 5) indicating continual and voluntary action. They are "to subject *themselves* to their *own* masters" as younger women were "to subject *themselves* to their *own* husbands."[14]

In v. 9 one is again faced with the dilemma of deciding whether "in everything" (ἐν πᾶσιν, *en pasin*) is to be taken with the preceding verb, "to subject," or the one that follows, "to please." While no conclusive arguments have been given, most favor taking "in everything" with the verb "to subject" for the following reasons: (1) in Col 3:22 Paul links a parallel phrase to the verb "obey" when used of slaves; (2) in the Pastoral Epistles "in everything" normally appears at the end of a clause; and (3) Paul links "in everything" to the verb "submit" in Eph 5:24.[15] Recognizing that the slave's submission to his master must always take second place to his submission to God, Knight says that "slaves are to subject themselves 'in all respects,' i.e., in all aspects of their service that a Christian slave can render without sinning."[16]

to try to please them, not to talk back to them,

Christian slaves are "to try to please" (literally "to be well pleasing to") their masters. "If Christian slaves could introduce into their lives so high a principle as this, it would do much

---

[13] Guthrie, p. 196.
[14] Once again the NIV has chosen not to translate the Greek word ἰδίοις *(idiois),* "their own."
[15] Knight, p. 314.
[16] *Ibid.*
[17] Guthrie, p. 196.

to lessen the evils of the system and to show the power of Christianity to transform the most difficult of relationships."[17]

2:10 and not to steal from them, but to show that they can be fully trusted, so that in every way they will make the teaching about God our Savior attractive.

Slaves are also to avoid two of the sins that so often plagued them: talking back and stealing or pilfering from their masters. Instead Christian slaves are "to show that they can be fully trusted" (literally "showing all good faith"). Again the reason for Paul's call for the Christian walk is the effect their behavior has on the neighboring pagans: "so that in every way" [literally 'in everything'; cf. v. 9] "they will make the teaching about God our Savior attractive" (cf. Paul's concern that the gospel not be blasphemed in v. 5). Here Paul's goal is that the behavior of slaves actually attract outsiders to the gospel message.

F. THE THEOLOGICAL BASIS FOR THE CHRISTIAN LIFE (2:11-15)

[11]For the grace of God that brings salvation has appeared to all men. [12]It teaches us to say "No" to ungodliness and worldly passions, and to live self-controlled, upright and godly lives in this present age, [13]while we wait for the blessed hope — the glorious appearing of our great God and Savior, Jesus Christ, [14]who gave himself for us to redeem us from all wickedness and to purify for himself a people that are his very own, eager to do what is good.

[15]These, then, are the things you should teach. Encourage and rebuke with all authority. Do not let anyone despise you.

In this section Paul gives the theological reason for his call for Christian living in the previous section. Here as in 1 Tim 2:3-7; 4:10 Paul appeals to the universal scope of salvation by grace which should produce an eagerness "to do what is good" (v. 14).

2:11 For the grace of God that brings salvation has appeared to all men.

The "for" which begins v. 11 clearly links vv. 2-10 with vv. 11-14. Paul explains why Christians should lead the Christian life. As Fee has noted, one must be careful not to misread v. 11. Paul does not say "the grace of God appeared bringing salvation to all men." Rather he says "the grace of God that brings salvation has appeared to all men."

2:12 It teaches us to say "No" to ungodliness and worldly passions,

When one understands God's grace, he faces certain ethical demands. There are things the Christian is compelled to avoid: "ungodliness" (ἀσέβεια, *asebeia*, the opposite of godliness which is so important in the Pastoral Epistles) and "worldly passions" (literally "worldly desires").

and to live self-controlled, upright and godly lives in this present age,

On the positive side he is compelled to live a life "in this present age" (to be contrasted with "the age to come"; cf. 1 Tim 1:16) which has Christian qualities. Christians' lives are to be "self-controlled" (σωφρόνως, *sōphronōs*, cf. vv. 2, 5, 6 above), "upright" (δικαίως, *dikaiōs*, see discussion in 1 Tim 6:11), and "godly" (εὐσεβῶς, *eusebōs*, a clear contrast with "ungodliness," ἀσέβεια, *asebeia*).

2:13 while we wait for the blessed hope —

In vv. 12-13 Paul contrasts the "present age" with the one to come. The Christian clearly looks to and waits for the future. "Hope" (ἐλπίς, *elpis*) throughout the NT refers to more than wishful thinking. It is always the anxious waiting for something that is assured. This hope is described as "blessed." Paul defines what the Christian hope is by the next phrase, namely, "the glorious appearing of our great God and Savior, Jesus Christ."

the glorious appearing of our great God and Savior, Jesus Christ,

The phrase "the glorious appearing of our great God and Savior, Jesus Christ" poses two difficulties for interpreters. The first problem has to do with how one understands "glory" in the verse. Is the text to be rendered "the glorious appearing of our great God" (KJV, NIV) or "the appearing of *the glory* of our great God" (RSV, NASB, NRSV)? As Lea and Griffin have noted, "Grammatically, this latter rendering is more natural and therefore slightly to be preferred."[18] This preference is due to the parallelism this will provide between the "appearing" of "the grace of God" in v.11 and "the appearing of the glory of God" here. Also this interpretation matches Jesus' own emphasis on his second coming demonstrating divine "glory" (Matt 16:27; Mark 8:38; Luke 9:26). The "grace of God" has appeared with the first advent of Jesus; the "glory" of God will appear in a definitive way with his second coming.

The second problem involves whether one would see one person or two in the final section of this verse: "the glorious appearing of our great God and Savior, Jesus Christ"; or "the glorious appearing of *the* great God and our Savior Jesus Christ." Although on the surface the difference seems to be only the placement of a comma, theologically there is a significant difference.[19] The former reading proclaims the deity of Jesus loudly and clearly. The following arguments may be made for this reading favored by the NIV:[20] (1) there is no definite article before "Savior," and normally, when two nouns are linked by "and" with a single article preceding the

---

[18]Lea and Griffin, p. 312.

[19]For a complete discussion of these two options and the current scholarship in the debate, see Murray J. Harris, "Titus 2:13 and the Deity of Christ," *Pauline Studies: Essays Presented to Professor F.F. Bruce on His 70th Birthday*, ed. D. Hagner and M.J. Harris (Grand Rapids: Eerdmans, 1980), pp. 262-277.

[20]Clearly the chosen reading of the NASB and the NRSV. Also the likely intention of the ASV, RSV, and NEB translators.

first, the nouns refer to a single entity; (2) the hope of Christians in Paul is centered in Christ and his return; (3) the Greek church fathers support this rendering; (4) no place in the NT does one find "the appearing of God";[21] (5) frequently in the pagan world the phrase "God and Savior" is used as a formula to apply to a single deity; (6) Paul's use of "who gave himself for us" can be seen as supporting this interpretation; and (7) the use of "great" can better be understood if both "our" and "great" modify the entire formula. Although there have been several attempts to explain each of these arguments,[22] it seems more reasonable to see the text as a Pauline statement of the deity of Jesus.[23] Paul's declaration of Jesus as divine can also be seen in the alternation of his use of "Savior" in Titus to refer first to God as Savior (1:3; 2:10; 3:4) then to Jesus as Savior (1:4; 2:13; 3:6).

2:14 who gave himself for us to redeem us from all wickedness and to purify for himself a people that are his very own, eager to do what is good.

In v. 14 Paul moves on to describe this Jesus Christ as the one "who gave himself for us." Christ's death is clearly seen as voluntary and "on behalf of (ὑπέρ, *hyper*) us" (cf. Mark 10:45). Paul here gives the twofold consequence of Jesus' death: "to redeem us" (or "set us free") "from all wickedness" (literally "lawlessness") and "to purify for himself a people that are his very own" (cf. 1 Pet 2:9 and Exod 19:5; Deut 7:6; 14:2; 26:18 in LXX; also Ezek 37:23). These people are to be "eager to do what is good" (literally "full of zeal for good works"; cf. Deut 26:18). Paul's concern in this entire section has been Christian living. He has now indicated that these good works are the natural response to the "grace of God" and are,

---

[21]In all other NT occurrences "appearing" is used of Jesus: four times of Jesus' second coming (2 Thess 2:8; 1 Tim 6:14; 2 Tim 4:1, 8); once of his first appearance (2 Tim 1:10).

[22]E.g., Kelly, pp. 246-247.

[23]Cf. Harris, pp. 262-277; Knight, pp. 322-326.

indeed, the reason Jesus has redeemed and purified them. They are saved to do "good" works.

2:15 These, then, are the things you should teach. Encourage and rebuke with all authority.

Paul now calls Titus to teach these things. Paul frequently used "these things" in his instructions to Timothy (1 Tim 4:6, 11, 15; 5:7, 21; 6:2, 11). Here "these things" may well refer to all the material from 1:10 to the current text. The word "teach" (λάλει, *lalei*) is literally "speak." He is to "encourage" (παρακάλει, *parakalei;* cf. 2:6) and "rebuke" (ἔλεγχε, *elenche*; 1:13) "with all authority." Paul's addition of the clause "with all authority" indicates the seriousness of this teaching. Titus is to deliver the message with *authority*, and the church at Crete is to accept it as authoritative.

Do not let anyone despise you.

Paul's final admonition, "Do not let anyone despise you," is similar to his instructions to Timothy (1 Tim 4:12). Although Paul says nothing of Titus' youth, he includes Titus in his instructions to "younger men" in 2:6-8. It is possible that Titus was a bit older than Timothy. Titus must not allow the Christians on Crete to disregard him or his message.

TITUS 3

IV. STANDARDS FOR CHRISTIAN BEHAVIOR (3:1-11)

A. RESPECT FOR GOVERNMENT AUTHORITIES (3:1)

¹Remind the people to be subject to rulers and authorities, to be obedient, to be ready to do whatever is good, ²to slander no one, to be peaceable and considerate, and to show true humility toward all men.

Paul now returns to the "good" works of 2:14 to emphasize the need for these deeds for the sake of the outsider (vv. 1-8). He then contrasts the Christian life and its works with that of the false teachers (vv. 9-11).

3:1 Remind the people

Paul's instruction for Titus to "remind" (literally "keep on reminding") the people is a natural transition from his instructions to "teach, encourage, and rebuke" in 2:15. The material Titus is to present is not new to his audience; he is to point out the implications of the gospel.

to be subject to rulers and authorities, to be obedient,

The people are "to be subject" (cf. 2:5, 9) "to rulers and authorities" and "to be obedient" (πειθαρχεῖν, *peitharchein*, literally "to be persuaded by" or "to listen to the advice of"). Although "rulers and authorities" may be used of angelic powers (Eph 3:10; 6:2; Col 1:16), here the phrase refers to secular governmental officials (cf. Luke 12:11). Paul expressed a similar concern for civic authorities in 1 Tim 2:2. Paul never addresses the issue of how the Christian should respond to officials who are hostile to and attempt to suppress the Christian faith. He is likely reflecting on a time when the government was relatively tolerant of Christianity (cf. Rom 13:1-8). Christians are called "to obey," or better perhaps "to heed" the laws of the land as long as those laws do not contradict the laws of God.

to be ready to do whatever is good,

Christians are "to be ready to do whatever is good" (literally "to be prepared for every good work"; cf. 2 Tim 2:21; 3:17). While some see this obligation as directed toward civic duty, i.e., good citizenship,[1] others would see the instruction as more general in nature.[2] Perhaps it is best to follow the lead of Knight and say that "the immediate context is with the government but the statement is not meant to be confined to that."[3] The obligation does provide the perfect transition to v. 2 and obligations "toward all men."

B. RESPECT FOR ALL (3:2)

3:2 to slander no one, to be peaceable and considerate,

Christians are "to slander no one" (cf. 1 Tim 6:5), a stark contrast with the false teachers who are involved in "foolish controversies" and "arguments" (v. 9). They are to be "peaceable" (ἀμάχους, *amachous*, better "uncontentious"; see discussion at 1 Tim 3:3) and "considerate"[4] (or perhaps "conciliatory"[5]), in contrast to the quarrels about the law (μάχας νομικάς, *machas nomikas*) of the opponents to the gospel.

---

[1] Kelly, p. 249; Guthrie, pp. 202-203; Hendriksen, p. 386.
[2] Fee, p. 201.
[3] Knight, p. 333.
[4] These two qualities — peaceable and considerate — are also given as qualifications for overseers in 1 Tim 3:3.
[5] Kelly, p. 249.

and to show true humility toward all men.

The final phrase may well be seen as the "key"[6] to the Christian lifestyle in a pagan world. "Humility" (πραΰτης, *praütēs*; cf. 1 Tim 6:11; 2 Tim 2:25), often rendered "meekness," "may best be understood by contrast to its opposites, roughness, bad temper, sudden anger, brusqueness."[7] In the original the word "humility" is qualified by the word "all" producing the "true humility" of the NIV. This humility is to be shown "toward all men," i.e., toward the world in general, toward Christians and non-Christians, toward enemies and friends.

C. THE THEOLOGICAL BASIS FOR LIVING WITH NON-CHRISTIANS (3:3-8)

³At one time we too were foolish, disobedient, deceived and enslaved by all kinds of passions and pleasures. We lived in malice and envy, being hated and hating one another. ⁴But when the kindness and love of God our Savior appeared, ⁵he saved us, not because of righteous things we had done, but because of his mercy. He saved us through the washing of rebirth and renewal by the Holy Spirit, ⁶whom he poured out on us generously through Jesus Christ our Savior, ⁷so that, having been justified by his grace, we might become heirs having the hope of eternal life. ⁸This is a trustworthy saying. And I want you to stress these things, so that those who have trusted in God may be careful to devote themselves to doing what is good. These things are excellent and profitable for everyone.

Paul now gives the theological basis for his earlier call for Christian living. The motivation for this life will be the believers' conversion experience.

---

[6]*Ibid.*
[7]Knight, p. 334.

3:3 At one time we too

The NIV does not translate the Greek word (γάρ, *gar*) "for" which provides the link to the previous section. The "we too" of v. 3 in no way indicates that the non-Christian lifestyle described there was characteristic of his Jewish background. Fee asserts, "One should note that whenever Paul is moved to speak about the gospel he takes up the personal self-identification of 'we too' (cf. 2:11-14; 2 Tim 1:9-10; Gal 1:4; etc.)."[8] The "we too were" may well be intended to imply that the outsiders still are bearing the sinful qualities that follow (i.e., "we too were . . . just as they now do").

were foolish, disobedient, deceived and enslaved by all kinds of passions and pleasures. We lived in malice and envy, being hated and hating one another.

The pre-Christian life was "foolish" ("without spiritual understanding"[9]), "disobedient" (cf. 1:16), "deceived" (or "led astray"; cf. 1 Tim 4:1-2; 2 Tim 3:13), and "enslaved by all kinds of passions and pleasures" (cf. Paul's description of the bondage of sin in Rom 6:6-7). The pre-Christian life was characterized by "malice" (or "badness") and "envy" (cf. 1 Tim 6:4). They were "being hated" (or "detestable") and "hating one another."

3:4 But when the kindness and love of God our Savior appeared,

In v. 4 Paul begins the contrast between the pre-regenerate life and the life of the Christian by rehearsing what God had done in Jesus. "Appeared" here refers to the incarnation of Christ (see discussion on 2:11). The incarnation demonstrates "the kindness" (in the list of the "fruit of the Spirit," Gal 5:22) and "love" (φιλανθρωπία, *philanthrōpia*, literally "love for mankind," cf. the English word "philanthropy") "of God." See the discussion of "God our Savior" at 1:3.

---

[8]Fee, p. 202.
[9]Guthrie, p. 203.

3:5 he saved us, not because of righteous things we had done, but because of his mercy.

God had, in the appearance of his "kindness" and "love," saved us. Paul paints the picture of that salvation much as he would in any of his letters. First Christians are saved "not because of righteous things [they] had done" (cf. Rom 4:4-5; Eph 2:8-9; Phil 3:9; 2 Tim 1:9). Salvation is rather "because of his mercy" (1 Tim 1:12-16). Paul generally talks of God's "grace" rather than his "mercy" as the cause of salvation, but the idea is really the same (cf. "his grace" in v. 7).

He saved us through the washing of rebirth and renewal by the Holy Spirit,

This salvation is then accomplished "through the washing of rebirth and renewal by the Holy Spirit." There has been considerable discussion in scholarly circles of this last phrase due to some grammatical ambiguities. If the word "through" (διά, *dia*) had been repeated with the second phrase, "renewal by the Holy Spirit," interpretation would have been relatively easy. Paul would then have been referring to two events: a "washing of rebirth" and a "renewal of the Holy Spirit."

Since, however, the word "through" does not appear before renewal of the Holy Spirit, two options exist. (1) Paul may be saying that God has saved us "through the washing," which is characterized by "rebirth and renewal," a washing which is accomplished "by the Holy Spirit." (2) Or, Paul may be understood as saying that God has saved us through an event that can be described both as "the washing characterized by rebirth" and as "renewal" either "characterized by or given by the Holy Spirit." The second option does have a sense of balance in its favor — two genitive words or phrases understood together before "and" (washing; rebirth) and two after (renewal; the Holy Spirit). The first option has much to be said in its favor. "Rebirth" is clearly dependent upon "washing." Considerable debate has occurred over whether "washing" (λουτροῦ, *loutrou*) should be seen as a reference to baptism or merely a metaphor for the cleansing of the Holy Spirit. If "washing" is seen as a clear reference to baptism, then it is relatively easy to argue that "rebirth" and "renewal" are accomplished at that point. If, however, "washing" is taken as initial cleansing from sin and "renewal" as sanctification which can be deemed progressive, then the second option above is more reasonable. Since "washing," even understood metaphorically, would have been seen by Paul as connected to baptism, it seems reasonable to assume that Paul had baptism in mind.[10]

Since the word "rebirth" (παλιγγενεσία, *palingenesia* and not ἀναγέννησις, *anagennēsis*) really does not convey the idea of birth, but rather of a "new genesis," Knight has suggested that the phrase should be translated "the washing of a new beginning" or "the washing of conversion."[11] The word "renewal" (ἀνακαίνωσις, *anakainōsis*) need not be seen as a process; it rather indicates "a making new."[12] "Rebirth" and "renewal" are thus "nearly synonymous metaphors."[13] However one understands "washing, rebirth, and renewal," emphasis clearly falls on the Holy Spirit as the source of the new life God has made available to believers.

3:6 whom he poured out on us generously through Jesus Christ our Savior,

In this verse Paul continues his discussion of the role of the Holy Spirit in the conversion and life of the believer. God has "poured the Holy Spirit out on us generously" (πλουσίως, *plousiōs*, literally, "richly" or "abundantly") "through Jesus Christ our Savior." It is significant that the Holy Spirit is given

---

[10]Lea and Griffin, pp. 323-324, have argued that Paul cannot have baptism in mind because this would be contradictory to Paul's understanding of works. If "washing" is to be understood as baptism, they say, it must be "Spirit baptism" at conversion and not "water baptism." They argue that in the New Testament, especially in Acts, there is no pattern or clear relationship between baptism and salvation. Here their theological presuppositions have, it would seem, caused them to jump to conclusions which the evidence will not support.

[11]Knight, p. 342.
[12]*Ibid.*, p. 344.
[13]Fee, p. 204.

by God "through Jesus." Paul's description of Jesus as Savior after using the term of God earlier in the chapter (v. 4) follows the alternating pattern of describing God and Jesus as Savior already noted in Titus (see discussion on 2:13).

3:7 so that, having been justified by his grace,

At this juncture Paul describes salvation using his common forensic or legal metaphor of justification: "having been justified by his grace." Christians have received a not-guilty verdict on the basis of God's "grace" and not on the basis of their own works, a theme common to Paul (Rom 3:24; 5:1, 9; 1 Cor 6:11; Gal 2:16-17; 3:24).

we might become heirs having the hope of eternal life.

The Spirit's work in the Christian's life has an eschatological or future, end-time effect: "that . . . we might become heirs" (cf. Gal 4:7; Rom 8:17) "having the hope" (see Titus 1:2; 1 Tim 4:10) "of eternal life" (see the discussion at 1 Tim 1:6; 6:12; Titus 1:2).

3:8 This is a trustworthy saying.

Here Paul proclaims the section above, likely 3:4-7, as another of the "faithful" or "trustworthy" sayings of the Pastoral Epistles (cf. 1 Tim 1:15; 3:1; 4:9; 2 Tim 2:11).[14] Paul's statement that the saving work of God in Jesus is accomplished by grace is reliable, and the Christians on Crete must live accordingly.

And I want you to stress these things, so that those who have trusted in God may be careful to devote themselves to doing what is good.

The "these things" which Titus is "to stress" (διαβεβαιόω, *diabebaioō*, also used by Paul of the false teachers in 1 Tim 1:7

---

[14]Vv. 4-7 lack the hymnic or creedal nature of some of the other "trustworthy sayings." No convincing arguments have been given to see something later in the text or some other portion of the preceding section as the "trustworthy saying." Cf. Fee, pp. 206-207; Guthrie, p. 207; Hendriksen, pp. 393-394; Kelly, p. 254; Knight, pp. 347-350; Lea and Griffin, p. 326.

where the NIV renders the verb "confidently affirm") is used at least in reference to vv. 4–7 and perhaps in reference to all of the good works Paul has called the Christians on Crete to do, i.e., the whole of the Christian lifestyle as prescribed in this letter. Paul's goal for Titus' preaching is "that those who have trusted in God may be careful to devote themselves to doing what is good" (literally "good works," the very purpose of God's redemptive act, 2:7, 14; 3:1).

These things are excellent and profitable for everyone.
Again one must decide to what "these things" refers. Although it is possible to see Paul as referring to the kindness of God and the gift of the Holy Spirit,[15] it is more reasonable to see a reference to "doing what is good" in the previous sentence, i.e., "good deeds," a theme which runs throughout.[16] Such deeds are intrinsically "excellent" (literally "good"), and they are "profitable" (or "beneficial") "for everyone" (literally "for human beings"). The Christian life lived in a pagan world has a positive effect on non-believers.

D. FINAL WARNINGS CONCERNING FALSE TEACHERS AND THE DIVISIVE (3:9–11)

9But avoid foolish controversies and genealogies and arguments and quarrels about the law, because these are unprofitable and useless. 10Warn a divisive person once, and then warn him a second time. After that, have nothing to do with him. 11You may be sure that such a man is warped and sinful; he is self-condemned.

Paul now turns in vv. 9–11 to warn Titus and the church on Crete of the corrupting influence of false teachers whose deeds are not "excellent and profitable" (v. 8) but rather are "unprofitable and useless" (v. 9).

---

[15]Hendriksen, p. 394; Kelly, p. 254.
[16]Fee, p. 208; Guthrie, p. 207; Knight, p. 352; Lea and Griffin, p. 326.

3:9 But avoid foolish controversies and genealogies and arguments and quarrels about the law, because these are unprofitable and useless.

Although the imperative "avoid" is second person singular addressing Titus, Paul's instructions are intended for all the Christians on Crete. He begins by spelling out four of the "unprofitable and useless" deeds of the false teachers from which Christians must steer clear: "foolish" (cf. 2 Tim 2:23) "controversies" (cf. 1 Tim 6:4; 2 Tim 2:23); "genealogies" (see the discussion of this term in 1 Tim 1:4); "arguments" (literally "strifes"; see discussion 1 Tim 6:4); and "quarrels about the law" (cf. 2 Tim 2:23; see also the discussion of "not quarrelsome" in v. 2 and 1 Tim 3:3; of "word battles" in 1 Tim 6:4; 2 Tim 2:14). The mention of "the law" here, of "the circumcision group" in 1:10, and of "Jewish myths" and "commands" in 1:14 help to establish the makeup of the false teachers as Hellenistic Jewish Christians.

3:10 Warn a divisive person once, and then warn him a second time. After that, have nothing to do with him.

After outlining the deeds of the false teachers that Titus, along with the other Christians on Crete, were to "avoid," Paul instructs Titus how he is to respond to the teachers themselves. Paul describes them as "divisive" (αἱρετικόν, *hairetikon*, thus the KJV translation "heretic"). Paul's use of this adjective does not indicate the nature of their teaching but rather their behavior (cf. 1 Cor 11:19; Gal 5:20 where the noun is used). He is concerned about the destructive nature of their teaching and their behavior (cf. 1:1). Titus is to "warn" (or "admonish") "a divisive person once" with the hope of redeeming them (the normal reason for correcting or taking disciplinary action in Paul; cf. 1 Tim 1:20; 2 Tim 2:25-26; 2 Cor 2:5-1; 2 Thess 3:14-15). The "divisive" are then given a second chance to repent. If that attempt is to no avail, Titus and the church are to "have nothing to do with him" (literally "reject"; see 1 Tim 5:11 where the same verb is used but rendered "do not put them on such a list" by the

NIV). The phrase "have nothing to do with him" represents a single Greek word (παραιτοῦ, *paraitou*). It is used in the same sense in Hebrews 12:25.

3:11 You may be sure that such a man is warped and sinful; he is self-condemned.

Paul wants Titus to realize that, without a doubt, divisive people are "warped" (a perfect tense verb in Greek, meaning "has gotten off track and remains so") "and sinful" (a present tense verb in Greek, probably intended by Paul to indicate "keeps on sinning"). Such a person is "self-condemned," i.e., his continued sinful behavior and rejection of correction indicate that he has put himself on the outside. Such a one is without excuse and is, therefore, to be rejected by Titus and the church.

V. PERSONAL DIRECTIONS AND CLOSING SALUTATIONS (3:12-15)

[12]As soon as I send Artemas or Tychicus to you, do your best to come to me at Nicopolis, because I have decided to winter there. [13]Do everything you can to help Zenas the lawyer and Apollos on their way and see that they have everything they need. [14]Our people must learn to devote themselves to doing what is good, in order that they may provide for daily necessities and not live unproductive lives.

[15]Everyone with me sends you greetings. Greet those who love us in the faith.

Grace be with you all.

Paul follows his normal custom of giving some final personal instructions and greetings at the end of his epistles. As Fee has noted, while both 1 Timothy and Titus are "all business," in Titus he takes time for the personal, something missing from the closing of 1 Timothy even though 1 Timothy has more frequent personal exhortations. This may indicate that the situation at Crete is less urgent and that Paul's goal is preventing fires rather than putting them out.[17]

3:12 As soon as I send Artemas or Tychicus to you,

Despite all his instructions to Titus about dealing with the Christians on Crete, Paul apparently intends for Titus to be replaced by either Artemas or Tychicus soon after he receives this letter which is likely carried by Zenas and Apollos (v. 13). As he writes this letter, Paul is uncertain who will replace Titus. Artemas appears nowhere else in Scripture. Tychicus travelled with Paul in Acts 20:4 and is mentioned in two of the prison epistles as one who will deliver the letter and bring news (Col 4:7; Eph 6:21). From 2 Tim 4:12 it is clear that Tychicus was sent by Paul to Ephesus and in 2 Tim 4:10 that Titus went to Dalmatia up the coast from Nicopolis. From this data one would assume that Artemas likely served as Titus' replacement.

do your best to come to me at Nicopolis, because I have decided to winter there.

Paul's desire was that Titus make every effort to join him at Nicopolis, where he had "decided to winter." It is impossible to know with any certainty where Paul was as he wrote Titus, but it is clear that he was not yet in Nicopolis. There are several ancient cities which bear the name "Nicopolis" ("victory city"). The most likely location is the one which served as the capital of Epirus. It would suit the mention of Titus being in Dalmatia in 2 Tim 4:10. The city was about 200 miles northwest of Athens. Spending the winter on land was the reasonable thing to do since travel by sea in winter was difficult if not impossible (see Paul's own travel pushing the fall envelope, Acts 27:12; 28:11).

3:13 Do everything you can to help Zenas the lawyer and Apollos on their way and see that they have everything they need.

Apparently Zenas and Apollos have been with Paul and

---

[17]Fee, p. 213.

will be traveling through Crete. They are apparently carrying the letter (cf. v. 14). Titus is to help them and see that their needs are met, a normal way to deal with traveling missionaries (cf. Acts 15:3; 21:5; Rom 15:24; 1 Cor 16:6, 11; 2 Cor 1:16; 3 John 6). Paul describes Zenas as "the lawyer" indicating that he serves as a Roman jurist. Apollos is undoubtedly the famous Alexandrian preacher (Acts 18:24-19:1; 1 Cor 1:12; 3:4-22; 16:12).

3:14 Our people must learn to devote themselves to doing what is good, in order that they may provide for daily necessities and not live unproductive lives.

Paul instructs Titus that "our people *too* [a word not translated in the NIV] must learn to devote themselves to doing what is good." The untranslated "too" (καὶ, *kai*) indicates that the people of the church must be devoted "to doing what is good" (again literally "good works") as Paul has instructed Titus to do with regard to Zenas and Apollos. Paul gives two reasons for these good works: to "provide for daily necessities," i.e., the pressing needs; and to "live lives" that are not "unproductive" (ἄκαρποι, *akarpoi*, literally "unfruitful").

3:15 Everyone with me sends you greetings. Greet those who love us in the faith.
Grace be with you all.

The letter ends with the normal greetings: first from "everyone with" Paul to Titus, and then from Paul to "those who love" him and his fellow workers "in the faith." Fee suggests that Paul's use of "those who love us in the faith" may be "an indirect reference to the fact that some in Crete have proven themselves disloyal to Paul and his gospel."[18] Paul closes with the normal farewell: "Grace be with you all" (cf. 1 Tim 6:21), a clear indication that Paul intended for the letter to be read by the church on Crete as well as by Titus.

---

[18]Fee, p. 216.

THE BOOK OF
2 TIMOTHY

INTRODUCTION

DATE AND PLACE OF ORIGIN

In 2 Timothy Paul finds himself in a Roman prison. Onesiphorus had searched for Paul and found him in Rome (1:16-17). Paul instructed Timothy to get Mark and bring him as he came (4:11). This indicates a time in Rome other than the imprisonment related at the end of Acts since both Timothy and Mark were with Paul when he wrote Colossians (Col 1:1; 4:10; Phlm 24). Paul had recently been in Asia Minor and left his cloak at Troas (4:13), stayed with Erastus at Corinth, and left Trophimus sick at Miletus (4:20).

Though Paul was imprisoned in Caesarea for two years before being sent on to Rome (Acts 24:27), it is unlikely that he was writing from Caesarea since Trophimus and Timothy were both with him in Jerusalem when he was arrested. It seems more likely that Paul was released from the imprisonment at the end of Acts, was involved in missionary activities, and then was subsequently arrested once again (probably in Troas).[1] 2 Timothy would then have been written during that second Roman imprisonment. Paul describes his situation in terms that indicate that he is in prison facing the prospects of a speedy execution.

The date of 2 Timothy depends largely upon one's view of the authorship of the book, the place of origin of the book, and Eusebius' date of the martyrdom of Paul. Those who deny Pauline authorship of the book class it with the other Pastoral Epistles and date it in the second century. Since

---

[1] See the discussion of 4:13.

Eusebius dates the martyrdom of Paul in A.D. 67, those who hold to Pauline authorship normally date the book in 66 or 67.

DESTINATION AND AUDIENCE

It appears from several references in 2 Timothy (2 Tim 1:18; 2:17; 4:9, 12, 14, 19; cf. 1 Tim 1:20; Acts 18:18-19, 24-26; 19:33-34) that Timothy is in Ephesus as Paul writes this book as he was when Paul wrote 1 Timothy (1 Tim 1:3). Again, as in 1 Timothy, while the book bears many personal notes intended for Timothy, Paul desires for this book to be read by the whole church.

THE CONTRIBUTION OF 2 TIMOTHY

The central message of 2 Timothy is Paul's desire for Timothy to suffer with him and endure hardship for the gospel. Timothy is to stand assured that God will provide him with strength (1:6-14; 2:1-13; 3:12; 4:5). Timothy is also urged to hold on to the apostolic message (1:13-14), to pass it on to others who can in turn share it with others (2:2), and to be careful to deal with it and the message of the Old Testament correctly (2:15; 3:10-17). Put simply, Timothy must fulfill his ministry (4:1-5); Paul is passing on the mantle to his young co-worker.

OUTLINE

I. SALUTATION — 1:1-2
II. THANKSGIVING — 1:3-5
III. PAUL'S APPEAL FOR ENDURANCE IN FACING SUFFERING — 1:6-2:13
   A. An Appeal for Loyalty in Facing Hardship — 1:6-14
   B. Examples of the Disloyal and the Loyal — 1:15-18
   C. Illustrations for Effective Ministry when Facing Hardship — 2:1-7
   D. The Basis of Effective Ministry when Facing Hardship — 2:8-13
IV. FALSE TEACHERS AND SOUND DOCTRINES — 2:14-4:8
   A. Dealing with False Teachers — 2:14-19
   B. Preparing for Noble Work — 2:20-26
   C. The Character of the Last Days — 3:1-9
   D. Further Exhortations for Timothy to Endure — 3:10-17
   E. A Final Charge to Timothy — 4:1-8
V. PERSONAL INSTRUCTIONS — 4:9-18
VI. FINAL SALUTATIONS — 4:19-22

2 TIMOTHY 1

Paul writes 2 Timothy from prison awaiting his likely death. His goal is to give Timothy the encouragement and stamina to withstand the hardships he is bound to face.

I. SALUTATION (1:1-2)

¹Paul, an apostle of Christ Jesus by the will of God, according to the promise of life that is in Christ Jesus,
²To Timothy, my dear son:
Grace, mercy and peace from God the Father and Christ Jesus our Lord.

Paul's salutation in 2 Timothy is very much like 1 Tim 1:1-2. The minor differences are, however, of some significance.

1:1 Paul, an apostle of Christ Jesus
In a letter so personal it seems a bit unusual for Paul to introduce himself as "an apostle." In 1 Tim 1:1 Paul needed to lend authority to the Ephesian Christians both for his letter and for Timothy and his ministry. Here, as Fee has suggested, although Paul may simply be acting out of habit, it is more likely that Paul's use of this self-designation reflects the urgent appeal for Timothy's loyalty to Paul and his message.[1]

---

[1] Fee, p. 219.

by the will of God, according to the promise of life that is in Christ Jesus,

In 2 Timothy Paul attributes his apostleship to "the will of God," a phrase which is parallel to "the command of God" in 1 Tim 1:1. Paul's apostleship and the suffering which accompanies it are all "by the will of God." With the next modifier Paul indicates that his apostleship is "according to the promise of life that is in Christ Jesus," a positive affirmation that does not occur in 1 Tim 1:1. For Paul, eternal life in the present and in the future resides *in Christ Jesus*.

1:2 To Timothy, my dear son:

Grace, mercy and peace from God the Father and Christ Jesus our Lord.

In 2 Tim 1:2 Paul addresses Timothy as "my dear" (ἀγαπη-τῷ, *agapētō*, "beloved") "son" (cf. 1 Cor 4:17) in contrast to "my true son in the faith" in 1 Tim 1:2. The note of intimacy adds an important emphasis to Paul's call for Timothy to endure suffering in 2 Timothy. His emphasis on his relationship to Timothy as legitimate in 1 Timothy gave authority to Timothy and his words.

Paul's words of greeting — "grace, mercy and peace from God the Father and Christ Jesus our Lord" — match 1 Tim 1:2.

II. THANKSGIVING (1:3-5)

³**I thank God, whom I serve, as my forefathers did, with a clear conscience, as night and day I constantly remember you in my prayers.** ⁴**Recalling your tears, I long to see you, so that I may be filled with joy.** ⁵**I have been reminded of your sincere faith, which first lived in your grandmother Lois and in your mother Eunice and, I am persuaded, now lives in you also.**

Paul normally follows the greeting in his letters with an expression of thanksgiving (cf. 1 Cor 1:4-9; Phil 1:3-11 for examples of extended sections of thanksgiving). The only exceptions to this pattern are found in 1 Timothy, Titus, and Galatians.

1:3 I thank God,
In this verse Paul does not specify the exact nature of his thanksgiving to God. Is it for God's gift of his ministry? Is it for "the promise of life in Christ Jesus" (v. 1)? Or is it for the "sincere faith" of Timothy?

whom I serve, as my forefathers did, with a clear conscience,
Paul connects his service to God with that of his "forefathers." He sees continuity in the faith of believers throughout the ages. For Paul there is a clear connection between Judaism and Christianity. Paul's service is "with a clear conscience" (see discussion at 1 Tim 1:5).

as night and day I constantly remember you in my prayers.
Although the KJV renders the word "constantly" (literally "without ceasing") with the verb "thank," the NIV is correct in taking it with "remember." Paul's prayer of thanksgiving becomes one of intercession for Timothy. Paul "constantly" remembers Timothy in his prayers "day and night" (see 1 Tim 5:5 where this is required of "widows indeed").

1:4 Recalling your tears, I long to see you, so that I may be filled with joy.
As Paul prays for Timothy he wishes to see him especially when he remembers Timothy's "tears." With the macho image of men, the American culture perhaps has little room for tears of a man like Timothy. Two options have been offered for the occasion of those tears. Some suggest that Paul is referring to his farewell to the elders at Ephesus on his trip to Jerusalem (Acts 20:37). Others suggest one should see Paul's leaving Timothy in Ephesus on his way to Macedonia as the occasion (1 Tim 1:3). The latter option is more likely. Seeing Timothy will fill Paul "with joy."

1:5 I have been reminded of your sincere faith, which first lived in your grandmother Lois and in your mother Eunice and, I am persuaded, now lives in you also.

Paul remembers Timothy's "sincere" (ἀνυποκρίτου, *anypokritou*, literally "unhypocritical") "faith." This faith "first lived in [Timothy's] grandmother Lois and in [his] mother Eunice" (cf. Acts 16:1). Their expression of "faith" was Timothy's heritage like Paul's heritage from his forefathers (v. 3). Paul is convinced that that faith is alive and well in Timothy.

III. PAUL'S APPEAL FOR ENDURANCE IN FACING SUFFERING (1:6–2:13)

Timothy's faith will sustain him through suffering. Paul knows that Timothy has much hardship ahead of him and sets out to prepare him to endure future suffering.

A. AN APPEAL FOR LOYALTY IN FACING HARDSHIP (1:6–14)

⁶For this reason I remind you to fan into flame the gift of God, which is in you through the laying on of my hands. ⁷For God did not give us a spirit of timidity, but a spirit of power, of love and of self-discipline.

⁸So do not be ashamed to testify about our Lord, or ashamed of me his prisoner. But join with me in suffering for the gospel, by the power of God, ⁹who has saved us and called us to a holy life — not because of anything we have done but because of his own purpose and grace. This grace was given us in Christ Jesus before the beginning of time, ¹⁰but it has now been revealed through the appearing of our Savior, Christ Jesus, who has destroyed death and has brought life and immortality to light through the gospel. ¹¹And of this gospel I was appointed a herald and an apostle and a teacher. ¹²That is why I am suffering as I am. Yet I am not ashamed, because I know whom I have believed, and am

convinced that he is able to guard what I have entrusted to him for that day.

¹³What you heard from me, keep as the pattern of sound teaching, with faith and love in Christ Jesus. ¹⁴Guard the good deposit that was entrusted to you — guard it with the help of the Holy Spirit who lives in us.

1:6 For this reason I remind you to fan into flame the gift of God,

Paul's conviction that Timothy has a living, "sincere faith" leads him to remind Timothy to "fan into flame the gift of God." The infinitive "to fan into flame" (ἀναζωπυρεῖν, *anazōpyrein*) is a present infinitive in Greek, indicating Paul's desire for Timothy "to keep fanning something into flame." As Knight has suggested, although to fan into flame represents a metaphor of the rekindling of a dying flame, Paul is not suggesting that Timothy's faith was dying.[2] He is simply calling Timothy to continue his faithful Christian life.

which is in you through the laying on of my hands.

The "gift of God" was given Timothy "through the laying on" of Paul's hands. The "gift" (χάρισμα, *charisma*) here need not be seen as a miraculous gift. It likely refers to Timothy's ministry (see the discussion of 1 Tim 1:18; 4:14) and to God's equipping him for that ministry. In 1 Tim 4:14 Timothy's gift is described as "given through a prophetic message when the body of elders laid their hands on" him. Paul's intent there was to emphasize for the church at Ephesus Timothy's authority. Here Paul speaks of his laying hands on Timothy because of the personal appeal he is making.

1:7 For God did not give us a spirit of timidity,

Paul describes this gift in terms of spirit God has given. Most translations and modern commentators understand "spirit" (πνεῦμα, *pneuma*) as some spirit or attitude (KJV, RSV, NIV,

---

[2]Knight, p. 370.

NASB, NRSV).[3] Fee and Hendriksen, however, take *pneuma* as "Spirit," i.e., the Holy Spirit.[4] Fee says that Paul's intent was "something like this: 'For when God gave us his Spirit, it was not timidity that we received, but power, love and self-discipline.'"[5] The strongest argument against this interpretation is the fact that Paul begins with the negative attribute — timidity. It also seems likely that the "us" (ὑμῖν, *hymin*) of the verse is Christians in general.[6] In reality the differences between the two interpretations are minimal.[7] With the gift of the Holy Spirit, a "spirit of timidity" is inappropriate. Perhaps, because of Timothy's own temperament as seen in both 1 and 2 Timothy, Paul sees the need to remind Timothy that timidity (or "cowardice") is inappropriate for his ministry.

but a spirit of power, of love and of self-discipline.

Timothy is rather to live out his God-given "spirit of power" (cf. Rom 15:13, 19; 1 Cor 2:4; Eph 3:16), "of love" (cf. Rom 5:5; 15:10; Gal 5:22; Col 1:8), and "of self-discipline" (σωφρονισμοῦ, *sōphronismou*, although this word appears only here in the NT, cf. 1 Tim 2:9, 14; 3:2 where cognates occur). This "spirit of power" is obviously connected to the indwelling Spirit in Timothy's life.

1:8 So do not be ashamed to testify about our Lord, or ashamed of me his prisoner.

On the basis of the "spirit" Timothy is to have (the "so," literally "therefore" of v. 8 makes this clear), Paul calls him to do two things: (1) "do not be ashamed" and (2) "join with me in suffering." Timothy is not to "be ashamed to testify about" the Lord. Appropriately Paul designates Jesus as "our Lord," indicating an element of intimacy. The NIV is correct in taking the genitive "of the Lord" as an objective genitive "the

---

[3]E.g., Kelly, p. 159; Knight, pp. 370-371; Lea and Griffin, pp. 188-189. Cf. 2 Cor 4:13 where *pneuma* is "spirit."
[4]Fee, pp. 226-227; Hendriksen, pp. 229-230; cf. TEV.
[5]Fee, p. 227.
[6]See Knight, p. 371.
[7]See Rom 8:15-16 where Paul moves from spirit to Spirit.

testimony *about* the Lord" rather than a subjective genitive "the testimony which the Lord gave." It is a call for Timothy to face the task of preaching the gospel with courage. Timothy is also called not to be ashamed of Paul "his prisoner" (cf. Eph 3:1; Phil 1:12-14).

But join with me in suffering for the gospel, by the power of God,
Notice that Paul emphasizes not that his imprisonment was imposed by the Roman government but that the Lord was in control and that Paul was in prison for him. Timothy is also called to "join with [Paul] in suffering." This suffering was "for the gospel" (i.e., because of his association with and for the spread of the gospel) and "by the power of God" (cf. v. 7).

1:9 who has saved us and called us to a holy life — not because of anything we have done but because of his own purpose and grace. This grace was given us in Christ Jesus before the beginning of time,
In typical Pauline fashion, Paul moves to describe God by indicating the grandeur of his work. He "has saved us and called us to a holy life."[8] Again Paul emphasizes that salvation and the Christian calling are "not because of anything we have done" (literally "not according to works") "but because of his own purpose and grace" (a theme already seen in the Pastoral Epistles, Titus 3:5).[9] Grace is not earned but "given in Christ Jesus." That gift was "determined"[10] or "became available"[11] "before the beginning of time" (literally "before the times of the ages"), speaking of "God's decision before time and the world began"[12] (cf. 1 Cor 2:7; Eph 1:4).

---

[8]To see Paul's understanding of the Christian calling, examine 1 Cor 1:9; Gal 1:6; Rom 8:28; 1 Thess 4:7.
[9]For Pauline texts that emphasize the *purpose* of God in the Christian calling, see Rom 8:28; 9:11; Eph 1:11. Cf. Eph 2:8-10 for salvation by grace through faith.
[10]Guthrie, p. 129.
[11]Lea and Griffin, p. 192.
[12]Knight, p. 375.

1:10 but it has now been revealed through the appearing of our Savior, Christ Jesus, who has destroyed death and has brought life and immortality to light through the gospel.

This grace "has now been revealed through the appearing" (ἐπιφάνεια, *epiphaneia*) "of our Savior, Christ Jesus." The appearance which Paul has in mind here is the incarnation. See Titus 2:11-13 where the same word "appearing" is used of the second coming (cf. Titus 3:4; 1 Tim 6:14). For a discussion of Jesus as "Savior" see Titus 1:4; 3:6. Christ Jesus is described as the one "who has destroyed" (literally "has rendered inoperative"; cf. 1 Cor 15:26) "death and has brought life and immortality" (literally "incorruptibility"; cf. 1 Cor 15:42; 50; 53; 54) "to light through the gospel."

1:11 And of this gospel I was appointed a herald and an apostle and a teacher.

It is for "this gospel," which has illuminated the world with regard to "life and immortality," and its proclamation that Paul "was appointed a herald" (i.e., "public proclaimer"; see discussion at 1 Tim 2:7) "and an apostle" (see discussion at 1 Tim 1:1) "and a teacher" (cf. 1 Tim 2:7). He was to be a bold messenger, commissioned by God, to share the gospel story.

1:12 That is why I am suffering as I am. Yet I am not ashamed, because I know whom I have believed, and am convinced that he is able to guard what I have entrusted to him for that day.

This task was the reason that Paul was enduring hardship. Despite the suffering, a reference to the indignity of his imprisonment, Paul was "not ashamed." The clause "yet I am not ashamed" may well function here as a *litotes* with Paul actually proclaiming that he is *proud* of the "suffering" and the "gospel" for which he suffers (cf. Rom 1:16). Paul is not ashamed because God, in whom Paul has put his trust, is sufficiently powerful to "guard" something dear to Paul. The question is what is the "entrusted" thing. The text literally says "because I know whom I have believed, and am convinced that he is able to guard my deposit (παραθήκη, *paratheke*) for that day." Some argue that "deposit" should be taken in the same way as it is used in v. 14 which refers to the "sound teaching" of v. 13, i.e., the "gospel" of v. 11. God has entrusted the gospel to Paul (v. 12), Paul has entrusted it to Timothy (v. 14; cf. 1 Tim 6:20), and Timothy is to entrust it to others who will be able to pass it on (2:2). The text is then rendered "he is able to guard what *has been entrusted to me*." This interpretation has attracted the majority of contemporary scholars and many modern translations.[13] God is then able to keep the gospel message alive and viable no matter what may happen to a Paul or a Timothy. This interpretation has the benefit of consistency.

The alternative is to take the more traditional interpretation as per the NIV, NASB, NRSV. God is able to keep secure what Paul has "entrusted to him," namely, his life or soul, his converts, and his work.[14] In favor of this rendering are (1) the fact that God, and not Paul, is the one who is portrayed as guarding the deposit; (2) the immediate context of Paul's suffering; and (3) the similarity to the idea expressed elsewhere in Scripture (Luke 23:46; 1 Pet 1:4; 4:19). Several factors distinguish the use of the word here from its use in 1 Tim 6:20 and 2 Tim 1:4. In the other passages Timothy is the one who is guarding the "deposit." That "deposit" is not personalized, i.e., "my deposit." Paul has already identified the nature of the "deposit" when he said "whom I have believed" ("in whom I have put my trust"). Paul has entrusted himself to God. This, by the way, also fits the direction of the entire epistle. Paul is calling Timothy to be ready to suffer for the cause. To do that he must, like Paul, entrust his life or soul to God's care. Paul's use of the phrase "for that day" also supports this interpretation. God "is able to guard" Paul's "deposit" until the last day.

---

[13]Cf. RSV, TEV, NEB. See Kelly, pp. 165-166; Guthrie, p. 132.

[14]Cf. NIV, NASB, NRSV; and marginal readings in the RSV, TEV, and NEB. See Fee, p. 232; Knight, pp. 379-380; Hendriksen, pp. 235-236.

1:13 What you heard from me, keep as the pattern of sound teaching, with faith and love in Christ Jesus.

In vv. 13-14 Paul appeals to Timothy in ways that parallel 1 Timothy. He is to keep the message he heard from Paul "as the pattern of sound [or 'healthy'] teaching" (see discussion at 1 Tim 1:10). Paul has modelled this "sound teaching" for Timothy (cf. 2:2; 3:10; 1 Tim 4:6). The word "pattern" (ὑποτύπωσιν, *hypotypōsin*) means an outline sketch or an architect's draft. The point in this text is not "pattern theology," as some would suggest, but rather that Timothy might preach the same message he had heard from Paul. While Paul's initial concern is the content of Timothy's teaching, he is also concerned with the manner in which that teaching is to be carried out — "with faith and love in Christ Jesus." Orthodoxy is important but so are faithfulness and compassion which are located "in Christ Jesus."

1:14 Guard the good deposit that was entrusted to you — guard it with the help of the Holy Spirit who lives in us.

Paul's final imperative in this section is an appeal for Timothy to "guard the good deposit that was entrusted to" him. This time the "deposit" is clear. It is the "sound teaching" which Paul had left with Timothy. Maintaining the purity of the gospel will require something bigger than the man Timothy. He is to rely upon "the help of the Holy Spirit who lives in us." The Holy Spirit lives within all believers and enables them to stand. He will enable Timothy in his ministry of the gospel.

B. EXAMPLES OF THE DISLOYAL AND THE LOYAL (1:15-18)

¹⁵You know that everyone in the province of Asia has deserted me, including Phygelus and Hermogenes.

¹⁶May the Lord show mercy to the household of Onesiphorus, because he often refreshed me and was not ashamed of my chains. ¹⁷On the contrary, when he was in Rome, he

searched hard for me until he found me. **[18]May the Lord grant that he will find mercy from the Lord on that day! You know very well in how many ways he helped me in Ephesus.**

In this section Paul begins by illustrating his call for Timothy to "guard the good deposit" by giving some examples of those who have not done so, Phygelus and Hermogenes. He then moves to one who has been faithful to that "good deposit," Onesiphorus.

1:15 You know that everyone in the province of Asia has deserted me, including Phygelus and Hermogenes.
Timothy is well aware of the fact that Christians from the province of Asia had "deserted" Paul. It is possible that some from Asia had travelled to Rome to be with Paul but had now returned leaving him alone. An alternate interpretation emphasizes Paul's use of the word "in" (ἐν, *en*) rather than "from" and suggests that at this time there was a major defection from the church "in the province of Asia." Since the next verses, 16-18, emphasize the help that Onesiphorus had rendered, it seems more likely that Paul intends to convey the idea that these people have abandoned him. The "all" should not be construed as "all people who are from Asia, without exception." Tychicus is clearly one from Asia who still stands by Paul (cf. Acts 20:2; 2 Tim 4:12; Titus 3:12). Onesiphorus is also from Asia. Whether Paul is reminding Timothy that some of his colleagues have deserted him, that some who are now in Asia failed to come to his aid, or that they have left to return to Asia, the modern reader cannot know with certainty. The situation was, however, clear to Timothy. The word translated "deserted" (ἀποστρέφω, *apostrephō*) also appears in 4:16 where Paul indicates that at his first defense all had deserted him.

No further information is given with regard to the two men in this group whom Paul singles out, Phygelus and Hermogenes. Later in the apocryphal work *The Acts of Paul and Thecla*, Hermogenes is mentioned with Onesiphorus.[15]

---

[15]*The Acts of Paul and Thecla* 14.

1:16 May the Lord show mercy to the household of Onesiphorus, because he often refreshed me and was not ashamed of my chains.

The mention of those who had deserted him brings to mind one who had helped him during his imprisonment and the family of that man. Onesiphorus had set the example of one who was loyal and who held as sacred the good deposit of the gospel. "He often refreshed" (ἀναψύχω, *anapsychō*; literally "to blow" or "to make cool") Paul. This refreshing could involve encouraging Paul, providing him with food, doing anything that would lift his spirits. Ellis has said, "When Onesiphorus came to see Paul in the stuffy dungeon, it was as if the air conditioning had been turned on."[16] Paul mentions the fact that "Onesiphorus was not ashamed of my chains" to drive home his call in v. 8 for Timothy "not to be ashamed" of him the Lord's "prisoner."

1:17 On the contrary, when he was in Rome, he searched hard for me until he found me.

Visiting and assisting a prisoner in Rome was not an easy task. Onesiphorus had "searched hard" for Paul "until he found" him. His assistance, though, did not begin when Paul went to prison. Timothy was well aware of all the assistance he had rendered to Paul earlier in Ephesus.

1:18 May the Lord grant that he will find mercy from the Lord on that day! You know very well in how many ways he helped me in Ephesus.

The language of vv. 16–18 may well indicate that Onesiphorus has died. Paul asked that the "Lord show mercy to the household of Onesiphorus" rather than to "Onesiphorus and his household." Fee has suggested that even the wish Paul expresses for Onesiphorus may indicate his death — "May the Lord grant that he will find mercy from the Lord on that

---

[16]Ralph Earle, *Word Meanings in the New Testament* (Grand Rapids: Baker, 1984), p. 404.

day!" Even if he was dead his memory was clear to Paul. He had "helped" (διακονέω, *diakoneō*; literally "served") in "many ways" when Timothy and Paul labored there (cf. 1 Cor 4:17; 16:8). Timothy needed to be like Onesiphorus and not like Phygelus and Hermogenes.

2 TIMOTHY 2

C. ILLUSTRATIONS FOR EFFECTIVE MINISTRY WHEN FACING HARDSHIP (2:1-7)

¹You then, my son, be strong in the grace that is in Christ Jesus. ²And the things you have heard me say in the presence of many witnesses entrust to reliable men who will also be qualified to teach others. ³Endure hardship with us like a good soldier of Christ Jesus. ⁴No one serving as a soldier gets involved in civilian affairs — he wants to please his commanding officer. ⁵Similarly, if anyone competes as an athlete, he does not receive the victor's crown unless he competes according to the rules. ⁶The hardworking farmer should be the first to receive a share of the crops. ⁷Reflect on what I am saying, for the Lord will give you insight into all this.

After giving examples of those who have and have not been loyal to him during his imprisonment (1:15-18), Paul resumes his appeal for Timothy to "endure hardship." Paul uses three analogies (the soldier, the athlete, and the farmer) to illustrate the need for endurance and the reward to those who do endure.

2:1 You then, my son, be strong in the grace that is in Christ Jesus.
The emphatic "you then" of v. 1 serves as the link to 1:6-14. Paul again recognizes Timothy as his "son" and calls him to "be strong in the grace that is in Christ Jesus." The imperative "be strong" is not unusual in Paul (cf. 4:17; 1 Tim

1:12; Eph 6:10; Phil 4:13). Here the phrase represents a present imperative in which Paul is calling Timothy to "continue to be strong." The prepositional phrase "in the grace" can be used to indicate either the place where Timothy is to be strong (the NIV rendering "in the grace"; cf. KJV, NASB, RSV, NRSV) or it can indicate the means by which Timothy is to be strong (i.e., "be strong by the grace"). While either option accords with the NT doctrine of grace, despite the tendency of most translations and commentators to assume that the phrase is locative, Kelly is probably right that "the force of in with grace is probably instrumental: 'by means of,' or 'in the power of.'"[1] This grace is located squarely "in Christ Jesus." In fellowship with Jesus one finds grace. He is the source of that grace.

2:2 And the things you have heard me say in the presence of many witnesses

Timothy is to "entrust" what he has "heard" from Paul (undoubtedly the "sound teaching" of 1:13) to others who can serve as "reliable" or "faithful" teachers. The verb to "entrust" (παρατίθεσθαι, *paratithesthai*) is related to the noun "deposit" (παραθήκη, *parathēkē*) in 1:12 and 14 (cf. 1 Tim 6:20). Timothy is to see the gospel as a sacred trust which must be passed on. Paul's message was delivered "in the presence of many witnesses." Although the word translated "in the presence of" (διά, *dia*) normally means "through," it is unlikely that Paul intends to represent his message as mediated through others to Timothy since Timothy had heard Paul directly. The suggestion that *dia* should be rendered "in the presence of" goes back to Chrysostom (d. A.D. 407) and is likely correct.[2]

entrust to reliable men who will also be qualified to teach others.

It should be noted that the word "men" (ἄνθρωποι, *anthrōpoi*) primarily indicates not "male persons" but "human beings" or

---

[1]Kelly, p. 172. Cf. Knight, p. 389.
[2]Fee, p. 241; Kelly, pp. 173-174; Knight, p. 390.

"people." Knight argues that the word is here to be understood as adult males in contrast to women, primarily on the basis of Paul's prohibition in 1 Tim 2:12 (cf. 1 Cor 14:34). He suggests that Timothy would have understood Paul's admonition as directed toward the instruction of elders/overseers.[3] While Knight's argument needs to be considered, he has pressed his conclusions further than the data allows. Paul's real concern here is that Timothy seek out "faithful" people who are able to share the gospel with others.[4] The setting here is not the public assembly. Paul would himself argue that older women need to be able teachers of the gospel and its implications for younger women (Titus 2:4-5). Priscilla had a part in the teaching of Apollos (Acts 18:24-26).

2:3 Endure hardship with us like a good soldier of Christ Jesus.

Paul's first analogy in his call for Timothy to "endure hardship" (συγκακοπαθέω, *synkakopatheō*, literally "take his share in suffering bad")[5] is that of the "soldier of Christ Jesus." Paul frequently uses military imagery (e.g., 1 Cor 9:7; 2 Cor 10:3-5; Eph 6:10-17; Phlm 2). Paul intends for Timothy to see some similarities between his ministry and the task of a soldier. It is to be expected that soldiers will face hardship.

2:4 No one serving as a soldier gets involved in civilian affairs — he wants to please his commanding officer.

Paul calls attention to two characteristics: (1) the soldier does not allow himself to get "involved" (or "entangled") in "civilian affairs"; (2) "he wants to please his commanding officer" (literally "the one who enlisted him as a soldier"). Paul's message to Timothy is that he must (1) give wholehearted devotion to his ministry and (2) seek to please the one who has enlisted him in that ministry.

---

[3]Knight, p. 391.
[4]Kelly, p. 174.
[5]Note Paul's use of an abbreviated form of this word (*kakopatheō*) in v. 9.

2:5 Similarly, if anyone competes as an athlete, he does not receive the victor's crown unless he competes according to the rules.

Paul's second analogy is that of "an athlete." When an athlete "competes," he must compete "according to the rules" (νομίμως, *nomimōs*; literally "lawfully"; cf. 1 Tim 1:8) if he wishes to "receive the victor's crown" (cf. 4:8). Paul does not specify what "rules" he intends Timothy to follow, perhaps simply the rule to endure hardship.

2:6 The hardworking farmer should be the first to receive a share of the crops.

Paul's final analogy depicts the minister as a "hardworking farmer." Interestingly Paul uses the same three analogies (the soldier, the athlete, and the farmer) in 1 Cor 9:7; 24–27. The "hardworking farmer" must also "endure hardship," but Paul's primary emphasis is on the reward for the faithful minister. Timothy must "work hard" (κοπιάω, *kopiaō*), a word already used by Paul of elders who are "working hard in the word" (1 Tim 5:17). The word "first" can be taken either with the verb "work hard" (i.e., the farmer who "first works hard" must receive) or with the verb "receive" (i.e., the hardworking farmer "must first receive"). The latter is more likely. As Fee has noted, "the point of his receiving the first share, therefore, is not about his making a living from the gospel, which is totally foreign to the context, but about his final reward for being hardworking."[6]

2:7 Reflect on what I am saying, for the Lord will give you insight into all this.

Finally Paul asks Timothy to "reflect on" the series of analogies he has given. Just in case Timothy misses his point, Paul expresses confidence that "the Lord will give [him] insight into all this."

---

[6]Fee, p. 243.

D. THE BASIS OF EFFECTIVE MINISTRY WHEN FACING HARDSHIP (2:8-13)

⁸Remember Jesus Christ, raised from the dead, descended from David. This is my gospel, ⁹for which I am suffering even to the point of being chained like a criminal. But God's word is not chained. ¹⁰Therefore I endure everything for the sake of the elect, that they too may obtain the salvation that is in Christ Jesus, with eternal glory.
¹¹Here is a trustworthy saying: If we died with him,
we will also live with him;
¹²if we endure,
we will also reign with him.
If we disown him,
he will also disown us;
¹³if we are faithless,
he will remain faithful,
for he cannot disown himself.

Paul gives both a fitting conclusion to his appeal for Timothy to endure hardship and the theological basis for that appeal in the gospel of Jesus Christ. Timothy's loyalty to Paul is connected to his loyalty to the gospel.

2:8 Remember Jesus Christ, raised from the dead, descended from David.
Paul moves from the analogies of vv. 3-7 to motivate Timothy by reminding him of the work of Jesus Christ. Paul rehearses the heart of his gospel: "Jesus Christ [was] raised from the dead [and] descended from David" (literally "of David's seed"). Jesus' victory over death in the resurrection should encourage and comfort Timothy as he faced suffering and the prospects of his own death. Timothy might well have reflected back on the words of Paul in 2:9-10 where Jesus is described as the one "who has destroyed death and has brought life and immortality to light." Paul may also be anticipating his description of the false teachers in vv. 14-18 as

those who argue that "the resurrection has already taken place." There is no obvious reason in the immediate context for Paul's addition of the phrase "descended from David." Likely the whole description — "Jesus Christ, raised from the dead, descended from David" — represents the common confession of Jesus as Messiah.

This is my gospel, 2:9 for which I am suffering even to the point of being chained like a criminal.

Paul's present suffering is a result of his ministry for that gospel. He describes suffering as being "even to the point of being chained like a criminal," "a clear indignity for one who was both a Roman citizen and innocent."[7] The word "criminal" (κακοῦργος, *kakourgos*) is used in Luke 23:32-39 to describe the two men who were crucified with Jesus and was reserved for burglars, murderers, traitors, and others who would have been deemed the worst of law breakers. Paul's description of his imprisonment here indicates a situation considerably more severe than the house arrest of Acts 28.

But God's word is not chained.

For Paul the point of importance is the fact that, although he is chained, the word of God remains unfettered. Paul's emphasis for Timothy is simple. "God's word" is what matters (cf. 4:2). Paul has been imprisoned and made to suffer. Timothy may face the same fate. But the gospel will go on (cf. Phil 1:12-18).

2:10 Therefore I endure everything for the sake of the elect, that they too may obtain the salvation that is in Christ Jesus, with eternal glory.

Paul indicates that he suffers (here "endures everything") "for the sake of the elect" (literally "the chosen"). As Fee has noted, "Far too much ink has been spilled on the theological implications of this term [i.e., the elect]."[8] For Paul the term

---
[7]Fee, p. 247.
[8]*Ibid.*

simply represents the people of God. Paul is clearly not saying that God elects some for salvation apart from their response to the gospel (see the phrase "that they too may obtain the salvation," v. 10). Paul will later use the word "endure" (ὑπομένω, *hypomenō*) in 4:5 when he exhorts Timothy to "endure hardship" in fulfilling his ministry (cf. 3:10; 1 Tim 6:11).

Paul does not see his suffering as salvific. Salvation is located "in Christ Jesus" and his work (cf. 2 Cor 5:17). Paul's suffering may provide people with opportunity to hear the gospel message. If his suffering enables the people of God "to obtain salvation," the suffering becomes almost unimportant. The "salvation of the elect" is accompanied by "eternal glory" (cf. Rom 5:1, 2; 8:21-25; 2 Cor 4:17; 2 Thess 2:13-14).

2:11 Here is a trustworthy saying:

In v. 11 Paul introduces yet another "trustworthy saying" (see discussion at 1 Tim 1:15; cf. 1 Tim 3:1; 4:10; Titus 3:8). The exact nature of this "saying" has been a matter of some debate. Is Paul referring to something in the previous section or to the poetic section which follows? Does the saying represent a fragment from an early Christian hymn or confessional statement? Is it composed by Paul or by some other early Christian author?

Although some (e.g., Ellicot, Fausset, Holtz, Ridderbos, Schlatter, von Soden, Weiss, and White) have suggested that Paul is referring to something in the previous material, this suggestion has not been widely accepted. As Knight has noted, it is unlikely that Paul would describe his statement about his gospel, his being chained, and his enduring as a "trustworthy saying."[9]

Paul introduces the poetic section with γάρ (*gar*; "*for* if we died with him"), which is not translated in the NIV. Some see Paul as pointing back to the introductory formula, "here is a trustworthy saying." Other suggest that the "for" is a part of the original hymn that referred to a previous section not cited

---

[9]Knight, p. 401.

by Paul.[10] Another alternative is to take the "for" as an intentional explanatory note added by Paul to refer back to 2:1-10 and call Timothy to endure his share of suffering.[11] Lenski suggests a final option by taking "for" as confirmatory and, therefore, better translated "indeed."[12] It would seem that the more likely options would involve either seeing "for" as a Pauline addition to the hymn fragment or poem tying to his declaration that it is a "trustworthy saying" or as a part of the original source which Paul simply preserves.

There is little question that this section bears some poetic qualities.[13] The section has many of the qualities one would expect to find in a hymn. It is not, however, as precise a match of those qualities as can be found elsewhere, e.g., 1 Tim 3:16.[14] The poetic nature can easily be seen in the strophic arrangement of the NIV. Each verse or strophe consists of a conditional sentence (if . . . , then). It may even be seen as two sets of couplets with the first two verses being positive and the last two negative. It is possible that Paul himself is the author of the material. After all, he did compose 1 Cor 13, and the material in vv. 11-13 sounds like Pauline preaching. Fee says that the saying is "perhaps an early poem or hymn, more likely from Paul himself or from his churches."[15]

If we died with him, we will also live with him;
The first line matches what Paul has said in Rom 6:8.

---

[10]Guthrie, p. 145; Hendriksen, p. 255; Kelly, p. 179; Knight, p. 401.
[11]Fee, p. 248.
[12]R.C.H. Lenski, *The Interpretation of St. Paul's Epistles to Colossians, to the Thessalonians, to Timothy, to Titus, and to Philemon* (Columbus, OH: Wartburg Press, 1946), p. 792.
[13]Few would agree with Spain, p. 127, who suggested that Paul may be "uttering some great truths without any effort to be poetic."
[14]Cf. Michael Moss, "Hymn Fragments in the New Testament and Their Implications for Hymnology Today," paper read at the Christian Scholars Conference, Harding University, July 23, 1993. See also W. Hulitt Gloer, "Homologies and Hymns in the New Testament: Form, Content and Criteria for Identification," *Perspectives in Religious Studies*, 11 (1984) pp. 116-130.
[15]Fee, p. 248.

Although some, like Hendriksen, would see Paul referring to martyrdom,[16] it is probable that he has in mind the believer's experience at his conversion and baptism.[17] This would agree with Paul's use of the argument in Rom 6:8-11 (cf. Col 3:3). It would also agree with Paul's use of the past tense "died." Although the primary intent is to emphasize the result of the Christian's baptismal experience, Fee may be correct that Paul may have intended the text to be "heard with the broader implications of Christian martyrdom," implications "not lost on Timothy."[18]

2:12 if we endure, we will also reign with him.
The second line provides the likely reason for Paul's use or construction of the text. Paul's appeal in the whole section (1:6-2:13) is for Timothy to "endure." Paul has just spoken of his own patient endurance of suffering in v. 10. If Christians endure, they will participate in the reign of the glorified Messiah they serve.

If we disown him, he will also disown us;
In v. 12b Paul turns to negative behavior and the results. Disowning Christ (the Greek literally says, "if we shall disown him") will result in Christ disowning that one. The language reflects the saying of Jesus in Matt 10:33 and Luke 12:9.

2:13 if we are faithless, he will remain faithful,
The final verse or line is the most problematic. Fee declares the line to be "full of surprises."[19] Most scholars see this line as negative corresponding to the line which precedes it. If Christians prove "faithless" (i.e., commit apostasy), God will still remain faithful to himself and will necessarily mete out judgment. The verb translated "will remain" (μένει, *menei*) by the NIV is, however, not a future tense but rather a present.

---

[16]Hendriksen, pp. 256-259.
[17]Cf. Fee, p. 249; Guthrie, p. 145; Kelly, pp. 179-180.
[18]Fee, p. 249-250.
[19]*Ibid.*, p. 250.

The text must then be understood as follows: "if we are faithless, God remains faithful" (i.e., he is still faithful to his nature and to his promises to his people). Fee suggests that the interpreter is left with two options. Either God can "override our infidelity with his grace," or God will in no way be rendered unfaithful to his promise of salvation to believers even though they are "faithless."[20] The latter option is the only one that fits the biblical doctrines of free will, grace, and human responsibility. It also fits the call Paul has made for Timothy and others to endure.

for he cannot disown himself.

The last clause "because he cannot disown himself" has been called the final coda.[21] Since this time the *protasis* (the "if" clause) does not give the reason for the *apodosis* (the "then" clause) as with the earlier lines, Paul provides the reason with a "because" or "for" (γάρ, *gar*) clause. God, or more likely as Knight suggests Christ, "cannot disown" (literally "deny"; cf. v. 12) "himself."[22] To be less than faithful to his promises and his people would be against Christ's very nature.

IV. FALSE TEACHERS AND SOUND DOCTRINES (2:14–4:8)

In this section Paul gives Timothy instructions for dealing with false teachers. He then appeals again for Timothy to persevere. He is to remain loyal to the Scriptures he has learned, to Paul's gospel, and to his own ministry.

A. DEALING WITH FALSE TEACHERS (2:14-19)

14Keep reminding them of these things. Warn them before God against quarreling about words; it is of no value, and only ruins those who listen. 15Do your best to present

---

[20]Fee, p. 251.
[21]*Ibid.*
[22]Knight, p. 407.

yourself to God as one approved, a workman who does not need to be ashamed and who correctly handles the word of truth. ¹⁶Avoid godless chatter, because those who indulge in it will become more and more ungodly. ¹⁷Their teaching will spread like gangrene. Among them are Hymenaeus and Philetus, ¹⁸who have wandered away from the truth. They say that the resurrection has already taken place, and they destroy the faith of some. ¹⁹Nevertheless, God's solid foundation stands firm, sealed with this inscription: "The Lord knows those who are his,"ᵃ and, "Everyone who confesses the name of the Lord must turn away from wickedness."

ᵃ*19* Num. 16:5 (see Septuagint)

Earlier Paul has given Timothy exhortations with regard to his life and ministry in a pagan world. Now he moves to continue the exhortations, but this time the context is false teachers and their teachings.

2:14 Keep reminding them of these things.
Paul now urges Timothy to "keep reminding them of these things." The word "them" does not occur in the original Greek text, but must be supplied for sense. It undoubtedly refers to Christians. The "things" of which Timothy is to remind them is perhaps the whole content of the epistle thus far but most likely refers in particular to the "faithful saying" of vv. 11-13. They must be reminded of the gospel and its implications.

Warn them before God against quarreling about words; it is of no value, and only ruins those who listen.
In addition to reminding them, Timothy must "warn them before God against quarreling about words" (λογομαχέω, *logomacheō*; a word Paul may have coined; cf. 1 Tim 6:4). This seems to be one of the primary characteristics of the false teachers at Ephesus (see the discussion at 1 Tim 2:8; 6:4-5; cf. Titus 3:9). These "word-battles" are "good for nothing" (cf. Titus 3:8). They lead only to the ruin of "those who listen."

213

The word "ruin" (καταστροφή, *katastrophē*) means literally "overturning" or "subverting." These "word-battles" produce "overturned" lives for those who give heed to them.

2:15 Do your best to present yourself to God as one approved,

In contrast to the false teachers who engage in those "word-battles," Timothy must "do his best" (σπούδασον, *spoudason*; cf. 4:9, 21; Titus 3:12) "to present [him]self as one approved" (i.e., "one who has been tested and met that test"; cf. 1 Cor 11:19; 2 Cor 10:18). Instead of "do your best" the KJV rendered *spoudason* as "study." Unfortunately a translation which originally meant to "give one's all" has misled many generations of Christians to assume that Paul was here calling Timothy to "get learning."

a workman who does not need to be ashamed and who correctly handles the word of truth.

Timothy must do his best to be "a workman who does not need to be ashamed." A workman might rightly be ashamed if his work were shoddy or lacked real effort. For Timothy to be an unashamed worker, he must handle "correctly the word of truth." The word translated "handles correctly" (ὀρθοτομέω, *orthotomeō*) appears only here in the NT and on two occasions (Prov 3:6 and 11:5) in the LXX. It means literally "to cut a straight path." The KJV rendering of the word as "rightly dividing" has produced some unusual dispensational and interpretive understandings which are foreign to Paul's intent. As Simpson has concluded, "It [this text] enjoins on every teacher of the Word straightforword exegesis."[23] It is a call for Timothy and all other workmen of God to be good exegetes of Scripture. Paul purposefully draws attention to Scripture as "the word of truth" to contrast it with the "word-battles" (v. 14) and the "godless chatter" (v. 16) of the false teachers Timothy must face.

---

[23]E.K. Simpson, *The Pastoral Epistles: The Greek Text with Introduction and Commentary* (London, 1954), p. 137.

2:16 Avoid godless chatter, because those who indulge in it will become more and more ungodly.

After instructing Timothy as to what he is to promote and do in vv. 14-15, in vv. 16-18 Paul instructs Timothy of the things he is to "avoid." The description of the banter of the false teachers as "godless chatter" (βεβήλους, *bebēlous*, literally "profane empty sounds") is identical to his depiction in 1 Tim 6:20 (cf. Titus 3:9; 1 Tim 1:6). Such godless chatter is to be avoided because it only causes people to "become more and more ungodly" (literally "to progress into more ungodliness"). See the discussion of "ungodliness," the opposite of the desired "godliness," in 1 Tim 2:2.

2:17 Their teaching will spread like gangrene.

The "teaching" of those who engage in "godless chatter" and are progressing in ungodliness "will spread" (literally "have pasture") "like gangrene." "Gangrene" (γάγγραινα, *gangraina*) is a medical term used for spreading sores or ulcers. The metaphor depicts in very descriptive language the advance of false teaching in a Christian community.

Among them are Hymenaeus and Philetus,

Two of those engaged in this false teaching are Hymenaeus and Philetus. Hymenaeus is not a common name, and it may, therefore, be assumed that this is the same man Paul had referred to in 1 Tim 1:20. There Paul stated that he had handed him, along with Alexander,[24] "over to Satan to be taught not to blaspheme." He is now joined in his false teaching by Philetus, about whom there is no further information.

2:18 who have wandered away from the truth. They say that the resurrection has already taken place, and they destroy the faith of some.

These two men seem to be leaders among a group of false teachers "who have wandered away from the truth" (cf. 1 Tim

---

[24]For a conjecture about Alexander see the discussion at 2 Tim 4:14.

1:6; 6:21 for a discussion of this phrase). The next phrase indicates the nature of this heresy: saying "that the resurrection has already taken place" (cf. 2 Thess 2:2 "saying that the day of the Lord has already come"). This text and 1 Tim 4:1ff are the only places in the Pastoral Epistles where the modern reader can ascertain with certainty the nature of the false teaching in Ephesus. Fee makes the following assessment of the false teaching: "This is probably some form of over-realized eschatology, that is, that the fullness of the End, especially the resurrection, has already been realized in our spiritual dying and rising with Christ (cf. v. 11; Rom 6:1-11; Col 2:20-3:4). Such an idea . . . was probably related to the Greek conception of the soul as immortal and released from physical existence at death. Such dualism . . . may also lie at the root of the asceticism in 1 Tim 4:3."[25] Such false teaching is very serious because it hits at the very heart of the Christian faith, "destroying" (literally "overturning"; cf. Titus 1:11) "the faith of some." To deny future bodily resurrection is to deny the Christian faith (cf. 1 Cor 15).

2:19 Nevertheless, God's solid foundation stands firm,
Despite (note the strong adversative μέντοι [*mentoi*], "nevertheless") the uncertainty that the false teaching might produce, Paul proclaims one thing as sure: "God's solid foundation stands firm." God "knows" his own. The exact nature of "God's foundation" has brought several conjectures. Is Paul referring to the church in general (cf. his description of the church as the pillar and foundation of the truth, 1 Tim 3:15), the faithful Christians in Ephesus, the deposit of faith, Christ (1 Cor 3:10-12), or the apostles and prophets (Eph 3:20)? In the light of what follows in this verse and in vv. 20-21, it seems likely that Paul is using the phrase in an even more general way. Paul can be seen as simply saying, "What God has founded is solid. What the false teachers say cannot thwart his work."

---

[25]Fee, p. 256.

sealed with this inscription: "The Lord knows those who are his," Inscriptions on foundation stones indicate either ownership or purpose of the structure. Here there are two inscriptions with which this foundation is "sealed." The first, "The Lord knows those who are his," is an almost exact quote of Num 16:5 in the LXX. The context is the rebellion of Korah, Dathan and Abiram against Moses and ultimately against God. There God clearly distinguishes between those loyal to him and those in rebellion. Paul contends that is what God will do in the church at Ephesus.

and, "Everyone who confesses the name of the Lord must turn away from wickedness."
Several OT passages have been suggested as the background for the second inscription, "Everyone who confesses the name of the Lord must turn away from wickedness" (e.g., Lev 24:16; Num 16:26; Josh 23:7; Isa 26:13; 52:11; Ps 6:8; 34:14; Prov 3:7). It likely represents a proverbial saying familiar to Timothy and the church at Ephesus. The true servant of the Lord demonstrates that he belongs to him by turning "away from wickedness," a direction opposite that of the false teachers and consistent with the noble work of vv. 20-21.

B. PREPARING FOR NOBLE WORK (2:20-26)

²⁰In a large house there are articles not only of gold and silver, but also of wood and clay; some are for noble purposes and some for ignoble. ²¹If a man cleanses himself from the latter, he will be an instrument for noble purposes, made holy, useful to the Master and prepared to do any good work.
²²Flee the evil desires of youth, and pursue righteousness, faith, love and peace, along with those who call on the Lord out of a pure heart. ²³Don't have anything to do with foolish and stupid arguments, because you know they produce

quarrels. ²⁴And the Lord's servant must not quarrel; instead, he must be kind to everyone, able to teach, not resentful. ²⁵Those who oppose him he must gently instruct, in the hope that God will grant them repentance leading them to a knowledge of the truth, ²⁶and that they will come to their senses and escape from the trap of the devil, who has taken them captive to do his will.

2:20 In a large house there are articles not only of gold and silver, but also of wood and clay; some are for noble purposes and some for ignoble.

Paul uses the various "articles" which could be found in a large house to illustrate the need to "turn away from wickedness." Paul's use of "a large house" and his reference to articles of gold and silver indicate that he has in mind a home with wealthy inhabitants. While some of the articles are expensive ("gold and silver"), others are everyday and inexpensive ("wood and clay"). The expensive ones would be used for meals, especially feasts, and "for noble purposes" (literally "for honor"). The inexpensive ones might be used for common meals but could also be used "for ignoble" (literally "for dishonor") tasks, including serving as containers for garbage or perhaps even bed pans. The use of the various types of vessels as an illustration is not unique to 2 Timothy (cf. Jer 18:1-11; the apocryphal work, the Wisdom of Solomon 15:7; Rom 9:19-24).

2:21 If a man cleanses himself from the latter, he will be an instrument for noble purposes, made holy, useful to the Master and prepared to do any good work.

Paul's point here is not that God can use any vessel (cf. 1 Cor 12:21-24) but rather that one must decide what kind of vessel he will be. Paul is calling for Timothy and others at Ephesus to "turn from wickedness" (v. 19) by cleansing themselves from wickedness and thus becoming "an instrument for noble purposes" (literally "a vessel for honor"), made "holy" (ἡγιασμένον, *hēgiasmenon*; literally "having been sanctified" or "set apart" like vessels designated for use in the Temple), "useful to the Master" (cf. 2:4). Paul concludes by saying that this cleansed vessel is "prepared to do any good work." Good works are an important theme throughout the Pastoral Epistles (cf. 1 Tim 2:10; 5:10; 6:18; Titus 1:16; 2:7, 14; 3:1, 8, 14; 2 Tim 3:17).

2:22 Flee the evil desires of youth,
In v. 22 Paul continues his personal instructions for Timothy begun in vv. 14-16. Timothy is instructed to "flee the evil desires of youth" (literally "continue to flee youthful desires"). Timothy is a young man, at least in comparison with Paul (see 1 Tim 4:12 for a discussion of Timothy's age). There is no way to determine exactly what desires Paul has in mind. The list of virtues to be pursued which follows is too general to give assistance in this regard.

and pursue righteousness, faith, love and peace, along with those who call on the Lord out of a pure heart.
Paul continues his instructions by listing four virtues Timothy should continue to "pursue" (the use of the present imperative implies the need for Timothy to continue in the pursuit). He must "pursue righteousness, faith, love and peace." Paul has already counselled Timothy to develop the first three virtues in 1 Tim 6:11. Now he adds "peace," something lacking in those who are involved in "foolish and stupid arguments" and "quarrels" (vv. 23-24). All "those who call on the Lord out of a pure heart" seek to develop these characteristics, which are missing in the false teachers.

2:23 Don't have anything to do with foolish and stupid arguments, because you know they produce quarrels.
If Timothy is to "pursue peace," he must "have nothing to do with" (cf. 1 Tim 4:7; 5:11 where the same verb is used) "foolish" (cf. Titus 3:9) and "stupid" (ἀπαίδευτος, *apaideutos*; literally "untrained" or perhaps "uneducated") arguments. Timothy must avoid the teaching of these people who are quibbling and

speaking as experts even though they are ill-informed. All of these foolish debates "produce" (literally "give birth to") "quarrels."

2:24 And the Lord's servant must not quarrel; instead, he must be kind to everyone, able to teach, not resentful.

In contrast to the false teachers, Timothy is to see himself as "the Lord's servant" (δοῦλος, *doulos*; literally "slave") and behave accordingly. He "must not quarrel." Not quarreling does not mean allowing false teaching to go unopposed. In a fashion much like the qualifications of elders (1 Tim 3:2-7; Titus 1:6-9), deacons (1 Tim 3:8-12), or widows to be enrolled (1 Tim 5:9-10), Paul gives the qualities one must have if he or she is to serve as an effective servant of the Lord. He must be "gentle" or "kind to everyone," including even the false teachers. "He must able to teach" (cf. 1 Tim 3:2 where the term is used of the overseer). Finally he is "not [to be] resentful" (ἀνεξίκακον, *anexikakon*; literally "holding up under bad"), a word rendered by the NASB "patient when wronged."

2:25 Those who oppose him he must gently instruct,

Timothy "must instruct those who oppose him gently." The word translated "instruct" (παιδεύω, *paideuō*) is used of training a child (cf. 1 Tim 1:20). In v. 23 Paul used the negation of this word (ἀπαίδευτος, *apaideutos*, rendered "stupid") to describe the arguments of the false teachers. This training is to be done "gently," a word often translated "meekness" (1 Tim 6:11; Titus 3:2).

in the hope that God will grant them repentance leading them to a knowledge of the truth,

The goal, when the "Lord's servant" instructs or corrects, is never to be getting even. He is to do so "in the hope that" (μήποτε, *mēpote*; literally "perhaps") "God will grant them repentance leading them to a knowledge of the truth." Repentance is here seen as the gift of God, resulting in their coming to "a knowledge of the truth" (cf. 1 Tim 2:4). This does not deny human decision in repentance but rather points to the fact that even our repentance is rooted in God's act and the opportunities granted by God.

2:26 and that they will come to their senses and escape from the trap of the devil, who has taken them captive to do his will.

The goal is also "that they will come to their senses" (literally "will return to their soberness") "and escape from the trap" (or "snare," παγίς, *pagis*; cf. Rom 11:9; 1 Tim 3:7; 6:9) "of the devil." Although the exact meaning of the final clause is uncertain,[26] the devil is depicted as having "taken them captive" (literally "having been captured alive by him") "to do his will."

Paul's message to Timothy is simple. He must refute false teachers and the error they propound (cf. 2:15), he must save sinners (1 Tim 4:16), and he must redeem the fallen.

---

[26]The last phrase — "who has taken them captive to do his will" (literally, "being taken captive by him to do the will of that one") — may be translated in at least three different ways. (1) Both "who" ("him") and "his" ("that one") could refer to "the devil." "The devil has taken captive" these false teachers "to do his (i.e., the devil's) will." (2) "Who" ("him") could refer to "the Lord's servant" and "his" ("of that one") to God. When the false teachers are brought to "repentance" they are "taken captive" by the "servant" of the Lord "to do [God's] will." (3) "Who" could refer to the devil and "his" could refer to God. "The devil has taken [them] captive," but God grants them "repentance to do his will." The first option, which is taken by the NIV, NASB and NRSV, is likely correct.

2 TIMOTHY 3

C. THE CHARACTER OF THE LAST DAYS (3:1-9)

¹But mark this: There will be terrible times in the last days. ²People will be lovers of themselves, lovers of money, boastful, proud, abusive, disobedient to their parents, ungrateful, unholy, ³without love, unforgiving, slanderous, without self-control, brutal, not lovers of the good, ⁴treacherous, rash, conceited, lovers of pleasure rather than lovers of God — ⁵having a form of godliness but denying its power. Have nothing to do with them.

⁶They are the kind who worm their way into homes and gain control over weak-willed women, who are loaded down with sins and are swayed by all kinds of evil desires, ⁷always learning but never able to acknowledge the truth. ⁸Just as Jannes and Jambres opposed Moses, so also these men oppose the truth — men of depraved minds, who, as far as the faith is concerned, are rejected. ⁹But they will not get very far because, as in the case of those men, their folly will be clear to everyone.

In this section, Paul shifts his focus from Timothy and his response to the false teachers to the relationship between the false teachers and "the last days." Only in v. 5 does Paul specifically give instructions to Timothy.

3:1 But mark this: There will be terrible times in the last days.

Paul now reminds Timothy of the common Christian conviction that "last days" would be characterized by "terrible" (literally "hard" or "difficult") times. "The last days" is used elsewhere in the NT to refer to the Messianic age from Jesus' coming until the final consummation at the end of time (cf. Acts 2:17; Jas 5:3; 2 Pet 3:3; Heb 1:2). The language and concept really represents an OT idea (cf. Joel 3:1; Isa 2:2). It does not, as some suggest, represent an assumption that the end of time is near. For example, in 1 John 2:18 the phrase "the last hour" is used of the author's own day. The future tense "will be" indicates certainty, and describes the same period of time as seen in 1 Tim 4:1.[1]

3:2 People will be lovers of themselves, lovers of money,

In vv. 2-4 Paul lists the characteristics of evil people living "in the last days." Five of the eighteen words occur only here in the NT, two more occur elsewhere only in the Pastoral Epistles, and three more are found only here and in Paul's similar list in Rom 1:29-31. These "people will be lovers of themselves" (in Titus 1:7 "not self-willed" is an important qualification for overseers), "lovers of money"[2] (a trait of false teachers in 1 Tim 6:5-10, see especially v. 10; cf. 1 Tim 3:3, 8; Titus 1:7, 11).

boastful, proud, abusive, disobedient to their parents,

"Boastful" and "proud" (two words which also appear together in Rom 1:30) emphasize arrogant and haughty attitudes and actions characteristic of the false teachers (cf. 1 Tim 1:7; 6:4). Such people will be "abusive" (a word usually rendered "blasphemers" or "slanderers"; cf. 1 Tim 1:13; 6:4; Titus 3:2), and "disobedient to their parents" (cf. Rom 1:30).

ungrateful, unholy, 3:3 without love, unforgiving,

The next four words in the list all begin with the Greek letter *alpha*, equivalent to the English prefix "un-." People of

---

[1]Knight, p. 429.
[2]Note the play on the Greek prefix *phil-* ("lovers of") which begins the list in v. 2 ("lovers of themselves," φίλαυτοι, *philautoi*; and "lovers of money," φιλάργυροι, *philargyroi*) and ends the list in v. 4 ("lovers of pleasure," φιλήδονοι, *philēdonoi*; and not "lovers of God," φιλόθεοι, *philotheoi*).

"the last days" will be "ungrateful" (Fee and Knight suggest this word coming after "disobedient to their parents" may indicate that they lack appreciation for what their parents have done[3]), and "unholy" (or "irreverent"), "without love" (ἄστοργοι, *astorgoi*; "without natural and/or expected affection"; cf. Rom 1:31) and "unforgiving" ("those who refuse to be reconciled").

slanderous, without self-control, brutal, not lovers of the good,
The list of *alpha* privative words is broken with the word "slanderous" (διάβολοι, *diaboloi*; cf. 1 Tim 3:11; Titus 2:5). Paul then resumes his list with three more "un-" words: "without self-control" (in Titus 1:8 and 1 Tim 3:3 elders/overseers must be self-controlled), "brutal" (although the word is not used in Titus 1:7, the requirement for elders is clearly that they not be brutal), and "not lovers of the good" (in Titus 1:8 elders are to be the opposite).

3:4 treacherous, rash, conceited, lovers of pleasure rather than lovers of God —
The next two words have the same Greek prefix (προ-, *pro-*) and seem to function together: "treacherous" (προδόται, *prodotai*, perhaps "readiness to betray";[4] a word used of Judas Iscariot in Luke 6:16) and "rash" (or "reckless" [προπετεῖς, *propeteis*], "a man who . . stops at nothing to gain his ends"[5]). These people will also be "conceited" (see 1 Tim 3:6; 6:4 where the same word is used). Paul closes his list in a way similar to the way he began it, with two words that use the same Greek prefix "lovers." In the last days people will be "lovers of pleasure" (only here in the NT; cf. Paul's description of the pre-Christian life of those at Crete in Titus 3:3) "rather than lovers of God" (also only here in the NT; a word which may summarize what Jesus, citing the OT, deemed the first commandment; cf. Matt 22:37-38; Mark 12:28-30; Luke 10:27-28).

---
[3]Fee, p. 270; Knight, p. 431.
[4]Kelly, p. 194.
[5]*Ibid.*

3:5 having a form of godliness but denying its power.
Paul concludes the description of the people of the last days by saying that they have "a form of godliness" (εὐσέβεια, *eusebeia*; the word used in the Pastoral Epistles for true religion; cf. 1 Tim 2:2; 3:16; 4:7, 8; 6:3, 5-6, 11; Titus 1:1) but "deny its power." These people will have all the outward characteristics one would expect of a religious person: asceticism, lots of religious discussions, etc. They are, however, really irreligious because they deny "its power," i.e., the gospel and the changed life it demands.

Have nothing to do with them.
Paul's instructions for Timothy to "have nothing to do with" such persons indicates that for Paul Timothy was indeed living "in the last days." Paul is in reality repeating the command he had given Timothy in 2:16.

3:6 They are the kind who worm their way into homes and gain control over weak-willed women,
In this verse Paul again indicates that the time described in vv. 2-5 is Timothy's own day by his use of present tense verbs. These people of v. 2 "are the kind" (literally "of such people" referring to vv. 2-5) "who worm their way into" (i.e., "enter through false pretenses") "homes" (literally "the homes"). Fee has suggested that the "into the homes" may indicate the homes about which Timothy already knows, and that it is likely that these were homes among some "well-heeled" younger widows where it would have been easier for the false teachers to spread their propaganda.[6] These false teachers "gain control" (αἰχμαλωτίζω, *aichmalōtizō*, literally "capture"; cf. Luke 21:24 where the word is used literally) "over weak-willed women" (literally "little women" indicating "childish women"). As Knight has noted, "Paul does not use the term 'weak-willed women' to derogate women but to describe a situation involving particular women. That he uses

---

[6]Fee, p. 271.

the diminutive form shows that he is not intending to describe women in general."[7]

who are loaded down with sins and are swayed by all kinds of evil desires,
Paul goes on to explain why these women are to be deemed "weak-willed." They "are loaded down" (a perfect participle which literally means "have been overburdened") "with sins." The perfect tense indicates that these women are currently overburdened. It can either indicate that they are currently engaged in these sins and are burdened by them or that they are burdened by their past sins (cf. NEB "burdened with a sinful past"). The latter is more likely.[8] These women "are swayed" (literally "are continually being led") "by all kinds of evil desires." Fee proposes that, if these desires are seen to have sexual overtones and if these women are sexually involved with some of the false teachers, this would shed additional light on texts in 1 Timothy like 2:9-10; 3:2; 5:2, 6, 11-15, 22. He does, however, admit "that there is a degree of speculation involved in this suggestion."[9] While his suggestion is interesting, it is very speculative and Paul's language would likely have been more specific if they were engaged in sexual immorality.

3:7 always learning but never able to acknowledge the truth.
Paul says that the women are "always learning" (apparently always anxious to learn something new like those in Athens who "spent their time doing nothing but talking about and listening to the latest ideas," Acts 17:21) "but never able to acknowledge the truth" (cf. 1 Tim 2:4).

3:8 Just as Jannes and Jambres opposed Moses, so also these men oppose the truth — men of depraved minds, who, as far as the faith is concerned, are rejected.
The false teachers who are leading these women astray are

---
[7]Knight, p. 433.
[8]Fee, p. 272; Knight, p. 434.
[9]Fee, p. 274.

like "Jannes and Jambres [who] opposed Moses." Although these two men are not mentioned by name in the OT, the reference is to Pharaoh's magicians who used sorcery to oppose Moses (Exod 7:11-12, 22; 8:7). Their names begin to appear in Jewish writings from the intertestamental period.[10] These men in Ephesus, like Jannes and Jambres, stand in opposition to "the truth"; they are "men of depraved minds" (cf. 1 Tim 6:5), "who, as far as the faith is concerned, are rejected" (ἀδόκιμοι, *adokimoi*; the opposite of "approved" in 2:15). Paul's use of the article "the" with both "truth" and "faith" indicates that he is using both words as equivalent to "the gospel."

3:9 But they will not get very far because, as in the case of those men, their folly will be clear to everyone.
Despite their efforts and their "badness," "they will not get" ("progress") "very far." The reason Paul gives is that "their folly will be clear to everyone." Jannes and Jambres were not successful in their stand against Moses. These people will not be successful as they "oppose the truth." The truth and the gospel will be victorious.

D. FURTHER EXHORTATIONS FOR TIMOTHY TO ENDURE (3:10-17)

[10]You, however, know all about my teaching, my way of life, my purpose, faith, patience, love, endurance, [11]persecutions, sufferings — what kinds of things happened to me in Antioch, Iconium and Lystra, the persecutions I endured. Yet the Lord rescued me from all of them. [12]In fact, everyone who wants to live a godly life in Christ Jesus will be persecuted, [13]while evil men and impostors will go from bad to worse, deceiving and being deceived. [14]But as for you, con-

---

[10]E.g., *Targum Pseudo-Jonathan* 1,3; 7.2; *Damascus Document* 5.18; cf. also references to the two in Pliny, *Natural History* 30.2.11 and Origen, *Against Celsus* 4.51.

tinue in what you have learned and have become convinced of, because you know those from whom you learned it, ¹⁵and how from infancy you have known the holy Scriptures, which are able to make you wise for salvation through faith in Christ Jesus. ¹⁶All Scripture is God-breathed and is useful for teaching, rebuking, correcting and training in righteousness, ¹⁷so that the man of God may be thoroughly equipped for every good work.

Paul's instructions to Timothy in this section are simple. He is to continue in what he has learned from and observed in Paul. He must recall what he learned from Paul, think about what he has seen in Paul's life, and pay attention to Scripture.

3:10 You, however, know all about my teaching, my way of life, my purpose, faith, patience, love, endurance,

This new section begins with an emphatic "you, however" (σὺ δέ, *su de*; cf. 2:1; 3:14; 4:5). Timothy, in contrast to the false teachers who really do not know what matters, has experience that should make him different. He knows "all about [Paul's] teaching" (i.e., his gospel), his "way of life" (only here in the NT; literally "leading"; cf. 1 Tim 4:12 for the concept), his "purpose" ("aim" or "resolve"), "faith" (cf. 1 Tim 4:12; 6:11; 2 Tim 2:22), "patience" (μακροθυμία, *makrothymia*; literally "longsuffering" with others; see discussion at 1 Tim 1:16; cf. 2 Tim 4:2), "love" (ἀγάπη, *agapē*; cf. 1 Tim 1:5; 4:12; 6:11; Titus 2:2; 2 Tim 2:22), "endurance" (ὑπομονή, *hypomonē*; "steadfastness" in a situation; cf. 1 Tim 6:11; Titus 2:2)

3:11 persecutions, sufferings — what kinds of things happened to me in Antioch, Iconium and Lystra, the persecutions I endured. Yet the Lord rescued me from all of them.

The virtues of Paul's way of life (v. 10) were accompanied by "persecutions" (διωγμοῖς, *diōgmois*) and "sufferings" (παθήμασιν, *pathēmasin*). Although Timothy had not personally seen the hardships Paul endured at Antioch (Acts 13:48-52) or Iconium (Acts 14:1-7), he had undoubtedly heard from Paul and others about those experiences. Timothy may have personally observed the things that happened to Paul at Lystra (Acts 14:8-20; 16:1-2) since Lystra was Timothy's hometown. From all these "persecutions [and] sufferings, the Lord [had] rescued" Paul. Fee ponders why Paul did not mention the persecution at other locations, especially Philippi (Acts 16:19-34) and Ephesus (2 Cor 1:1-11) and Rome (Phil 1:1, 12-18). Fee conjectures that it is Paul's aim to call Timothy to loyalty so he picks those times closest to Timothy's conversion.[11]

3:12 In fact, everyone who wants to live a godly life in Christ Jesus will be persecuted,

Paul reminds Timothy that the persecutions he had endured were not unique to him. "In fact, everyone who wants to live a godly life" (εὐσεβῶς, *eusebōs*; see the discussion at 1 Tim 2:2) "in Christ Jesus will be persecuted." For Paul life is clearly to be located "in Christ Jesus" (cf. 1 Tim 1:14; 2 Tim 1:2).

3:13 while evil men and impostors will go from bad to worse, deceiving and being deceived.

At this point Paul again turns to the false teachers. Although believers will suffer, "evil men" (see the description in vv. 2-5) and "impostors" (γόητες, *goētes*, literally something like "enchanters"; perhaps "charlatans"[12]) "will go from" (literally "progress"; cf. 1 Tim 4:15; 2 Tim 2:16; 3:9) "bad to worse." Their sins will lead them even deeper into a sinful lifestyle, "deceiving and being deceived" (cf. Titus 1:10; 3:3).

3:14 But as for you, continue in what you have learned and have become convinced of, because you know those from whom you learned it,

---

[11]Fee, p. 277.
[12]*Ibid.*

Again Paul contrasts his wishes for Timothy with the practice and lives of the false teachers ("but as for you"). Timothy must "continue in what [he has] learned [and has] become convinced of," undoubtedly a reference to the gospel he had learned and in which he had put his faith. After all, Timothy knew the character and life of those from whom he had learned the gospel. Although "those from whom you learned it" may be a possible reference to the "many witnesses" of 2:2, here it probably is a reference to Paul (cf. vv. 10-11) and to Timothy's mother and grandmother.

3:15 and how from infancy you have known the holy Scriptures, which are able to make you wise for salvation through faith in Christ Jesus.

From his infancy Timothy had been taught "the holy Scriptures" (obviously a reference to the OT). In addition to knowing the character of those who taught him, Timothy also has "known the holy Scriptures" and their character. They "are able to make" the believer "wise" (a contrast to the "depraved minds" of the false teachers in v. 9) resulting in "salvation through faith in Christ Jesus." It is perhaps worth noting, as does Fee, that "salvation lies not in the Scriptures themselves, but only as they are properly understood to point to Christ. Always for Paul salvation is through faith in Christ Jesus."[13]

3:16 All Scripture is God-breathed

Having reminded Timothy of his knowledge of Scripture and indicated its connection with salvation, Paul concludes his appeal by discussing the origin of Scripture and its import for Timothy's ministry. V. 16 is a sentence "which commentators have found bafflingly ambiguous."[14] The first difficulty rests in the fact that, because Paul uses the singular word for "Scripture," there has been some debate about the translation of the word "all" (πᾶσα, *pasa*). Is Paul saying that "all Scripture"

---

[13]Fee, p. 279.
[14]Kelly, p. 202.

or "every" Scripture is of divine origin? Knight states, "In final analysis there is no essential difference in meaning."[15] Since Paul will go on to say that "Scripture is" useful in many ways, it seems likely that he is using the word in a collective sense and that the correct translation is "all Scripture."

The second problem has to do with whether one understands "God-breathed" (θεόπνευστος, *theopneustos*) as a predicate adjective or as an attributive adjective. The first "is" in v. 16 does not represent a Greek word in the original but rather has been supplied by the NIV translators. The first part of the verse can be rendered either "all Scripture is God-breathed and is useful" (KJV, NASB, RSV, TEV, NIV, NRSV), or "all God-breathed Scripture is *also* useful" (ASV, NEB). Because of the placement of the adjective and Paul's general argument, the rendering of the NIV is likely correct.

A third issue is the meaning of "God-breathed" (*theopneustos*). If the verbal adjective is understood in a passive sense, "all Scripture" is the product of God's breath or Spirit, the result of God's action. If understood in an active sense, "all Scripture" is filled with and exudes the breath or Spirit of God. Warfield has effectively argued that the adjective should be understood in a passive sense, the first option.[16]

and is useful for teaching, rebuking, correcting and training in righteousness,

Paul's first affirmation that "all Scripture is God-breathed" leads to an affirmation of the usefulness of Scripture, particularly for Timothy's ministry and his dealings with the false teachers at Ephesus. Scripture "is useful for teaching" (Timothy's primary task; cf. 1 Tim 4:6, 13, 16; 6:3), "rebuking" (ἐλεγμός, *elegmos*; only here in the NT; in the LXX "convicting" one engaged in error), "correcting" (ἐπανόρθωσις, *epanorthōsis*; also only here in the NT; "setting straight") and

---

[15]Knight p. 445.
[16]B.B. Warfield, *Inspiration and Authority of the Bible* (Philadelphia: Presbyterian and Reformed, 1948), pp. 245–296.

"training" (παιδεία, *paideia*; cf. 2:25; Titus 2:12) "in righteousness" (here "uprightness" or "right conduct").

3:17 so that the man of God may be thoroughly equipped for every good work.
In this verse Paul gives the purpose or perhaps the result of this proper use of Scripture: "so that the man of God" (here the more general word for man, ὁ τοῦ θεοῦ ἄνθρωπος, *ho tou theou anthrōpos*, therefore "person of God" or as the NRSV rendering "everyone who belongs to God"; cf. 1 Tim 6:11) "may be thoroughly equipped" (ἄρτιος, *artios*, "able to meet all the demands," BAGD) for every good work (cf. 2:21; Titus 1:16; 3:1).

2 TIMOTHY 4

E. A FINAL CHARGE TO TIMOTHY (4:1-8)

¹In the presence of God and of Christ Jesus, who will judge the living and the dead, and in view of his appearing and his kingdom, I give you this charge: ²Preach the Word; be prepared in season and out of season; correct, rebuke and encourage — with great patience and careful instruction. ³For the time will come when men will not put up with sound doctrine. Instead, to suit their own desires, they will gather around them a great number of teachers to say what their itching ears want to hear. ⁴They will turn their ears away from the truth and turn aside to myths. ⁵But you, keep your head in all situations, endure hardship, do the work of an evangelist, discharge all the duties of your ministry.

⁶For I am already being poured out like a drink offering, and the time has come for my departure. ⁷I have fought the good fight, I have finished the race, I have kept the faith. ⁸Now there is in store for me the crown of righteousness, which the Lord, the righteous Judge, will award to me on that day — and not only to me, but also to all who have longed for his appearing.

Paul now brings to a conclusion his appeal to Timothy. He began that appeal in 1:6 and then picked it up again in 3:10. The appeal in this section takes the form of a solemn charge, almost an oath which Timothy is to take. In vv. 1-5 alone, Paul uses nine imperatives concerning Timothy's ministry and his commitment to the Lord. Paul is certain that he is about to die. He is now handing the gauntlet to Timothy. He must carry on the ministry which is everything to Paul.

4:1 In the presence of God and of Christ Jesus, who will judge the living and the dead, and in view of his appearing and his kingdom, I give you this charge:
Paul begins his final charge to Timothy with the single Greek word (διαμαρτύρομαι, *diamartyromai*; literally "I testify") rendered "I give you this charge" (cf. 1 Tim 5:21; 2 Tim 2:24). The language of a "charge" in this verse is very similar to the language in 1 Tim 5:21 and 6:13. Although the NIV makes it difficult for the modern reader to discern, the basis of the charge is fourfold: "in the presence" (or "in view") (1) "of God," (2) "of Christ Jesus," (3) "of his appearing" (1:10; 4:8; Titus 2:13), and "of his kingdom." To emphasize the eternal nature and significance of the charge, Paul describes Christ Jesus as the one "who will judge" (literally "is going to judge") "the living and the dead" (cf. Acts 10:42; 1 Pet 4:5). The reference to the judgment of "the living and the dead," the two classes of people at the second coming, provides a very natural link to the third witness of his appearing and his reign.

4:2 Preach the Word; be prepared in season and out of season;
The first imperative in the charge is "preach" ("herald" or "publicly proclaim") "the Word" (a reference to the gospel; see the discussion at 1 Tim 4:5). Next Paul charges Timothy to "be prepared in season and out of season." "Be prepared" is the rendering of a Greek word (ἐφίστημι, *ephistēmi*) which literally means "stand by" or "be at hand." In v. 6 the perfect tense of the verb is rendered "has come." Kelly suggests that the word be translated "keep at it."[1] Guthrie elucidates the meaning when he says, "the Christian minister must always be on duty."[2] The phrase "in season and out of season" may

---

[1]Kelly, p. 205.
[2]Guthrie, p. 166.

refer to either Timothy's circumstance or his audience or perhaps to both. It indicates that Timothy must be ready to minister whether or not circumstances are favorable, whether or not the audience is receptive.

correct, rebuke and encourage — with great patience and careful instruction.
Kelly suggests that the next three imperatives illustrate the preacher's appeal to reason, conscience, and will.[3] Timothy is to "correct" (ἔλεγξον, *elengxon*, perhaps better "rebuke" as in 3:16; Titus 1:13; 2:15), "rebuke" (ἐπιτίμησον, *epitimēson*, a near synonym to the last word; perhaps "censure"; Fee suggests "warn"[4]), and "encourage" (παρακάλεσον, *parakaleson*, better "exhort" or "urge"; see the discussion at 1 Tim 2:1; 5:1; 6:2). These three tasks are to be done "with great" (literally "all" which goes with both objects) "patience" (a quality especially needed by Timothy toward those who do not respond to his message; cf. 3:10; 1 Tim 1:16) "and careful" (literally "all") "instruction" (literally "teaching").

4:3 For the time will come when men will not put up with sound doctrine.
With the "for" of v. 3, Paul indicates that he is about to give the reason for the urgency of his charge in vv. 1-2. Again Paul contrasts the gospel message with the teaching of the false teachers. "For the time will come when men will not put up with" (literally "will not hold up") "sound doctrine" (literally "healthy teaching"; see discussion at 1 Tim 1:10).

Instead, to suit their own desires, they will gather around them a great number of teachers to say what their itching ears want to hear.
In the place of healthy teaching, these people "will heap up a great number of teachers" according to "their own desires." As Knight has said, "In other words, they have

---
[3]Kelly, p. 206.
[4]Fee, p. 285.

made themselves the measure of who should teach them and what teaching is acceptable."[5] These teachers will "say what their itching ears want to hear" (literally "being tickled or scratched with reference to their hearing"; cf. the "weak-willed women" of 3:6-7). The latter metaphor expresses a "curiosity, that looks for interesting and spicy bits of information" (BAGD).

4:4 They will turn their ears away from the truth and turn aside to myths.

Instead of seeking "healthy teaching," these people "will turn their ears away from the truth," i.e., the gospel (cf. 1 Tim 3:15; 6:5; Titus 1:14; 2 Tim 2:18; 3:7-8). They will "turn aside to myths" (cf. 1 Tim 1:4-6; 4:7; Titus 1:14).

4:5 But you, keep your head in all situations,

As he does throughout his epistles to Timothy, Paul makes the transition from instructions about the false teachers back to instructions for Timothy with "but you" (σὺ δέ, *su de*; cf. 2:1; 3:10, 14; 1 Tim 6:11). Paul now resumes his final "charge" with four more imperatives. First, Timothy must "keep [his] head in all situations" (literally "be sober in everything"; see cognate word in qualifications of overseers and deacons in 1 Tim 3:2, 11).

endure hardship, do the work of an evangelist, discharge all the duties of your ministry.

He must "endure hardship." This represents an important theme in 2 Timothy (cf. 1:8; 2:3; 3:10, 12). He must also "do the work of an evangelist." The noun "evangelist" (εὐαγγελίστης, *euangelistēs*) appears only here, and in Eph 4:11 and Acts 21:8. Paul began his charge to Timothy in v. 2 with words which carry the same idea: "preach the Word." Finally, he must "discharge all the duties of" (literally simply "fulfill") his "ministry" (διακονία, *diakonia*).

---

[5]Knight, p. 455.

4:6 For I am already being poured out like a drink offering, and the time has come for my departure. Up to this point Paul has not indicated his expectations with regard to his imprisonment. He has indicated that he is a prisoner in chains and that he is suffering like a criminal (1:8, 12, 16; 2:9). In this paragraph (vv. 6-8) and in the final section (vv. 9-22), Paul says that he expects this imprisonment to result in his death. He is aware that his ministry is coming to an end. Timothy must carry on the work.

Paul uses two metaphors to describe his expected death. First, he says that he is "already being poured out like a drink offering." Libations or drink offerings are taken from OT sacrificial imagery of pouring out wine (cf. Exod 29:40-41; Lev 23:13; Num 15:1-10; 28:4-8). Paul had used the same metaphor in Phil 2:17 where he says that, even if this were to happen in his service to the Philippians, he would still rejoice. The use of the present tense verb and the word "already" indicates that Paul was aware that the wheels were already in motion that would lead to his death. The second metaphor is that of a ship lifting its anchor to leave harbor or of a group of soldiers breaking camp: "the time has come for my departure." Interestingly, in Phil 1:23, Paul had used the cognate verb "to depart." "Departure" was a common euphemism for death.

4:7 I have fought the good fight,
Paul uses three very graphic expressions to describe what he perceives as the conclusion to his ministry. The first two represent athletic metaphors. "I have fought the good fight" (ἀγῶνα, *agōna*) does not, as the English translation might suggest, refer to a military conflict. It is rather a metaphor from athletic competition.[6] See 1 Tim 6:12 where Paul used the

---

[6]Knight, p. 459, argues that one need not decide whether Paul has in mind athletic or military struggle. Most commentators today, however, argue that the metaphor is athletic. The exact nature of the athletic competition still remains a matter of some debate. Kelly, p. 208, thinks Paul has in mind a wrestling match; Fee, p. 289, thinks a race; and yet others boxing (cf. Hendriksen, p. 315).

same figure. Paul's designation of the "fight" or "contest" as "good" (or "noble") in no way indicates that his effort has been good, but rather that the task, namely his ministry, is a noble one.[7]

I have finished the race,
Paul continues by saying that he has "finished the race" (cf. Acts 20:24), indicating that his life, and more particular his ministry, is almost over. Both verbs in the first two metaphors are in the perfect tense indicating a completed task and an ongoing effect. The contest and the race are over, and Paul is ready to enjoy the rewards of the competition.

I have kept the faith.
Finally, Paul says that he has "kept the faith." Paul's keeping "the faith" in this final statement can either mean that Paul has "kept on believing" (a subjective use of the word "faith") or that he has kept "the faith" (this body of material believed, i.e., the gospel). The latter choice fits the most frequent usage of "faith" in the Pastoral Epistles (see comments at 1 Tim 1:19). It also would make this final statement by Paul match the first two where the object of the verb refers to his ministry in and for the gospel. It also fits very well the context of 2 Timothy with Paul's call for Timothy to remain true to the gospel and to refute those who do not. Paul has again, as with the first two metaphors, used the perfect tense of the verb. He is saying, "I have loyally held on to the gospel which has been entrusted to me and the consequences of that are ongoing. I know the final result." Some have sought to see Paul's third statement as a metaphor after the sort of the first — either an athlete's promise to compete by the rules, a soldier's oath of fidelity, or a steward's care for the deposit he has received.[8] It is better to see the final statement as an explanation or clarification of the first two analogies.

---

[7]Fee, p. 289.
[8]Guthrie, pp. 169-170.

4:8 Now there is in store for me the crown of righteousness,
Because Paul has competed in this noble contest, "finished the race," and "kept the faith, there now is in store for me the crown of righteousness." The word "now" in the NIV represent a Greek word (λοιπόν, *loipon*) which indicates what remains or is left, drawing a contrast between what Paul has already accomplished and what is to come. The "crown" (στέφανος, *stephanos*) refers not to a royal diadem (διάδημα, *diadēma*) but to a victor's crown or garland reserved for those who compete victoriously in athletic events, who return victorious from battle, or who have done something noble for a sovereign. With the two athletic analogies which precede this statement, it would seem that Paul is continuing the illustration. There are two ways of understanding the phrase "the crown of righteousness." "Righteousness" may stand in apposition to "crown," i.e., "the crown which is righteousness" (or "right standing before God"), much like the phrase "crown of life" in Jas 1:12 and Rev 2:10. One may also understand "righteousness" as a simple possessive, i.e., "the crown which belongs to righteousness" (or "right living"). This final option results in Paul's discussion of a crown which belongs to those who have lived righteous lives.[9] Although the final choice is possible, the first option best fits Paul's argument and his usage of the victor's crown elsewhere in his writings (cf. 1 Cor 9:24-25; Phil 4:1; 1 Thess 2:19).[10]

which the Lord, the righteous Judge, will award to me on that day — and not only to me, but also to all who have longed for his appearing.
This crown is to be awarded by "the Lord, the righteous Judge." Some have seen a reference to the judges or referees in athletic events, people who are not always impartial. Others have suggested a reference to the wrong and perverted judgments of the emperor Nero. There is a certain pun on the

---

[9]Fee, p. 290.
[10]For further information about this decision, see Knight, p. 461.

words "righteousness" and "righteous." If Paul does intend Timothy to see a continuation of the Olympic metaphor, there is a major difference. The reward will not be immediate but must wait for "that day," a clear reference to the second coming or "appearing" of Jesus in v. 1. With this Paul concludes his admonition to Timothy and perhaps sets up the contrast in v. 9 with Demas who has "loved this [present] world."

V. PERSONAL INSTRUCTIONS (4:9-18)

⁹**Do your best to come to me quickly, ¹⁰for Demas, because he loved this world, has deserted me and has gone to Thessalonica. Crescens has gone to Galatia, and Titus to Dalmatia. ¹¹Only Luke is with me. Get Mark and bring him with you, because he is helpful to me in my ministry. ¹²I sent Tychicus to Ephesus. ¹³When you come, bring the cloak that I left with Carpus at Troas, and my scrolls, especially the parchments.**

¹⁴Alexander the metalworker did me a great deal of harm. The Lord will repay him for what he has done. ¹⁵You too should be on your guard against him, because he strongly opposed our message.

¹⁶At my first defense, no one came to my support, but everyone deserted me. May it not be held against them. ¹⁷But the Lord stood at my side and gave me strength, so that through me the message might be fully proclaimed and all the Gentiles might hear it. And I was delivered from the lion's mouth. ¹⁸The Lord will rescue me from every evil attack and will bring me safely to his heavenly kingdom. To him be glory for ever and ever. Amen.

This section of Paul's epistle follows the normal pattern of a Hellenistic letter. One would expect final greetings and personal instructions at the end of the letter before the final farewell. Paul's appeal for Timothy's loyalty to the gospel and to him take on special meaning with the final information. Tychicus is likely carrying this letter (v. 12) and will replace Timothy. Paul had earlier indicated his desire for Timothy to join him in the thanksgiving section at the beginning of the epistle (1:4).

4:9 Do your best to come to me quickly,
After announcing his impending death in vv. 6-8, Paul makes a heartfelt and urgent request for Timothy to "do [his] best" (σπούδασον, *spoudason*, the word rendered "study" in KJV of 2:15; cf. 2:15; 4:21; Titus 3:12) "to come quickly" (cf. Paul's intense desire to see Timothy in 1:4). Paul will repeat the request in v. 21. Paul's request for Timothy to "come quickly" may well indicate his concern that, if Timothy did not hurry, he would never again see him. At best, several months would elapse between the time this letter was dispatched to Timothy and the time it would require for Timothy to make his way to Rome. Paul's mention of his first defense in vv. 16-17 indicates that he is well aware of the slowness of the political processes in Rome.

4:10 for Demas, because he loved this world, has deserted me and has gone to Thessalonica.
Paul is anxious for Timothy to join him because all of his co-workers except Luke have left him — one dishonorably and others for various reasons. The departure of Demas was a sad one for Paul. He had been a close associate of Paul during his first imprisonment in Rome (Col 4:14; Phlm 24). Demas is described as one who "loved this world" (αἰῶνα, *aiōna*, literally "the now world" or "age"). Paul may be purposefully contrasting Demas with "all who have longed for his appearing," i.e., the age to come. He has now "deserted" (or "forsaken"; cf. Matt 27:46; Mark 15:34) Paul and gone on to Thessalonica. There is no indication as to why Demas chose Thessalonica. Perhaps that was home for him.

Crescens has gone to Galatia, and Titus to Dalmatia.
After mentioning the departure of Demas, Paul turns to two other co-workers who have left. There is no indication of

any ill motives for these two men. They have likely gone on to other ministry efforts. The modern reader knows nothing more from the biblical text of Crescens. Some traditions connect him with churches in Vienne and Mayence in Gaul, probably due to a textual variant that has "Gaul" rather than "Galatia" in v. 10. In all likelihood he went to minister to the churches in the province of Galatia in central Asia Minor, a major emphasis in the Pauline mission. Titus had gone "to Dalmatia," the coastal region of ancient Illyricum, just up the Adriatic from Nicopolis (cf. Titus 3:12).

4:11 Only Luke is with me. Get Mark and bring him with you, because he is helpful to me in my ministry.
Only Luke ("the beloved physician" of Col 4:14; cf. Phlm 24 and the "we" sections of Acts) has remained with Paul. Timothy is to bring along Mark. Here as in Col 4:10 during Paul's earlier imprisonment in Rome, John Mark is a part of the Pauline circle. Both texts provide interesting insights into a relationship that had earlier caused dissension between Paul and Barnabas (Acts 15:37-41). Mark is now described as one who "is helpful" to Paul in his "ministry" (or "service," διακονία, *diakonia*). It is interesting that, despite his impending death, Paul saw his "ministry" as ongoing.

4:12 I sent Tychicus to Ephesus.
Paul tells Timothy that he has sent Tychicus to Ephesus, presumably to deliver this letter and to relieve Timothy. Tychicus appears frequently in Pauline epistles as a trusted co-worker and messenger (Eph 6:21; Col 4:7; Titus 3:12; cf. Acts 20:4).

4:13 When you come, bring the cloak that I left with Carpus at Troas, and my scrolls, especially the parchments.
Paul's request for his "cloak," "scrolls," and "parchments" is such an incidental and personal note that it speaks against pseudonymity. Paul likely left his things at the house of Carpus in Troas as he was on his way back to Ephesus, apparently being arrested either in Miletus (v. 20) or in Troas. Paul

assumes that Timothy will be traveling the same basic route as he comes to Rome. Paul's "cloak" would have been a warm woolen garment, used especially by travelers and now of special value to Paul in a cold, dark, damp prison. There has been considerable debate as to the nature of Paul's "scrolls" (βιβλία, *biblia*) and "parchments" (μεμβράνας, *membranas*). The two words may represent two different classes of documents or writing materials. On the other hand, the NIV translation, by the rendering "especially (μάλιστα, *malista*) the parchments," makes the second term a narrower class of the first. Another option is to see the term translated "especially" as "an equating-defining term" — "the books, I mean by that the parchment notebooks."[11] Skeat has provided substantial information from the Pastoral Epistles as well as other literature that makes the final option most likely.[12] The content of these materials is still open to debate. The terms could refer to sacred Scripture (i.e., the OT), to written accounts of Jesus' sayings and doings, or to Paul's legal papers (e.g., his certificate of Roman citizenship). Any of the above conjectures or even a combination of those conjectures is possible. Whatever their contents, they were especially valued by Paul.

4:14 Alexander the metalworker did me a great deal of harm. The Lord will repay him for what he has done.

Now Paul moves to warn Timothy of an opponent, "Alexander the metalworker" (a term which may well indicate that he was a "coppersmith"[13]), who had done "a great deal of harm" to Paul. This man "strongly opposed" (cf. 3:8 where the verb is used of Jannes and Jambres) the "message" of Paul and his co-workers. Exactly who "Alexander the metalworker" was has been a matter of some debate. Is he (1) the Alexander of 1 Tim 1:19-20 who was linked with Hymenaeus, (2) the

---

[11]T.C. Skeat, "'Especially the Parchments': A Note on 2 Timothy IV.13," *Journal of Theological Studies* 30 (1979) p. 174; cf. Fee, p. 295; Knight, p. 467.
[12]Skeat, pp. 173-177.
[13]Knight, p. 467.

Jew who tried to end the riot in Ephesus (Acts 19:33-34), or (3) some otherwise unknown metalworker? It is likely that the third alternative is best.

4:15 You too should be on your guard against him, because he strongly opposed our message.
Timothy may well meet up with this character in Troas when he stops to gather Paul's cloak and parchments. Therefore, Timothy "too should be on [his] guard against him." Paul has complete confidence that God can handle the wrongdoer and his sins, either in this life or in the life to come — "the Lord will repay (cf. v. 8) him for what he has done."

4:16 At my first defense, no one came to my support, but everyone deserted me. May it not be held against them.
Paul's urgency in his request for Timothy to come is explained in v. 16. At his "first defense, no one" has come to his "support, but everyone deserted" him. It is unlikely that the "first defense" would refer to Paul's earlier imprisonment in Rome at the end of Acts since Timothy would have been well aware of that situation. Rather Paul must be referring to a preliminary hearing, a *prima actio* of the Roman judicial system, during this imprisonment. After this hearing, Paul would then face the trial. During Paul's first imprisonment in Rome (Acts 28:16, 30), this period stretched out for two years. During that time Paul was held under house arrest. Despite his being "rescued from the lion's mouth" (v. 17), he is now in chains (1:16; 2:9) and expects to die. Paul's claim that "no one came to [his] support" (from παραγίνομαι, *paraginomai*, literally "became beside" him) and that "everyone deserted" him may well be seen as a slight hyperbole allowing for Tychicus and Luke to still be at his side. Whatever the case, Paul felt very much alone. Paul's language, "May it not be held against them," is reminiscent of the words of Jesus from the cross in Luke 23:34 (cf. the words of Stephen in Acts 7:60).

4:17 But the Lord stood at my side and gave me strength, so that through me the message might be fully proclaimed and all the Gentiles might hear it.

While others may have deserted Paul (notice the adversative but, δέ, *de*), "the Lord stood at [his] side and gave [him] strength" (1 Tim 1:12). The "strength" which he had received Timothy would need (2:1). God had given Paul strength in order that through him "the preaching might be fulfilled." Paul saw himself as the agent by which God would accomplish this most important proclamation. Also through him "all the Gentiles might hear it." There is little question that Paul saw his ministry as clearly to "the Gentiles." Now even his imprisonment had become the means through which God could catch the ears of the Gentiles in the chief city of the empire.

And I was delivered from the lion's mouth.

Paul proclaims that he had been "delivered from the lion's mouth." Interpreters have been divided regarding whether the lion of v. 17 represents the literal lions of Nero's amphitheater or Satan. Paul may well be reflecting on Psalm 22. There the psalmist pleads with God to rescue him "from the lion's mouth" (Ps 22:21). The context here (vv. 9-18) bears several similarities to that psalm. Paul was "deserted" (vv. 10, 16), and the psalmist feels "forsaken" or deserted by God (Ps 22:1). Paul has been "delivered" (v. 17) and indeed will be brought to safety (v. 18), and the psalmist proclaims that God has "delivered" those who put their trust in him and will save them (Ps 22:4-5).[14] "The lion's mouth" it would seem is a simple metaphor for death; God has delivered him from death.

4:18 The Lord will rescue me from every evil attack and will bring me safely to his heavenly kingdom.

Reflecting on the deliverance which the Lord has recently given, Paul moves to the larger significance of that fact. "The

---

[14]See W.A. Lock, *A Critical and Exegetical Commentary on the Pastoral Epistles*, International Critical Commentary (Edinburgh, 1924), p. 116, for a careful look at the similarities between this passage and Ps 22.

Lord will rescue [him] from every evil attack" (literally "every evil deed"). Since Paul fully expects the current situation to lead to his death, it seems likely that he is here expressing his confidence that he will triumphantly overcome all the forces of evil in the end. As Kelly puts it, "[Paul] is affirming his confidence that no assault of his enemies will undermine his faith or his courage, or cause him to lapse into disastrous sin."[15] Put another way, if he endures and remains faithful to God who has called him, God will take care of the rest. Paul goes on to declare that God "will bring [him] safely to his heavenly kingdom." God will complete the work that he has begun in Christ.

To him be glory for ever and ever. Amen.
In typical fashion the note of final victory and triumph leads Paul to break into a doxology (cf. 1 Tim 1:17; 6:15-16). "To him be glory for ever and ever. Amen" (see especially Phil 4:20).

VI. FINAL SALUTATIONS (4:19-22)

[19]Greet Priscilla[a] and Aquila and the household of Onesiphorus. [20]Erastus stayed in Corinth, and I left Trophimus sick in Miletus. [21]Do your best to get here before winter. Eubulus greets you, and so do Pudens, Linus, Claudia and all the brothers.
[22]The Lord be with your spirit. Grace be with you.

[a]*19* Greek *Prisca*, a variant of *Priscilla*

Paul concludes his letter with greetings to Timothy and others in Ephesus. He cannot close without making one more appeal for Timothy to come to him in haste. He then sends final greetings from those with him to Timothy and closes with a simple benediction.

---

[15]Kelly, p. 220.

4:19 Greet Priscilla and Aquila

Paul begins by sending greetings to Priscilla and Aquila, two old friends and co-workers, both in the tent-making business and in the cause of Christ. Despite the rendering of the NIV, in reality Paul follows his normal custom and addresses Priscilla here as "Prisca," the more formal name. It is Luke who consistently calls her "Priscilla." It is striking that Priscilla and Aquila are now back in Ephesus. Paul had first met them in Corinth after they had been expelled from Rome under the edict of Claudius (Acts 18:1-3). They then accompany Paul to Ephesus (Acts 18:18-26), and the church meets in their home (1 Cor 16:19). By the time Paul writes Romans, they are in Rome, and again a church meets in their home (16:3-4).

The exact circumstances that have brought them back to Ephesus are uncertain. Aquila is clearly a Jew from Pontus. We know nothing for certain of Priscilla's origin. Fee assumes that she was also Jewish.[16] Ramsey has argued that by Luke's emphasizing that Aquila was a Jew, he has implied that Priscilla was not (Acts 18:2).[17] It is noteworthy that, in four out of the six times when her name is mentioned, her name precedes her husband's, a phenomenon unusual in the ancient world. Ramsey has assumed that this may be due to her being of noble birth. He argues that, while her name was that of a prominent Roman family, the name Aquila was frequently used of freemen.[18] Others have assumed that she may well have been the more dominant personality. Whatever the case, Paul cannot pass up the opportunity to greet this special couple.

and the household of Onesiphorus.

Paul also sends greetings to "the household of Onesiphorus." Paul had earlier mentioned Onesiphorus in 1:16-18. The

---

[16]Fee, p. 300.
[17]William M. Ramsey, *St. Paul the Traveller and the Roman Citizen* (1897 reprint; Grand Rapids: Baker Book House, 1966), pp. 268-269.
[18]*Ibid.*

fact that Paul does not mention him in connection with his family indicates that he is not with them and may indicate that he has died (see the discussion at 1:16-18).

4:20 Erastus stayed in Corinth,
At this point Paul stops to give some information about some mutual friends. Erastus is the name of one of Timothy's companions in Acts 19:22. It is also the name of a city offical in Corinth in the mid-fifties (Rom 16:23). It is unlikely that the two accounts refer to the same man. While one cannot say with certainty that either of these men is the Erastus of 2 Tim 4:20, the Erastus of Acts 19 is the better candidate. He was, after all, well known to Timothy. Paul could be simply trying to catch Timothy up on his whereabouts and his ministry. Paul informs Timothy that Erastus had "stayed in Corinth." Perhaps Timothy had expected him to join Paul in Rome, and Paul was explaining where he was.[19]

and I left Trophimus sick in Miletus.
Next Paul mentions Trophimus whom he had "left sick in Miletus." If Erastus was the former associate of Acts 19, then the mention of Trophimus which follows is logial. Trophimus was also an old associate. He had been a part of the group who brought the Gentile contribution to Jerusalem and the mistaken supposition that Paul had taken him into the temple was the reason for Paul's seizure by a mob there (Acts 20:4; 21:29). The reason for Paul's visit to Miletus which resulted in Trophimus's being left there is unknown. As Lea and Griffin have indicated, the passage provides some insights into the nature of miraculous healings in the NT: "The passing reference to Trophimus's sickness indicates that miracles of healing were not produced at the demand of an apostle but were evidences of divine power carried out by the will of God."[20]

---

[19]Fee, p. 301.
[20]Lea and Griffin, p. 261; cf. Hendriksen, p. 332.

4:21 Do your best to get here before winter.
Paul makes a final request of Timothy: "Do your best to get here before winter." Transportation on the Mediterranean stopped from November until March. Paul is likely writing this letter in the late spring or early summer. If Timothy missed the window of opportunity, there was no guarantee that he would arrive in time to see his father in the faith alive. Missing the window might well mean nearly a year's delay in arriving in Rome.

Eubulus greets you, and so do Pudens, Linus, Claudia and all the brothers.
Paul sends greetings to Timothy from Eubulus, Pudens, Linus, Claudia, and "all the brothers." All of the names in the list except Eubulus are Latin names. There is no further information available about Eubulus. Tradition, however, provides some interesting conjectural data regarding the others. The only one about whom this data has any likely validity is Linus. Irenaeus said that, after the death of Peter and Paul, Linus became an important leader in the church at Rome.[21] According to less reliable legends, Pudens was a Roman senator converted by Peter, and Claudia was the mother of Linus. There is really no reliable data to provide additional information regarding these Roman Christians. Paul concludes the list of those who send greetings with "and all the brothers." The term "brothers" need not be taken as sexually exclusive. The NRSV conveys the correct understanding in rendering the text "all the brothers and sisters." It is Paul's way of saying "all the Christians here."

4:22 The Lord be with your spirit. Grace be with you.
Paul closes with a brief benediction — "The Lord be with your spirit" — and a closing salutation — "Grace be with you." The "your" of the benediction is singular and is a personal reference to Timothy. It is Paul's prayer that "the Lord" will

---

[21]Irenaeus, *Against Heresies* III.iii.3. Cf. Eusebius, *Ecclesiastical History* III.iv.

grant him strength to stand and strength to endure suffering (cf. Gal 6:18; Phil 4:23; Phlm 25). In the closing salutation, Paul broadens his audience. The "you" is there plural. Paul apparently expects the church at Ephesus also to read and learn from his letter.

SELECTED BIBLIOGRAPHY

Allan, J.A. "The 'In Christ' Formula in the Pastoral Epistles," *New Testament Studies* 10 (1963) 115-121.

Barclay, William. *The Letters to Timothy, Titus, and Philemon* (DSB rev. ed.). Philadelphia: Westminster, 1975.

―――――. "Paul's Certainties VII. Our Security in God — 2 Timothy 1,12," *Expository Times* 69 (1958) 324-327.

Barnett, Paul W. "Wives and Women's Ministry (1 Timothy 2:11-15)," *Evangelical Quarterly* 61 (1989) 225-238.

Barrett, C.K. *The Pastoral Epistles* (NCB). Oxford: Clarendon, 1963.

Berdot, D.N. *Exercitatio theologica-exegetica in epistulam Pauli ad Titum.* 1703.

Bernard, J.H. *The Pastoral Epistles.* Thornapple Commentaries, 1899; reprinted Grand Rapids: Baker, 1980.

Bratcher, R.G. *A Translator's Guide to Paul's Letters to Timothy and Titus.* New York: United Bible Society, 1983.

Cadbury, H.J. "Erastus of Corinth," *Journal of Biblical Literature* 50 (1931) 42-58.

Carson, D.A.; Douglas J. Moo, and Leon Morris, *An Introduction to the New Testament.* Grand Rapids: Zondervan, 1992.

Colson, F.H. "'Myths and Genealogies' — A Note on the Polemic of the Pastoral Epistles," *Journal of Theological Studies* 19 (1917/18) 265-271.

Cook, D. "The Pastoral Fragments Reconsidered," *Journal of Theological Studies* 35 (1984) 120-131.

Cottrell, Jack. "1 Timothy 2:12 and the Role of Women," *Christian Standard* (Jan. 17, 1993) 5.

Deer, D.S. "Still More about the Imperatival *hina*," *Bible Translator* 30 (1979) 148.

Dibelius, M. and H. Conzelmann, *The Pastoral Epistles*, tr. P. Buttolph and A. Yarbro. Hermeneia; Philadelphia: Fortress Press, 1972.

Dodd, C.H. "New Testament Translation Problems II," *Bible Translator* 28 (1977)112-116.

Doty, W.G. "The Classification of Epistolary Literature," *Catholic Biblical Quarterly* 31 (1969)183-199.

Earle, Ralph. "1 Timothy," *Evangelical Bible Commentary*, vol 11. Grand Rapids: Zondervan, 1978.

_____. "2 Timothy," *Evangelical Bible Commentary*, vol 11. Grand Rapids: Zondervan, 1978.

_____. *Word Meanings in the New Testament*. Grand Rapids: Baker, 1984.

Easton, B.S. *The Pastoral Epistles*. New York: Scribners, 1948.

Ellicott, C.J. *The Pastoral Epistles of St. Paul.* 2nd ed. Andover: Draper, 1897.

Ellingworth, P. "The 'True Saying' in 1 Timothy 3.1," *Bible Translator* 31 (1980) 443-445.

Ellis, E. Earle. *Paul's Use of the Old Testament.* London, 1957; reprinted Grand Rapids: Eerdmans, 1981.

_____. "The Problem of Authorship: First and Second Timothy," *Review and Expositor* 56 (1959) 343-354.

_____. "Traditions in the Pastoral Epistles," in *Early Jewish and Christian Exegesis: in Memory of William Hugh Brownlee,* ed. C. Stephens and W. F. Stinespring. Atlanta: Scholars Press, 1987.

Falconer, Robert, "1 Timothy 2:14, 15. Interpretive Notes," *Journal of Biblical Literature* 60 (1941) 375-379.

Fee, Gordon D. *1 and 2 Timothy, Titus* (NIBC). Peabody, MA: Hendrickson, 1988.

_____. "Issues in Evangelical Hermeneutics, Part III: The Great Watershed Intentionality and Particularity/Eternity: 1 Timothy 2:8-15 as a Test Case," *Crux* 26 (1990) 31-37.

Ferguson, Everett. "τοπος in 1 Timothy 2:8," *Restoration Quarterly 33* (1991) 66-73.

Furfey, P.H. "PLOUSIOS and Cognates in the New Testament," *Catholic Biblical Quarterly* 5 (1943) 241-263.

Gealy, F.D. "The First and Second Epistles to Timothy and the Epistle to Titus," *Interpeters Bible XI,* 341-551.

Gloer, W. Hulitt. "Homologies and Hymns in the New Testament: Form, Content and Criteria for Identification," *Perspectives in Religious Studies,* 11 (1984) 118-130.

Grayston, K. and G. Herdan, "The Authorship of the Pastorals in the Light of Statistical Linguistics," *New Testament Studies* 6 (1960)1-15.

Gromacki, Robert G. *Stand True to the Charge: An Exposition of I Timothy*. Grand Rapids: Baker, 1982.

Gundry, R.H. "The Form, Meaning and Background of the Hymn Quoted in 1 Timothy 3:16," *Apostolic History and the Gospel*, ed. W. W. Gasque and R. P. Martin. Grand Rapids: Eerdmans, 1970, 203-222.

Guthrie, Donald. "The Development of the Idea of Canonical Pseudepigrapha in New Testament Criticism," *Vox Evangelical.* 1 (1962) 43-59.

_____. *The Pastoral Epistles: An Introduction and Commentary* (TNTC). Grand Rapids: Eerdmans, 1957.

_____. *New Testament Introduction*. 3rd ed. Downers Grove: InterVarsity Press, 1979.

Hanson, A.T. *The Pastoral Epistles* (NCBC). Grand Rapids: Baker, 1982.

_____. *Studies in the Pastoral Epistles*. London: SPCK, 1968.

Harris, Murray J. *Jesus as God: The New Testament Use of "Theos" in Reference to Jesus*. Grand Rapids: Zondervan, 1992.

_____. "Titus 2:13 and the Deity of Christ," *Pauline Studies: Essays Presented to Professor F. F. Bruce on His 70th Birthday*, ed. D. Hagner and M. J. Harris. Grand Rapids: Eerdmans, 1980.

Harrison, P.N. "Important Hypotheses Reconsidered: III. The Authorship of the Pastoral Epistles," *Expository Times* 67 (1955-56) 77-81.

_____. *Paulines and Pastorals*. London: Oxford University Press, 1964.

_____. *The Problem of the Pastoral Epistles*. London: Oxford University Press, 1921.

Hebert, G. "'Faithfulness' and 'Faith,'" *Theology* 58 (1955) 373-379.

Hendriksen, William *Thessalonians, Timothy and Titus* (NTC). Grand Rapids: Baker, 1979.

Hiebert, D.E. "Titus," *Evangelical Bible Commentary*, vol. 11. Grand Rapids: Zondervan, 1978.

Hommes, N.J. "Let Women Be Silent in Church . . ." *Calvin Theological Review* 4 (1969) 5-22.

Houlden, J.L. *The Pastoral Epistles: I and II Timothy, Titus* (PNTC). London: Penguin Press, 1976.

House, H.W. "Biblical Inspiration in 2 Timothy 3:16," *Bibliotheca Sacra* 137 (1980) 54-63.

Hull, W.E. "The Man — Timothy," *Review and Expositor* 56 (1959) 355-366.

Hultgren, Arland J. *I and II Timothy, Titus*. Minneapolis: Augsburg, 1984.

Hurley, J.B. *Man and Woman in Biblical Perspective*. Grand Rapids: Zondervan, 1981.

Johnson, Luke T. *1 Timothy, 2 Timothy, Titus*. Atlanta: John Knox Press, 1987.

Johnson, P.F. "The Use of Statistics in the Analysis of the Characteristics of Pauline Writings," *New Testament Sudies* 20 (1974) 92-100.

Karris, Robert J. "The Background and Significance of the Polemic of the Pastoral Epistles," *Journal of Biblical Literature* 92 (1973) 549-564.

_____. *The Pastoral Epistles*, New Testament Message 17. Wilmington: Michael Glazier, 1979.

Kelly, J.N.D. *A Commentary on the Pastoral Epistles*. Black's New Commentary. New York, 1960; reprinted Thornapple Commentaries. Grand Rapids: Eerdmans, 1981.

Kenny, Anthony John Patrick. *A Stylometric Study of the New Testament*. Oxford: Clarendon Press, 1986.

Kent, H.A. *The Pastoral Epistles: Studies in I and II Timothy and Titus*. Chicago: Moody, 1958.

Kidd, R.M. *Wealth and Beneficence in the Pastoral Epistles*. Society of Biblical Literature Dissertation Series 122. Atlanta: Scholars Press, 1990.

Knight, George W., III. "ΑΥΘΕΝΤΕΩ in Reference to Women in 1 Timothy 2.12," *New Testament Studies* 30 (1984) 143-157.

_____. *Commentary on the Pastoral Epistles* (NIGTC). Grand Rapids: Eerdmans, 1992.

_____. *The Faithful Sayings in the Pastoral Letters*. Kampen, 1968; reprinted Grand Rapids: Baker, 1979.

_____. "The New Testament Teaching on the Role Relationship of Male and Female with Special Reference to the Teaching/Ruling Functions in the Church," *JETS* 18 (1975) 81-91.

_____. *The Role Relationship of Men and Women*. Revised ed. Phillipsburg, NJ. 1985.

Kroeger, Catherine C. "1 Timothy 2:12 – A Classicist's View" in *Women, Authority and the Bible*, ed. A. Mickelsen. Downers Grove: InterVarsity Press, 1986.

Kroeger, Richard Clark and Catherine C. Kroeger. *I Suffer Not a Woman: Rethinking 1 Timothy 2:11-15 in Light of Ancient Evidence.* Grand Rapids: Baker, 1992.

Lane, W.L. "First Timothy IV.1-3: An Early Instance of Over-realized Eschatology?" *New Testament Studies* 11 (1965) 164-167.

Lea, Thomas D. and Hayne P. Griffin. *1, 2 Timothy, Titus* (NAC). Nashville: Broadman Press, 1992.

Leaney, A.R.C. *The Epistles to Timothy, Titus, and Philemon: Introduction and Commentary* (TBC). London: SMC Press, 1960.

Lenski, R.C.H. *The Interpretation of St. Paul's Epistles to the Colossians, to the Thessalonians, to Timothy, to Titus and to Philemon.* Minneapolis: Wartburg Press, 1937.

Lewis, Robert M. "The 'Women' of 1 Timothy 3:1," *Bibliotheca Sacra* 136 (April-June 1979) 167-175.

Lock, W. *A Critical and Exegetical Commentary on The Pastoral Epistles* (ICC). Edinburgh: T&T Clark, 1924.

Malherbe, A.J. "'In Season and Out of Season': 2 Timothy 4:2," *Journal of Biblical Literature* 103 (1984) 235-243.

McEleney, N.J. "The Vice Lists of the Pastoral Epistles," *Catholic Biblical Quarterly* 36 (1974) 203-219.

Meade, David G. *Pseudonymity and Canon. An Investigation into the Relationship of Authorship and Authority in Jewish and Earliest Christian Tradition.* Grand Rapids: Baker, 1987.

Metzger, Bruce M. "A Reconsideration of Certain Arguments against the Pauline Authorship of the Pastoral Epistles," *Expository Times* 70 (1958) 91-94.

Michaelson, S. and A.Q. Morton. "Last Words: A Test of Authorship for Greek Writers," *New Testament Studies* 18 (1972) 192-208.

Mickelsen, A. ed. *Women, Authority and the Bible*. Downers Grove: InterVarsity Press, 1986.

Moellering, H. Armin. *1 Timothy, 2 Timothy, Titus*. Concordia Commentary. Saint Louis: Concordia Publishing House, 1970.

Moo, D.J. "1 Timothy 2:11-15: Meaning and Significance," *Trinity Journal* new series 1(1980) 62-83.

_____. "The Interpretation of 1 Timothy 2:11-15: A Rejoinder," *Trinty Journal* new series 2 (1981) 198-222.

Morris, Leon, *The Apostolic Preaching of the Cross*, 3rd ed. London: Eerdmans, 1965.

Morton, A.Q. *Literary Detection: How to Prove Authorship and Fraud in Literary Documents*. New York: Scribner, 1978.

_____. and J.J. McLeman. *Paul, the Man and the Myth*. New York: Harper and Row, 1966.

Moss, C. Michael. "Hymn Fragments in the New Testament and Their Implications for Hymnology Today," unpublished paper read at Christian Scholars Conference, Harding University, Searcy, AR, July 23, 1993.

Moule, C.F.D. "The Problem of the Pastorals: A Reappraisal," in *Essays in New Testament Interpretation*. Cambridge: Cambridge University Press, 1982.

Moule, H.C.G. *Studies in II Timothy*. London, 1905 (as *The Second Epistle to Timothy: Short Devotional Studies on the Dying Letter of St. Paul)*; reprinted Grand Rapids: Eerdmans, 1977.

Neumann, K.J. *The Authenticity of the Pauline Epistles in the Light of Stylostatistical Analysis.* Society of Biblical Literature Dissertation Series 120. Atlanta: Scholars Press, 1990.

Norbie, D.L. "The Washing of Regeneration," *Evangelical Quarterly* 34 (1962) 36-38.

Oden, Thomas C. *First and Second Timothy and Titus.* Louisville: John Knox Press, 1989.

Osburn, Carroll D. *"Authenteō* (1 Timothy 2:12)," *Restoration Quarterly* 25 (1982) 1-12.

_____. ed. *Essays on Women in Earliest Christianity.* Joplin: College Press, 1993.

Padgett, Allan. "The Pauline Rationale for Submission: Biblical Feminism and the *Hina* Clauses of Titus 1:1-10," *Evangelical Quarterly* 59 (1987) 39-52.

Payne, Philip B. "Libertarian Women in Ephesus: A Response to Douglas J. Moo's Article '1 Timothy 2:11-15: Meaning and Significance,'" *Trinity Journal* new series 2 (1981) 169-197.

Pherigo, L.P. "Paul's Life After the Close of Acts," *Journal of Biblical Literature* 70 (1951) 277-284.

Piper, John, and Wayne Grudem, eds. *Recovering Biblical Manhood and Womanhood.* Wheaton, IL: Crossway Books, 1991.

Plummer, Alfred. *The Pastoral Epistles.* The Expositor's Bible. New York: A.C. Armstrong, 1889.

Quinn, J.D. "The Last Volume of Luke: The Relation of Luke-Acts to the Pastoral Epistles," *Perspectives on Luke-Acts,* ed. C.H. Talbert. Macon: Mercer Press, 1978.

_____. *The Letter to Titus: A New Translation with Notes and Commentary and an Introduction to Titus, I and II Timothy, the Pastorals*. The Anchor Bible. New York: Doubleday, 1990.

Ramsay, William M. "A Historical Commentary on the Epistles to Timothy," *Expositor* 7/7 (1909) 481-494; 7/8 (1909) 1-21, 167-185, 264-282, 339-357, 399-416, 557-668–7/9 (1910) 172-187, 319-333, 433-440; 8/1 (1911) 262-273, 365-375.

_____. *St. Paul the Traveller and the Roman Citizen*. 1897 reprint; Grand Rapids: Baker, 1966.

Roberts, Mark D. "Women Shall Be Saved: A Closer Look at 1 Timothy 2:15," *The Reformed Journal* (1983) 18-22.

Roberts, J.W. "The Bearing of the Use of Particles on the Authorship of The Pastoral Epistles," *Restoration Quarterly* 2 (1958) 132-137.

_____. "Every Scripture Inspired of God," *Restoration Quarterly* 5 (1961) 33-37.

_____. "Note on the Adjective after πᾶς in 2 Timothy 3^{16}," *Expository Times* 76 (1965) 359.

Robertson, A. T. *The Epistles of Paul (Word Pictures in the New Testament, IV)*. Nashville, 1931.

_____. "The Greek Article and the Deity of Christ," *Expositor* 8/21 (1921) 182-188.

Robinson, J.A. T. *Redating the New Testament*. Philadelphia: Westminster Press, 1976.

Scholer, David M. "1 Timothy 2:9-15 and the Place of Women in the Church's Ministry," in *Women, Authority and the Bible*. ed. A. Michelsen. Downers Grove: InterVarsity Press, 1986.

Scott, Ernest Findlay. *The Pastoral Epistles* (MNTC). London: Hodder and Stoughton, 1936.

Simpson, E.K, *The Pastoral Epistles: The Greek Text with Introduction and Commentary.* Grand Rapids: Eerdmans, 1954.

Skeat, T.C. "'Especially the Parchments': A Note on 2 Timothy IV.13," *Journal of Theological Studies* 30 (1979) 173-177.

Smith, R.E. and Beekman, J. *A Literary-Semantic Analysis of Second Timothy,* ed. M. F. Kopesec. Dallas, 1981.

Spain, Carl. *The Letters of Paul to Timothy and Titus* (LWC). vol 14; Austin: R. B. Sweet, 1970.

Spence, R.M. "2 Timothy iii.15, 16," *Expository Times* 8 (1896-1897), 564f.

Spenser, Aida Besançon. *Beyond the Curse: Women Called to Ministry.* Nashville: Thomas Nelson, 1985.

Stott, John R.W. *Guard the Gospel: The Message of 2 Timothy.* Downers Grove: InterVarsity Press, 1973.

Swete, H.B. "The Faithful Sayings," *Journal of Theological Studies* 18 (1917) 1-7.

Thrall, M.E. "The Pauline Use of Συνείδησις," *New Testament Studies* 14 (1967-68) 118-125.

Towner, Philip H. *1-2 Timothy & Titus.* IVP New Testament Commentary Series. Downers Grove: InterVarsity Press, 1994.

_____. "The Present Age in the Eschatology of the Pastoral Epistles," *New Testament Studies* 32 (1986) 427-448.

Van der Jagt, Krijn. "Women Are Saved Through Childbearing," *The Bible Translator* 39 (1988) 201-208.

Verner, D.C. *The Household of God: The Social World of the Pastoral Epistles.* Society of Biblical Literature Dissertation Series 71. Chico, CA: Scholars Press, 1983.

Vine, W.E. *The Epistles to Timothy and Titus.* London, 1965.

Wallis, W.B. "The First Epistle to Timothy," "The Second Epistle to Timothy," "The Epistle to Titus," *The Wycliffe Bible Commentary*, ed. C.F. Pfeiffer and E.F. Harrison. Chicago: Moody Press, 1975.

Ward, Ronald A. *Commentary on 1 & 2 Timothy & Titus.* Waco: Word Books, 1974.

Warfield, B.B. *The Inspiration and Authority of the Bible.* Philadelphia: Presbyterian and Reformed, 1948.

White, Newport John Davis. "The Pastoral Epistles," *Expositor's Greek Testament IV*, reprint; Grand Rapids: Eerdmans, 1983.

Wilshire, L.E. "The TLG Computer and Further Reference to ΑΥΘΕΝΤΕΩ in Timothy 2.12," *New Testament Studies* 34 (1988)120-134.

Wilson, Stephen G. *Luke and the Pastoral Epistles.* London: SPCK, 1979.

Winter, Bruce W. "Providentia for the Widows of 1 Timothy 5,3-16," *Tyndale Bulletin* 39 (1988) 83-99.

Witherington, Ben, III. *Women in the Earliest Churches.* Society for New Testament Studies Monograph Series 59. Cambridge: Cambrige University Press, 1988.

Wright, D.F. "Homosexuals or Prostitutes? The Meaning of ΑΡΣΕΝΚΟΙΤΑΙ (1 Cor. 6:9; 1 Tim. 1:10)," *Vigilae Christianae* 38 (1984) 125-153.

Wuest, K.S. *The Pastoral Epistles in the Greek New Testament.* Grand Rapids: Eerdmans, 1952.